Dear Leon,

A happy

Thank you

♡ Carol.

xxx

The Owl **HOUSE**

The Owl **HOUSE**

ANNE EMSLIE

with photographs by **ROY ZETISKY**

VIKING

VIKING

Published by the Penguin Group
Penguin Books Ltd, 27 Wrights Lane, London W8 5TZ, England
Viking Penguin, a division of Penguin Books USA Inc., 375 Hudson Street, New York, New York 1004, USA
Penguin Books Australia Ltd, Ringwood, Victoria, Australia
Penguin Books Canada Ltd, 2801 John Street, Markham, Ontario, Canada LR3 1B4
Penguin Books (NZ) Ltd, 182-190 Wairau Road, Auckland 10, New Zealand
Penguin Books, Amethyst Street, Theta Ext 1, Johannesburg, South Africa

Penguin Books Ltd, Registered Offices: Harmondsworth, Middlesex, England

First published 1991

ISBN 0 670 83368 1

Design and typesetting by Press Books, Johannesburg
Printed and bound by Creda Press

To the memory of **HELEN MARTINS**

CONTENTS

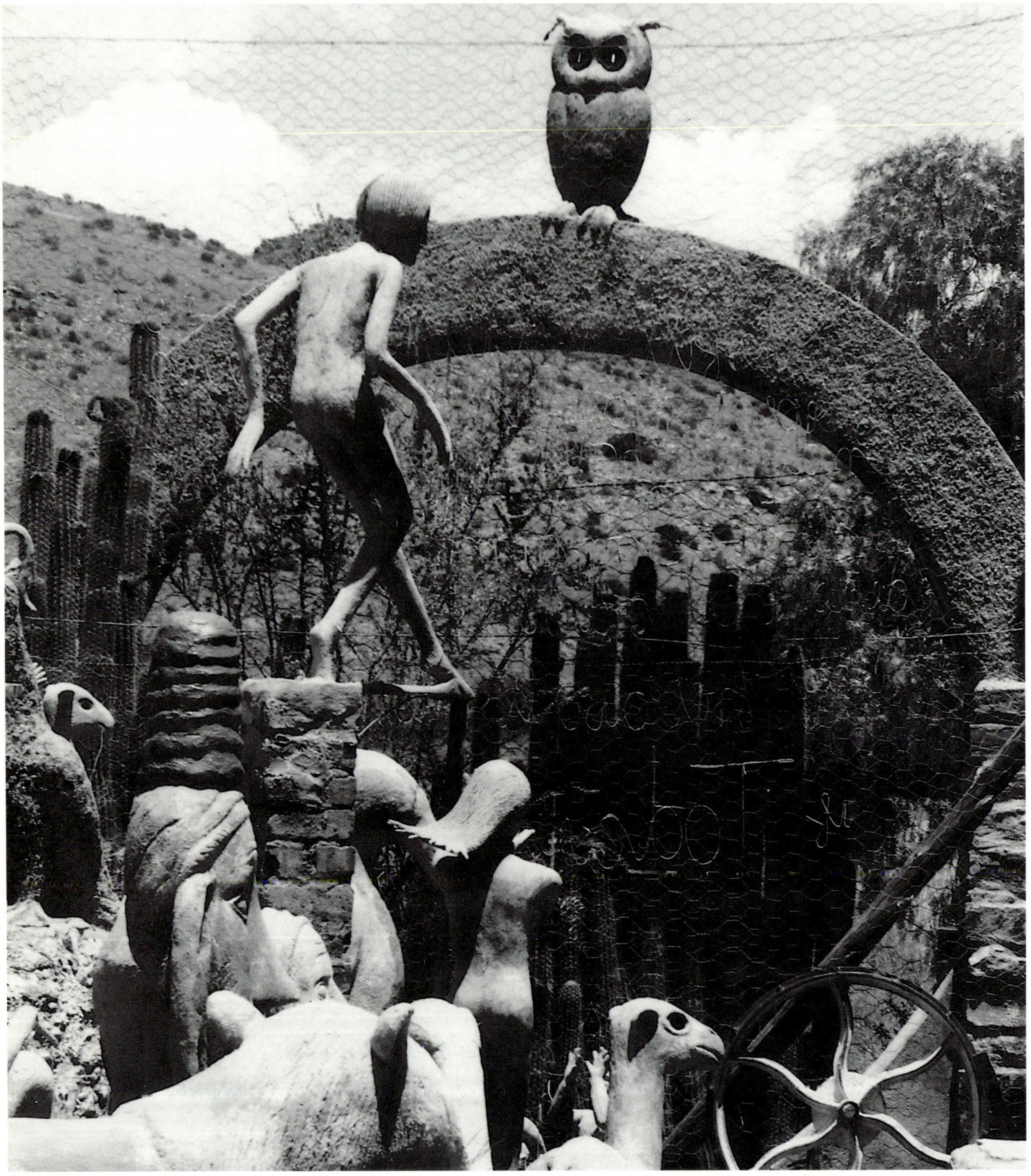

PREFACE

Miss Helen's Owl House is a remarkable achievement. It is as unexpected as it is moving. What started off as an ordinary house, home of Helen Martins, was slowly transformed over the years into a strange and intense art world. The work challenges definitions of art, just as Miss Helen herself challenges conventional notions of the artist. She had no formal training in art. She employed others to build her statues. She used humble means. Cement and other people's rubbish, such as discarded bottles, were her materials. With these she created a space which speaks movingly about the human predicament. She was able, through her art, to transcend her very limited circumstances.

Miss Helen received little by way of praise or acknowledgement during her lifetime, although there were some who recognised her ability. The writer Don Maclennan visited and befriended Helen. In a copy of the *Rubáiyát of Omar Khayyám*, which he gave to Helen, he inscribed the words 'From one artist to another'. Another visitor, John Moyle,observed that Miss Helen had 'the authentic soul of an artist'. He recalls how she would deprecate herself and her work, saying things like 'What a silly old woman I am!' and then the very next moment she would be turning the mirror on a window ledge in the house to reflect a beam of light onto her glass-encrusted walls. Suddenly she would be transported with rapture, entirely engrossed in the world she was creating. At other times of the day the sheen she picked up from a metallic garden star, or the sunshine glinting off a glass mosaic would spark off her excitement, while all the time her fertile mind would be seeing further possibilities for creation and transformation. She thought as an artist thinks, and she created a space that has astonishing complexity and beauty.

Part of the motivation for writing this book was to record an environment of artistic interest and merit that is intrinsically impermanent in nature. The Owl House was an inhabited environment, the home of Helen Martins. It never remained exactly the same from one day to the next, and over the years changing circumstances have altered it continually.

The Owl House evolved through a number of stages during the years that Helen Martins spent beneath its roof. At one time, for instance, the entire yard had a roof of chicken-wire, turning the area into a vast cage. It was always a living, changing space. Objects and statues were frequently moved around and new combinations tried out. As one idea sparked off another, the Owl House grew organically and its meanings shifted. Helen herself was very much a part of the art environment she created. Her personality, the way she chose to show visitors around, the remarks she made, the specific occasions, such as Christmas Eve or full moon, when she would light up the house at night and invite company around, all contributed to the nature of the experience that the environment offered. Partly for this reason and partly, too, to discover more about the nature of the driving force behind the building of such an elaborate and unusual fantasy environment, it seems important to attempt to understand Helen's character.

PREFACE

Helen no longer lives at the Owl House. The statues have ossified in their places, and ornaments and other objects remain where they were when her death stopped the clock in 1976. Thus one would suppose that the visitor to the Owl House encounters it, these days, as it was at that one frozen point in time. Yet even this is not altogether true, for deleterious changes have set in since then, changes which obscure her original intentions. The space is considerably shabbier now and numerous items have been removed. Various ornaments, lamps, mirrors, pieces of furniture, even statues, have disappeared. The birds that once inhabited the yard have long since flown, and the dammetjies that were meticulously kept filled with water are now dry, sunken pits. In attempting to reconstruct the intricate web of interconnecting thoughts that were spun throughout the space, linking one part to the next, one idea to another, it is important to be aware of the alterations and shifts that have occurred. This book attempts to draw attention to the significant changes which may detract from Helen Martins' primary objectives.

The Owl House is not an easy environment to preserve. The cement mix used in the construction of the garden statuary has not stood up well to the ravages of time. Many statues have crumbled, many have collapsed. Funds have not always been available for restoration, and where restoration work has taken place, this has not always been faithful to the original. A recent surge of interest in the Owl House has fuelled a good deal of debate as to how the space should be preserved. The issue is complex and opinions differ.

The Friends of the Owl House, a group formed as a result of popular interest in preserving this unique place, has many deserving plans and is attempting to co-ordinate a conservation effort. Hopefully their action and their fundraising will give the Owl House a new lease of life. However, whether it can be preserved indefinitely is uncertain. This is an important reason for a book. It is able to record for posterity, in images and in words, an environmental art experience that ultimately may not otherwise survive.

ACKNOWLEDGEMENTS

I wish to thank the many people who so generously shared with me their thoughts and memories of Helen Martins and the Owl House:

Koos Malgas, Piet van der Merwe, Jonas Adams, Anna Adams, Jill Wenman, Francie Lund, Peggy Delport, Johann Potgieter, Johan van Meyeren, John Moyle, Matie Cupido, Cynthia Craig, Gertie Retief, Rosemary van der Merwe, Ouma Mollie, Mrs Cloete, and Hugo van der Westhuisen.

I wish, too, to thank Johann Potgieter, Johan van Meyeren and Ian Ballantine for allowing me to reproduce their photographs. Johann Potgieter has an especially interesting collection of pictures taken at the Owl House during the early seventies. They provide a valuable visual documentation of the art environment as it was during Helen Martins' lifetime. The hermit-like Miss Helen disliked being photographed and not many pictures of her exist. Johann Potgieter's photographs of Miss Helen and her Owl House therefore give us a rare glimpse of the elderly artist and the world of her making.

I wish to express my thanks to my husband Trevor, who conceived the idea that I should write this book, and to our four children, Stephen, Clare, David and James, who created the space for me to spend solitary time and energy on this undertaking.

I wish to express my appreciation to Alison Lowry of Penguin for her assistance and, especially, for her faith in the merit of publishing a book on Helen Martins' Owl House.

Anne Emslie
CAPE TOWN
JANUARY 1991

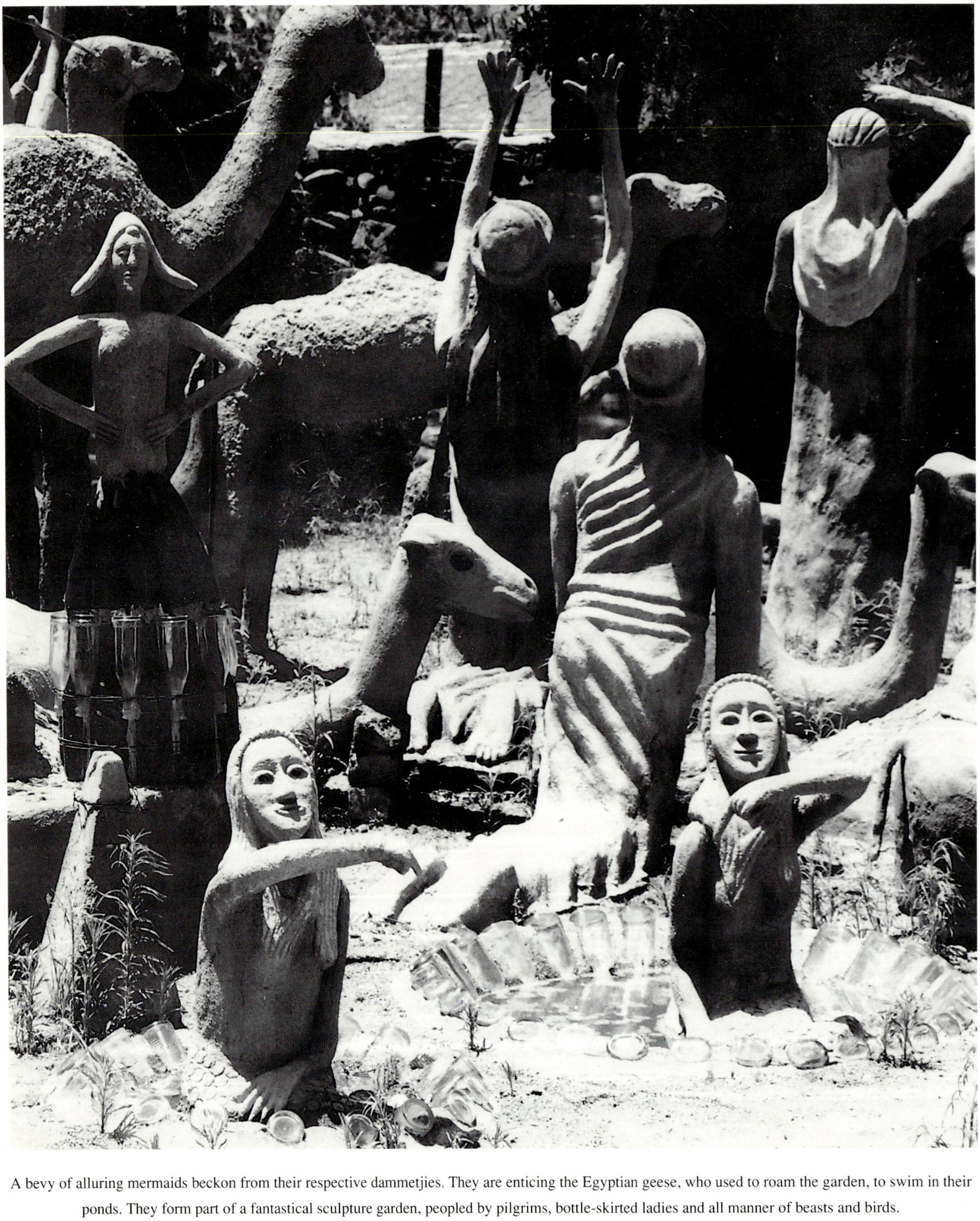

A bevy of alluring mermaids beckon from their respective dammetjies. They are enticing the Egyptian geese, who used to roam the garden, to swim in their ponds. They form part of a fantastical sculpture garden, peopled by pilgrims, bottle-skirted ladies and all manner of beasts and birds.

Part One: MISS HELEN'S WORLD

One cold day in the winter of 1976 Koos Malgas returned to the Owl House. He had been absent for only an hour or so, doing chores for his employer. She was Helen Martins, the owner of the Owl House, and known locally as 'Miss Helen'. Koos had an unusual job. He built statues in Miss Helen's garden. On this fateful winter's day he knew something was wrong the moment he arrived at the house. A neighbour, Mrs Hartzenberg, was waiting outside on the stoep. 'Where have you been?' she exclaimed. 'Your madam has done a terrible thing!' He followed her through to the kitchen where they found the dominee and his wife, as well as the district nurse, Sister Alice.

Miss Helen was being supported on a couch. She looked ashen and frightened and blood oozed from her mouth. Her tongue was swollen and she could not speak, but she beckoned to Koos and indicated that she wanted him to open the drawer of the kitchen dresser where she kept her letter-writing paper. Koos opened the drawer and found a letter. Koos, however, had never learned to read. He therefore handed the letter to Dominee Cloete, who read it silently to himself and then passed it on to his wife. In it Miss Helen had left instructions as to where she had hidden her money, but Mrs Cloete did not pass this information on to Koos. For years he wondered about that letter and what Miss Helen might have written, but no one ever told him.

Koos had noticed, when he entered the kitchen, a number of items on the table. There was a spoon and a cup. Next to these were a bottle of castor oil and a packet of the caustic soda that Miss Helen used to clean her floors.

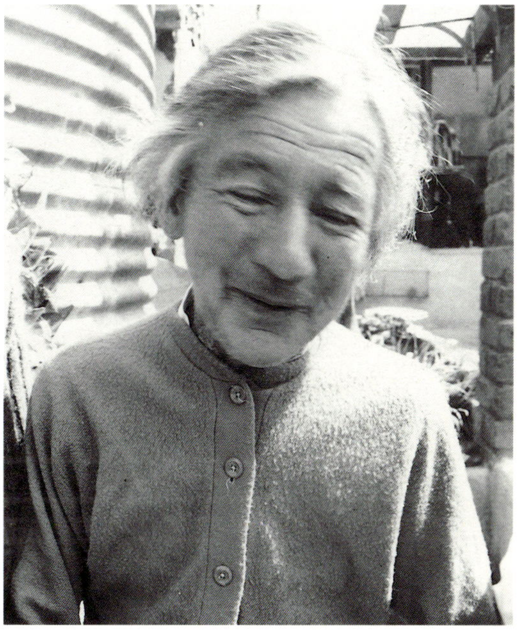

Johann Potgieter photographed the elderly Helen Martins at the Owl House. He describes her: 'She smelt of ginger and had a slight stubbly moustache.'

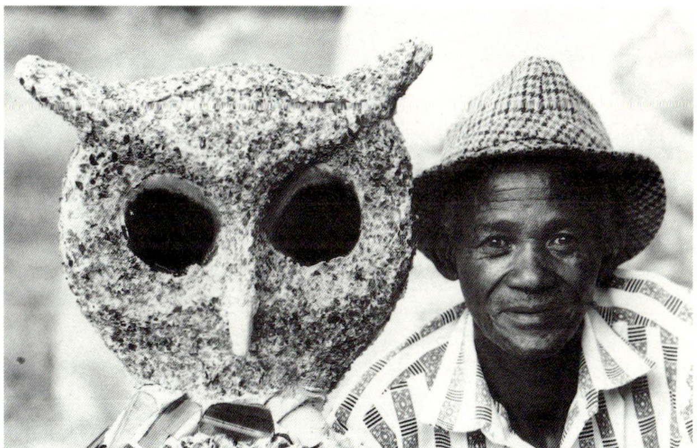

Koos Malgas, alongside one of the owls he built in Miss Helen's yard.

Koos knew what Miss Helen had done. Earlier that morning she had said to him: 'Koos, if I had a gun, I'd ask you to shoot me.'

'You want me to land in jail, and be accused of murder? No, Miss Helen must not say such things!'

He had tried to talk her out of her suicidal thoughts. But when he went out later to pay her insurance and collect some groceries, he was worried enough to stop off at the police station and ask the officer on duty to drive over to the Owl House and check up on Miss Helen. To this day, Koos feels bitter that the policeman first went home for lunch. Koos had wrapped Miss Helen in a blanket and was gently carrying her out to the waiting car when the police vehicle drew up. Miss Helen, accompanied by the local nursing sister, Alice Meyer, was taken to the hospital in Graaff-Reinet.

She died in hospital three days later, from caustic soda poisoning. It was 1976 and she was seventy-eight years old.

The village was shocked. Mrs Cloete thinks back to that time:

> *We could not imagine why she should have taken her life, but it was believed that she feared she was turning blind and did not want to be dependent on others. We honestly never realised she was so deeply depressed. We visited her in hospital. She was unconscious but she appeared serene, dressed in a blue nightie. My husband offered a prayer for her and after that we left.*

At that time not many people knew about Miss Helen and her Owl House. She had lived an isolated, reclusive life in the remote dorp of Nieu Bethesda in the heart of the South African Great Karoo.

Nieu Bethesda was first founded as a centre of worship for the local farmers. The Dutch Reformed Minister, Ds Charles Murray, on seeing the valley with its plentiful supply of water, is reported to have said, 'Let there be a new Bethesda here.' Bethesda, meaning 'house of the stream', was a pool in Jerusalem visited by the Jews for its healing powers. In Miss Helen's youth Nieu Bethesda was a thriving community, but times change and lack of opportunity led to a gradual exodus of residents in search of employment in the larger towns. Since 1961 there has not even been a permanent minister in town.

The skyline of Nieu Bethesda is still dominated by the fine spire of the local Dutch Reformed church, but it is another, smaller spire, a miniature version of the town's, built in the back garden of Miss Helen's house on River Street, which now attracts more attention, for Miss Helen's Owl House has become well known and today visitors come from far and wide to see it.

The Owl House is a strange place, a place unlike any other. First, there is the cage of cement owls on the front veranda. In stony, perpetual silence, they stare outwards with large, all-seeing glass eyes. They are the guards. From the beak of one owl, ghoulish, hangs the limp body of its prey. Above the front door another owl is perched with wings outstretched, as if ready to swoop.

Further along, adjacent to the front veranda, is a moon-shaped gateway. Before it a high fence has been erected which effectively seals off the gateway, so that no entry is possible.

On top of the Moon Gate is perched yet another cement owl. This one is two-faced, looking both inwards towards the garden and outwards towards the road and the river. It is an ever-watchful, all-seeing presence that guards both ways. The Owl House is well fortified. It is also aptly named.

Behind the protective wire fencing and a row of tall cactus plants with menacing thorns stands the miniature church. Its spire is visible from the road outside. It is part of a sculpture garden that might be someone's private dreamscape. The garden is peopled with a surging throng of pilgrims, ecstatic figures in acrobatic poses, elegant, wide-skirted ladies and a bevy of alluring mermaids. A

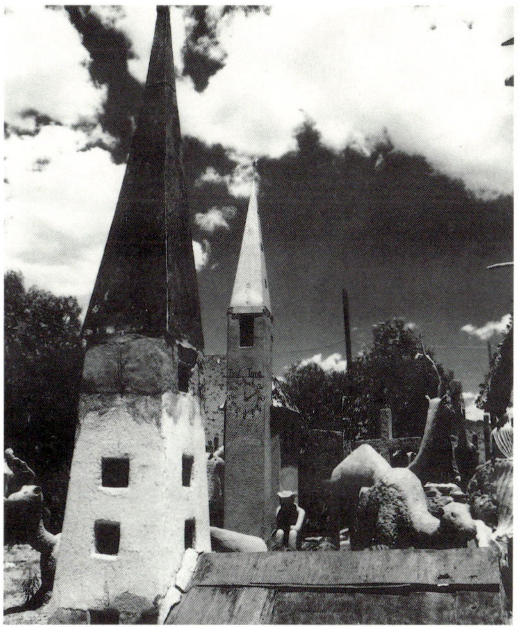

Leading the life of a recluse, and never attending the local church, Miss Helen built her own churches and spires as part of her self- contained sculptural world.

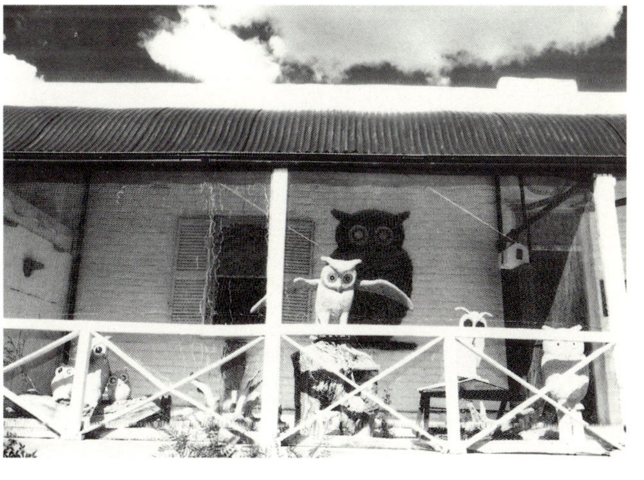

A cage of cement owls with large glass eyes staring outwards from the front veranda. Never off guard, they are a perpetually watchful and vigilant presence.

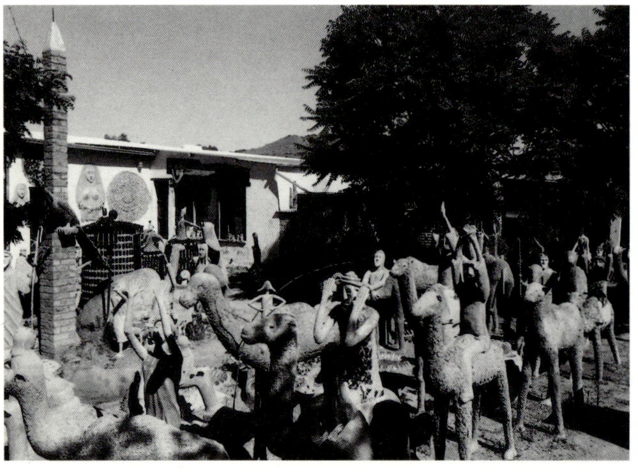

Numerous, nearly life-size camels form a caravan that travels through the part of Miss Helen's backyard that she thought of as Egypt.

multitude of beasts and birds are all crammed together: peacocks, herons, a lion, giraffes, camels and owls. There is one fabulous creature that is half-owl and half-camel. Miniature buildings and other architectural edifices are scattered among the people and the creatures. They, too, are a part of this beautiful and bizarre world.

When Miss Helen committed suicide the Owl House was not complete. Still in Miss Helen's fertile and active mind were a number of schemes which never came to fruition. There was the plan to create hollowed-out niches in her sculptured pyramids where she intended to insert statues. Another plan involved the painting of the cement camels and their riders. The paint for this project still stands in the storeroom. A friend, Jill Wenman, who accompanied her to the nearby town of Graaff-Reinet to buy it remembers vividly the look of bemusement and incredulity on the face of the salesman. He saw before him a diminutive, wrinkled old lady, with a few grey wisps of old-woman's beard and startlingly large and lively blue eyes, requesting paint for her camels. On discovering that there were about three dozen nearly life-size cement camels in her back yard, the salesman could not contain his astonishment.

His astonishment might have been even greater had he realised how many more cement statues Miss Helen's back garden boasted. The space is so claustrophobically crowded, it is perhaps not surprising that, after her death, there were people who came to believe she committed suicide simply because she ran out of space and there was nothing more for her to do. The truth was far more desperate. With old age came the increasingly crippling arthritis from which she suffered, and she had reached a point where she was unable to care for herself properly. However, it was the increasing lassitude which affected her daily activities and the very real problem of failing eyesight that finally caused intolerable depression. Shortly before she ended her life, she wrote to a friend, Francie Lund:

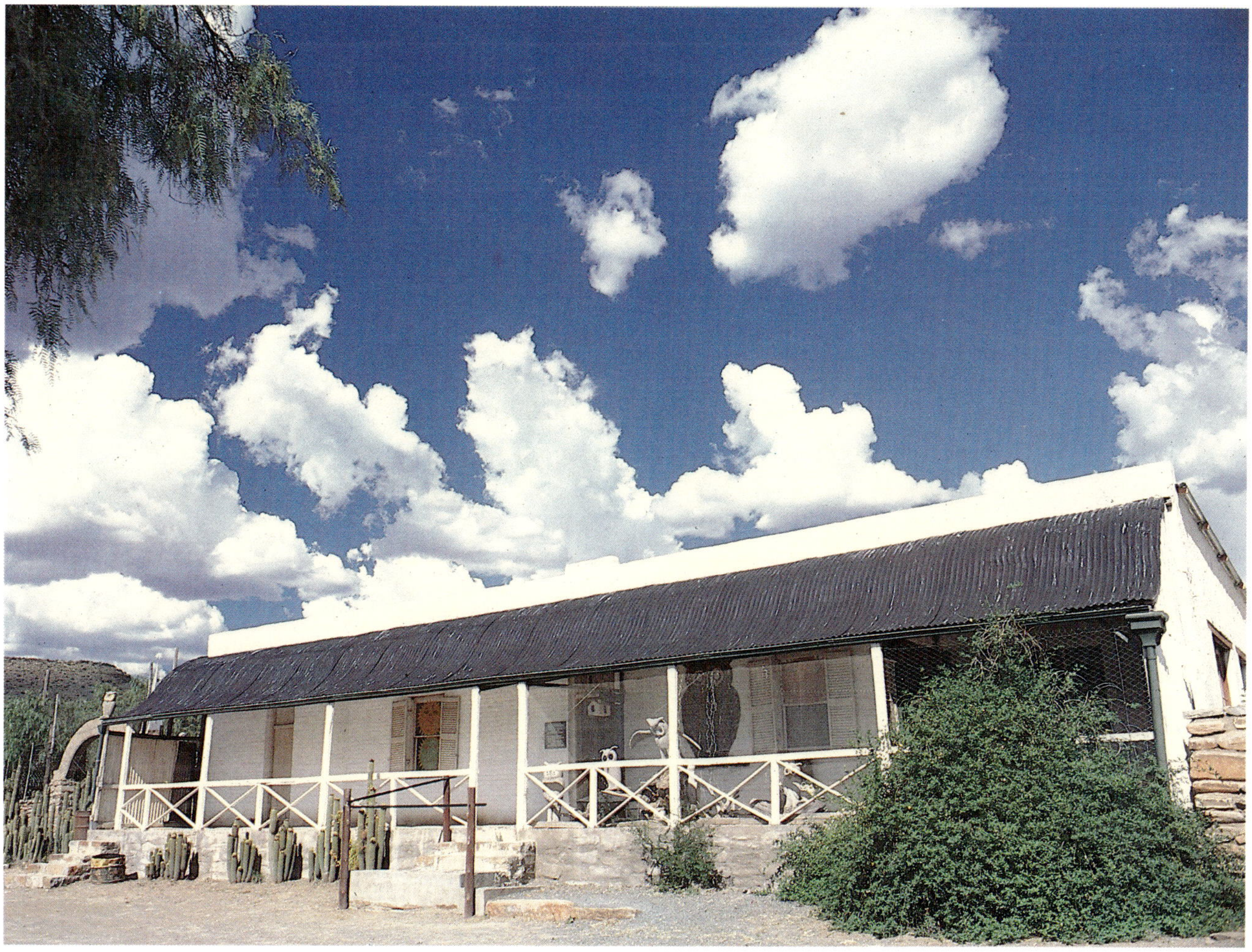

The front façade of *the Owl* **HOUSE** is typical of many Karoo dwellings, but there are certain oddities which hint at this being no ordinary residence. There is a cage of cement owls on the front stoep, and on the front windows are frosted suns, made from glass dust glued to the panes. They are an example of one of Miss Helen's reversals of the natural order of things, shining out brightly only at night, when the rooms are lit up from behind.

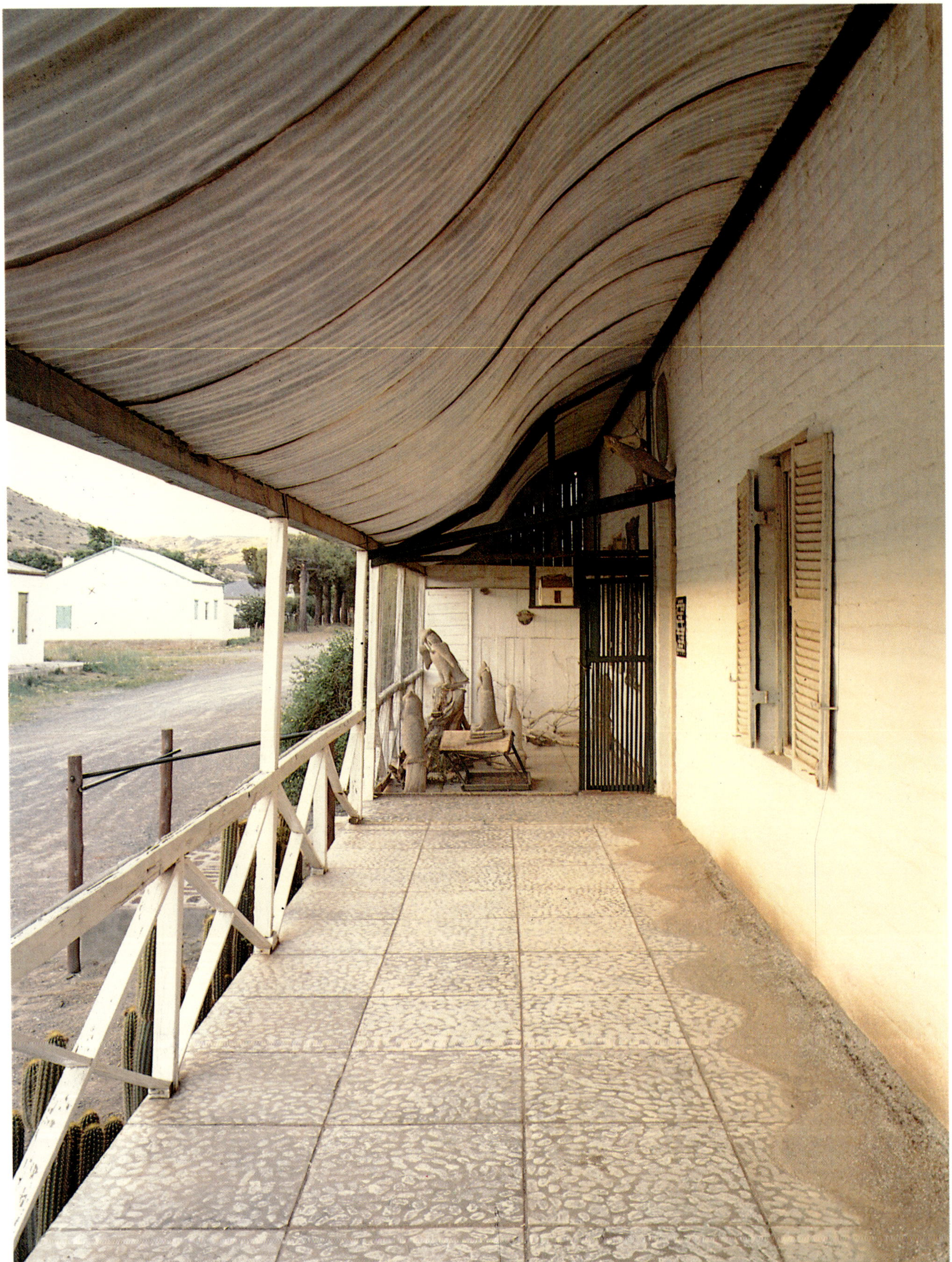

A view of the front veranda with the owl cage at one end. The cement floor has been festooned with a wavy shoreline of seasand that runs along the wall of the house. The smattering of white flecks denote the surf of a tide. They may also be interpreted as snowflakes which have drifted down on some cold and bleak winter's day. The shutters and doors facing onto the veranda are also covered with a thick coating of snow, made from finely crushed glass mixed with cement. It is clear that Helen Martins wished to indicate that the world outside *the Owl* **HOUSE** was very cold and very bleak. She wished, too, with the imagery of the sea and sand, to indicate that arriving at *the Owl* **HOUSE** was akin to coming in from the vast ocean and arriving at some welcome shore.

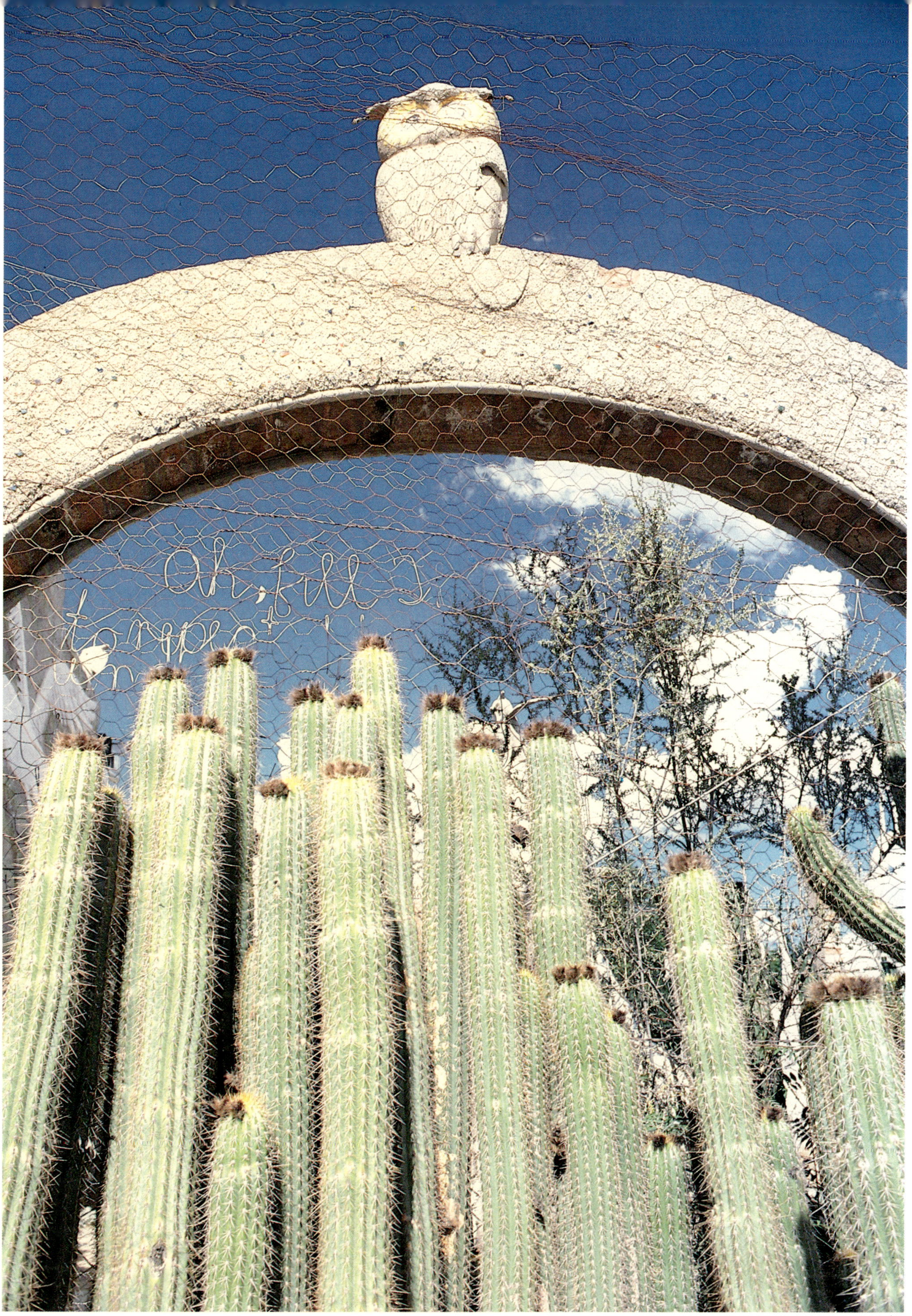

Alongside the veranda is the Moon Gate. Sitting on the crest of its arch is a double-faced owl. One of Miss Helen's guards, he is staring outwards towards the road, as well as keeping a watchful eye over the Camel Yard, in the other direction. A tantalising glimpse through the fence, of steeples and statuary, is the first indication that an extraordinary fantasy world lies beyond, built largely from glass and cement. On the wire of the fence is a quatrain, taken from the *Rubáiyát*, extolling the virtue of grasping present pleasures and living in the moment. Against the wire fence is a thick cluster of Queen of the Night cactus plants, with their vicious thorns. Helen planted these to form a protective barricade for the sculpture garden. This was an important plant for Helen, and is also in evidence amongst the statues. The flower of the cactus, with its perfumed, lotus-like blooms, flowers around Christmas time. It lends an air of festivity to *the Owl* **HOUSE** at this significant time of the year for Helen Martins, whose sculpture garden, on one level, is a vast celebratory tribute to the birth of the Divine child.

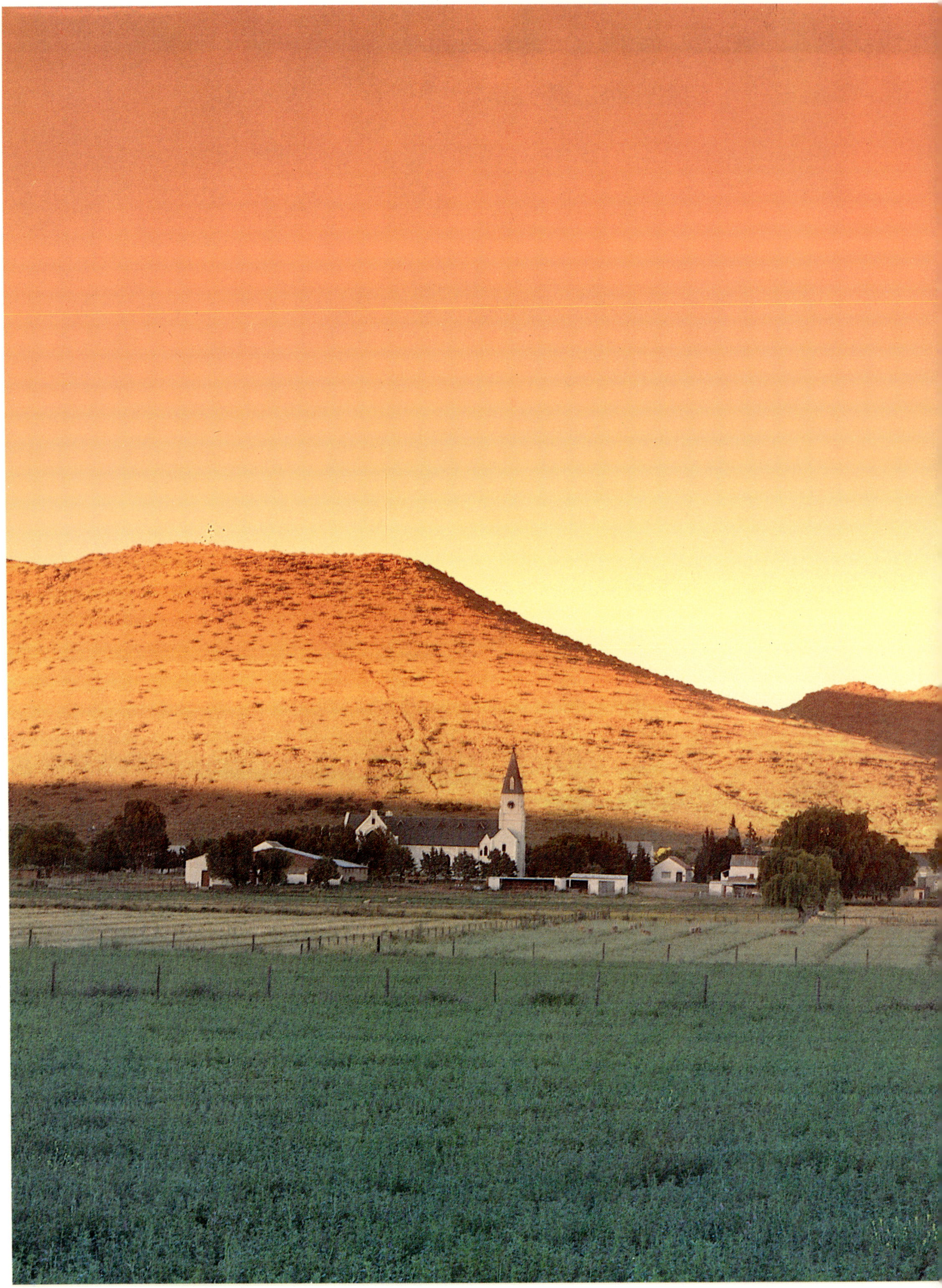

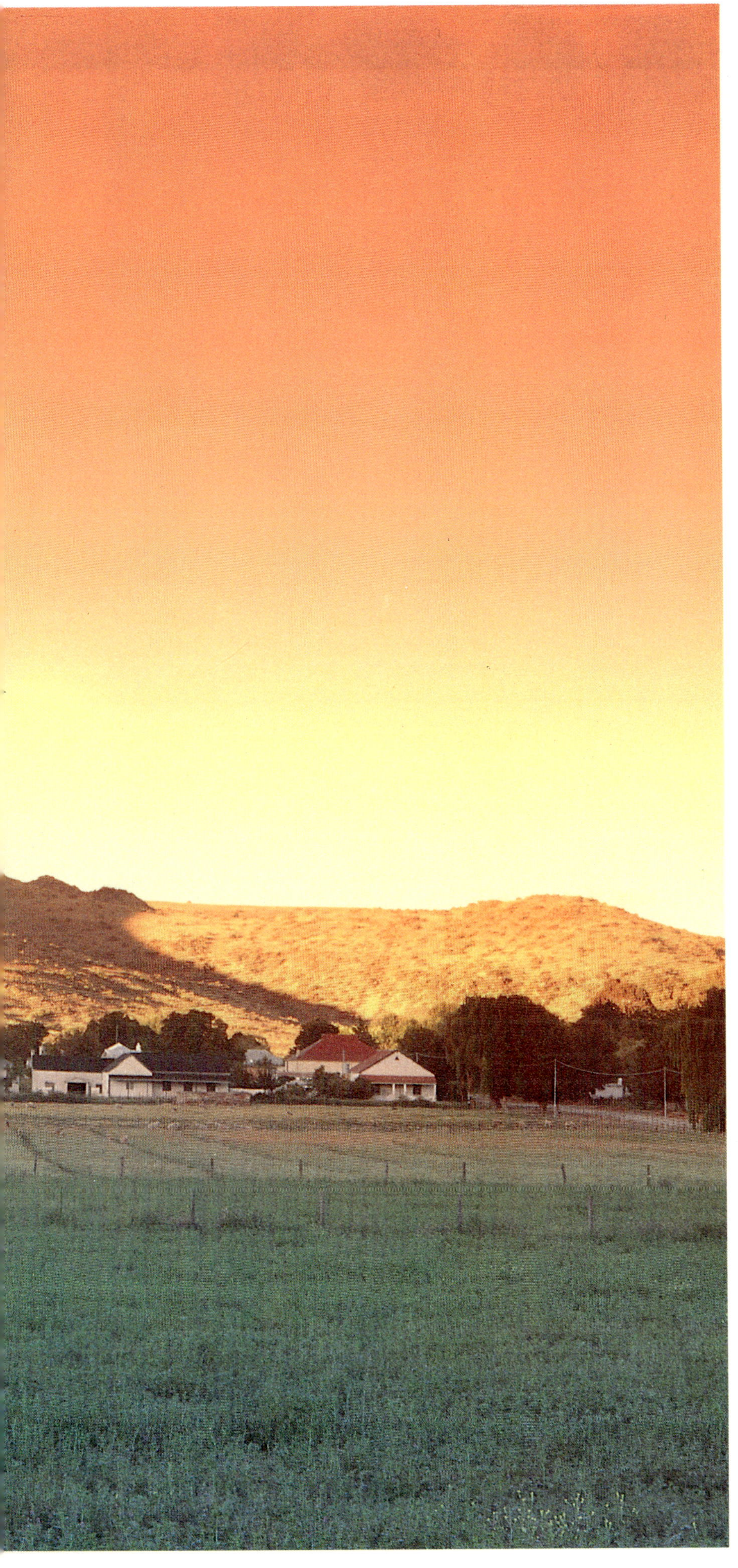

The Owl **HOUSE** is situated in the small and isolated Karoo village of Nieu Bethesda. The surrounding countryside, for this part of the world, is surprisingly lush and verdant, being irrigated by water that is channeled down from mountain springs. The local Dutch Reformed church, with its imposing spire, has for many years been the centre of worship for the local community. The steeple in Miss Helen's Camel Yard resembles, in miniature, that of the village church. This is one of the innumerable ways in which the environment influenced Miss Helen's artistic imagery.

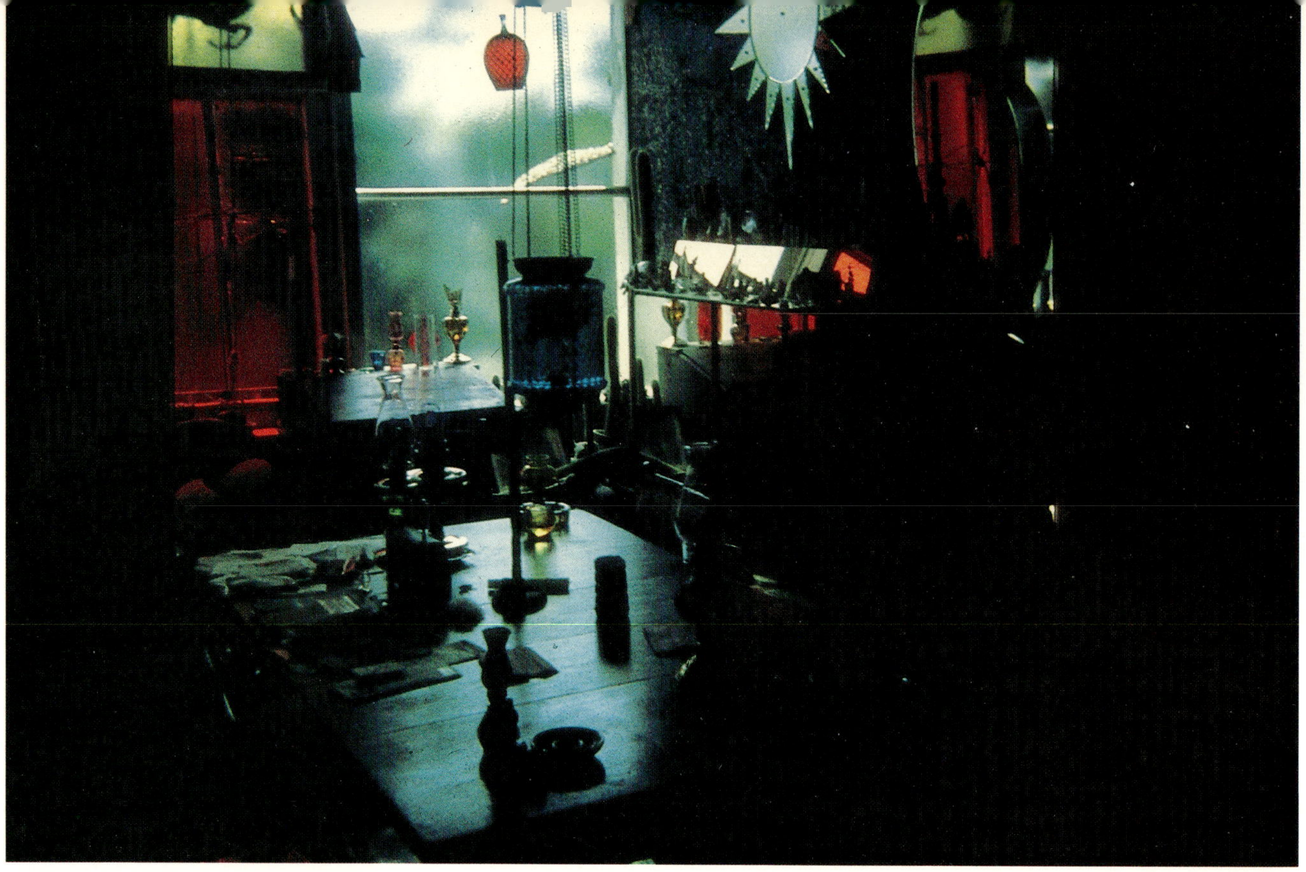

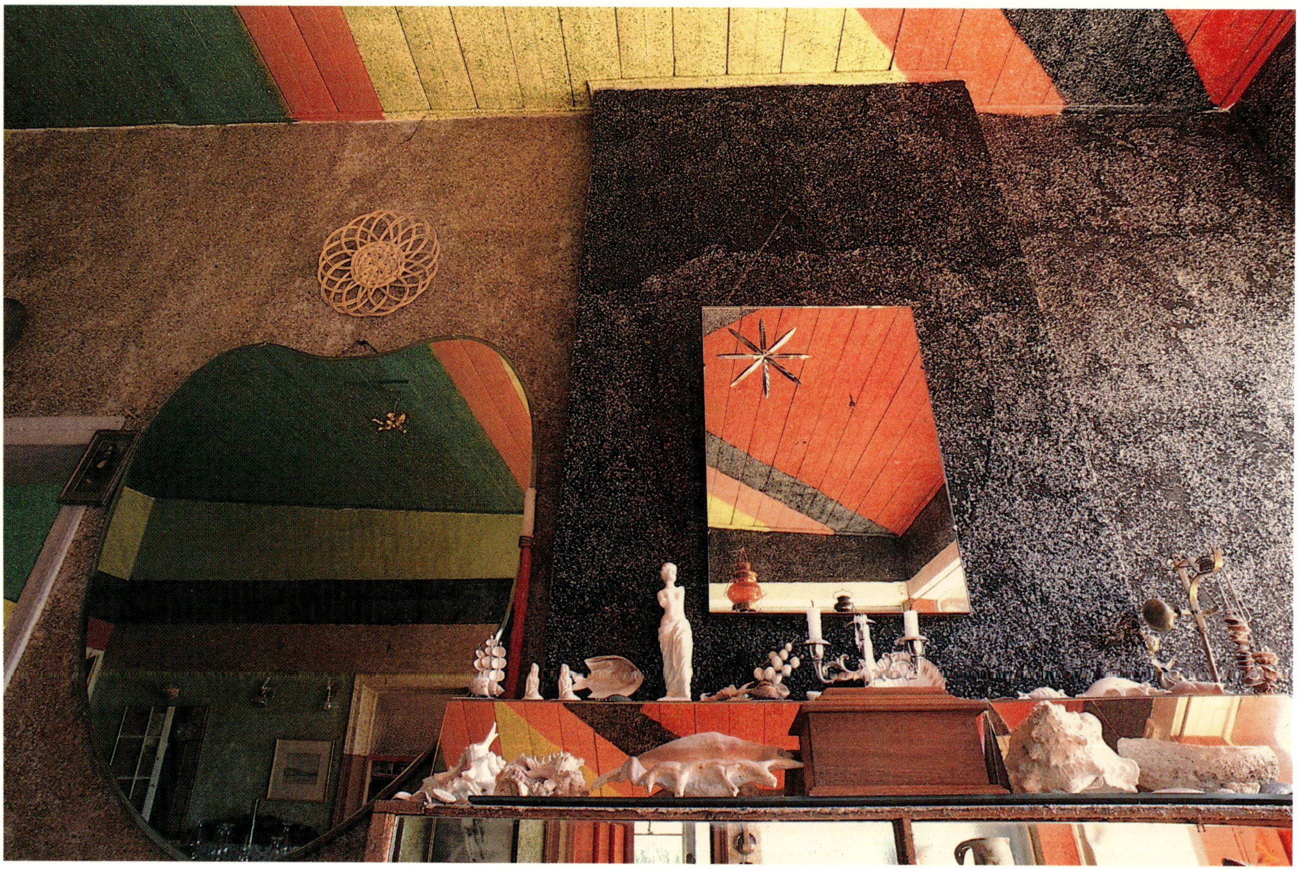

Top: The main living-room as it looked when Helen lived at *the* **OWL HOUSE**. It can be seen that the room once held a fine old table upon which many lamps were displayed. Other lamps were suspended from the ceiling. A large sun mirror, now gone, hung against the dark, crushed glass surface of the wall. The extensive use of mirrors, lamps and coloured glass lent a rich, sparkling and bejewelled quality to the interior.

(*Photograph*: **J VAN MEYEREN**)

Above: Mirrors on the wall of the main living-room reflect fragments of the colourful ceiling geometry. Walls and ceiling have been coated with patchwork colours of paint to which myriad glass particles adhere, shimmering when they catch the light. The mirrored shelf supports many shells, indicative of Helen's preoccupation with seaside imagery. It also holds a wooden casket. This contains Helen's ashes; the ashes that she had hoped might one day be sprinkled and glued over her favourite cement owl, Oswald.

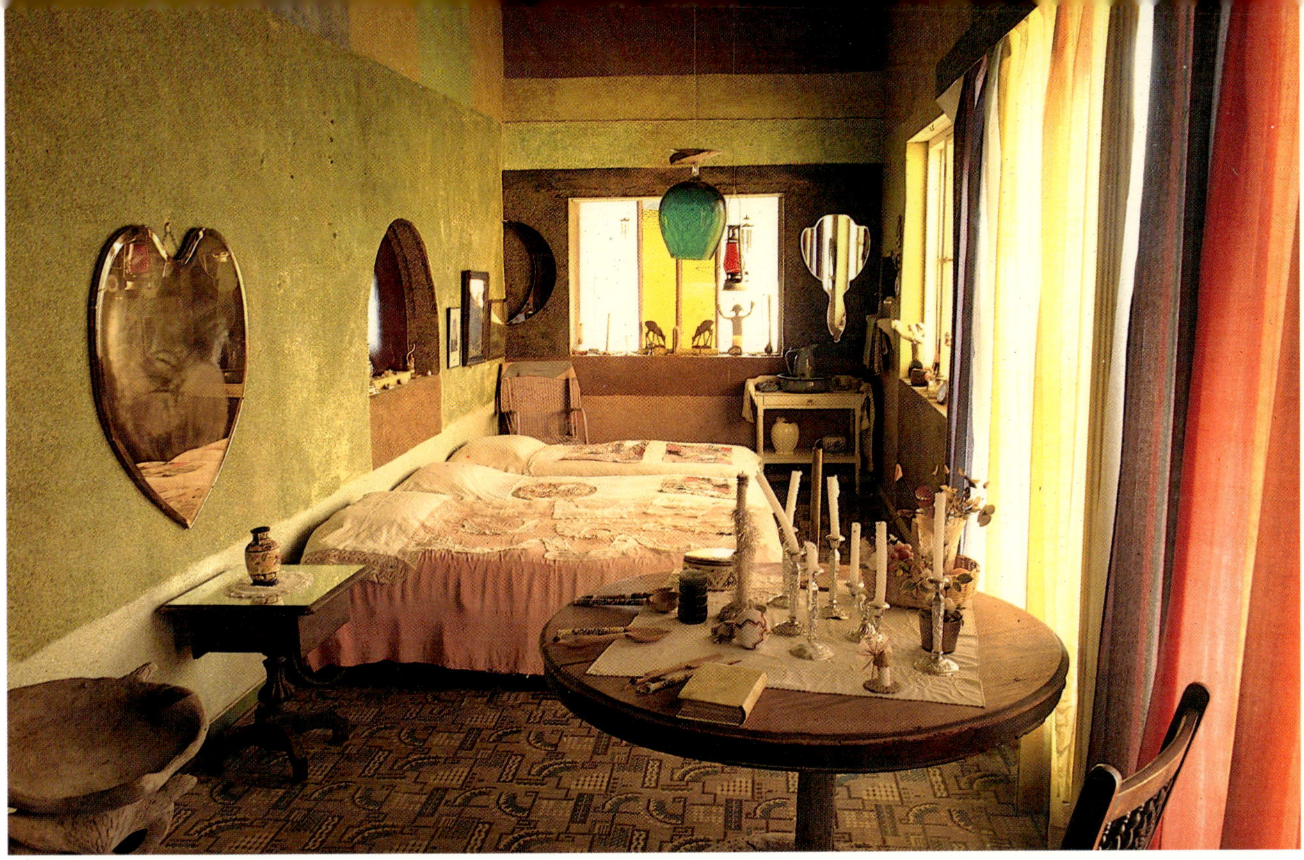

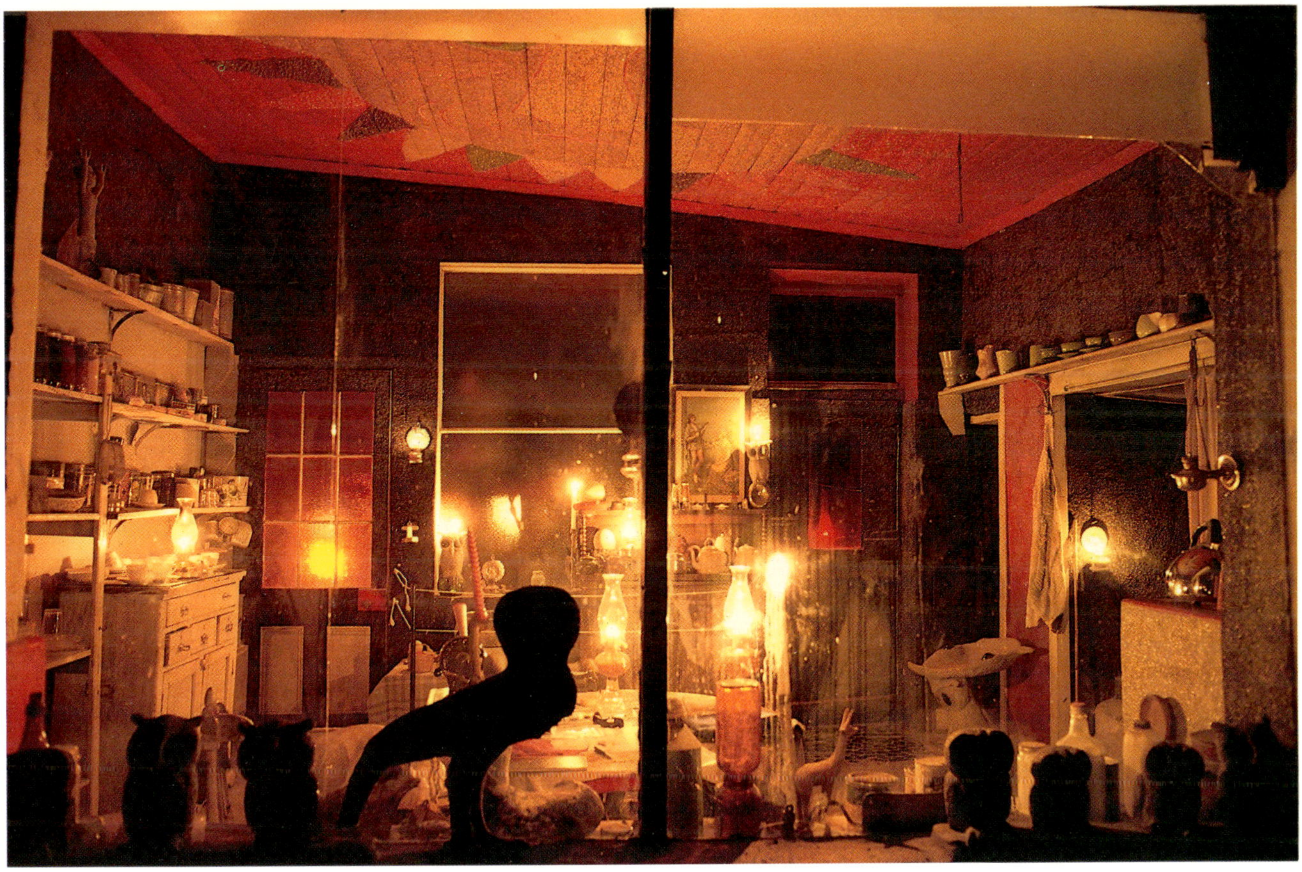

Top: This long bedroom, once a porch, is where Miss Helen slept. Fine lace and satin covers displayed on the beds, lend an air of opulence to the room. Multi-hued sun-filter curtains and a glittering length of tinselled nylon fabric hang at the windows. Miss Helen's love of sparkling light effects is also evident in her use of an upturned green glass vase that hangs from the ceiling. Many more of these upturned vases used to be suspended from the ceilings of the house. The glass shone in the sunlight, creating the equivalent of day-time lamps. As in this room, hanging from the walls of the house are an inordinate number of mirrors, many of which she requested the supplier to shape to her specifications. Favourite shapes were the heart and the giant hand-mirror, as well as stars, suns and moons.

Above: At night, by star and lamplight, both the garden and the house take on an aura of enchantment.

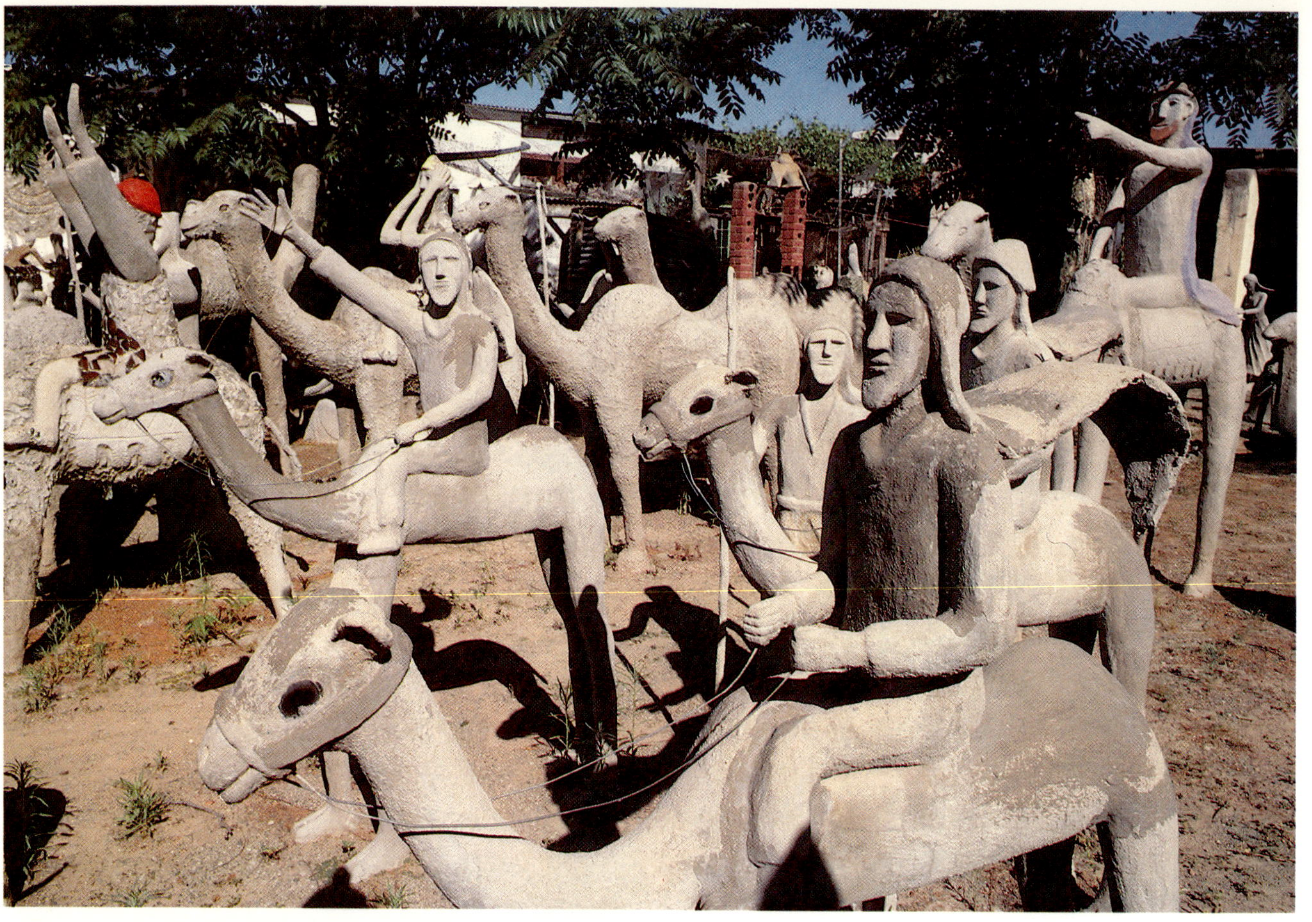

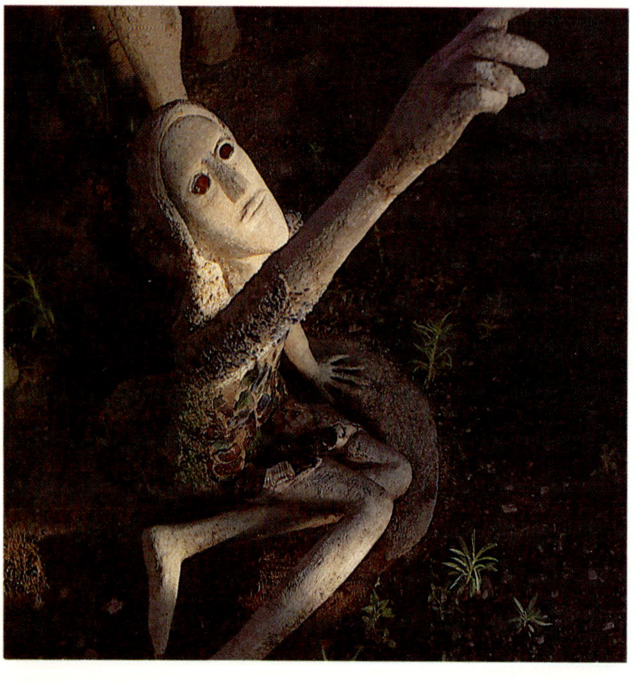

A surging mass of pilgrims presses forward, filled with fervour. The garden is crammed with statues and infused with a sense of spiritual urgency. 'There is no rest in it,' recalls Peggy Delport, who knew Miss Helen, 'and it all made me feel quite claustrophobic.'

A seated figurine, encrusted with glass, points upwards towards the sign on the fence which reads 'East/Oos'. The absence of baby toes on the feet, an autobiographical detail, suggests that Helen Martins had chosen to place herself in the garden. Helen had once undergone an operation to have the deformed small toes of both feet amputated.

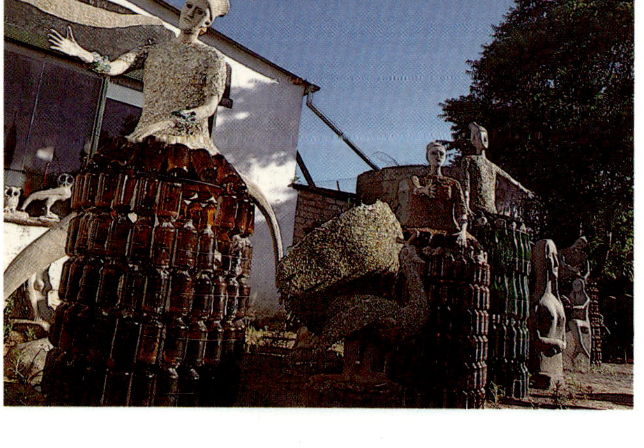

Gracious bottle-skirted hostesses, whom Miss Helen referred to as her *meisies*, guide the way to the Pool of Healing.

... my strength seems to have given in: a dead sleepiness overwhelms me. I cannot keep my eyes open, not for anything — should the doctor advise that I should leave off working, then I shall die; and directly.

In a letter to Jill Wenman she expressed fears about her fading sight:

I am prey of deep depression which I cannot shake off — hence the reason why I cannot and do not write to you. I have lost my eyesight. I do not know what it is — I seem to see through a mist. I feel frightfully worried.

She was concerned about the consequences if her approaching blindness should become public knowledge:

The darkness is gathering around me — I am so depressed. I beg you, breathe it to no one — to NO ONE — if you do it will make matters worse for me. I have done nothing wrong. I have harmed no one; I am only very depressed. Oh, why should this have come over me? I wonder if Nortjie could have felt worse — if only I had the little yellow pill.

Nortjie was a promising young South African poet who committed suicide in his early twenties. He wrote a poem entitled *Notes From the Middle of the Night* in which the idea of blotting out fear with a little yellow pill appears in the second verse:

inside me blooms a sudden wish
to calm fright with a little yellow pill,
lull it to a predawn slumber,
escape by soporific in an orange capsule.
There blows a flowering death release
in winds from Lethe, Styx or anywhere
forgetfulness resides.

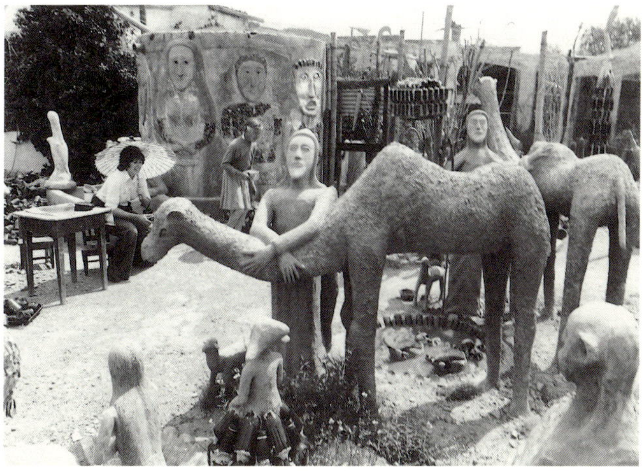

Miss Helen and Francie Lund in the sculpture garden. Miss Helen's work was the prime focus of her life, into which she channelled all her time, energy and money. Francie remembers a visit to the Owl House with Jill Wenman, when a kindly neighbour had brought Helen a cake. Helen became 'silly, senile, giggly. She put herself right down.' Afterwards she explained her behaviour: 'That's why they think I am crazy, the village idiot. And behaving like that keeps them away and I can get on with my work.' (Photograph: Johann Potgieter)

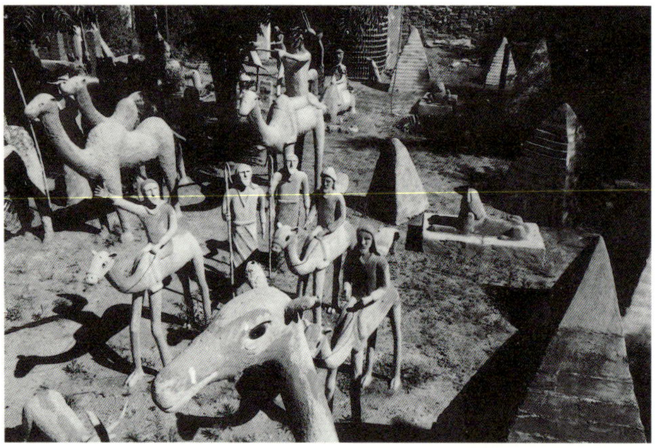

Wise men and their camels march to the East with purposeful intent. When Helen first started making her camels, she realised that she had orientated them wrongly. She simply put a bilingual sign on the fence, saying East/Oos, adjusting the world to her creatures. John Moyle remembers his response when Helen pointed out and explained her sign. 'I found it quite uncanny, the literal consistency of her vision. This was indeed her world and she, as creator and operator of it, felt entitled even to manipulate the cardinal points of the compass; crazy but a kind of Divine craziness.'

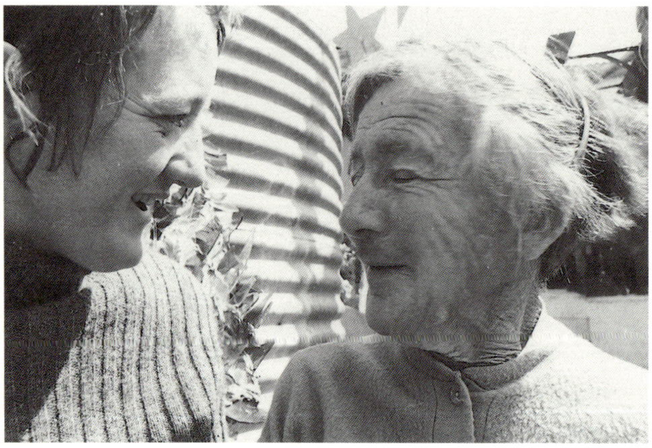

Jill Wenman (left) and Helen became close friends. Jill drove up from Cape Town to visit Helen at intervals, and they corresponded frequently. The friendship, support and encouragement of both Jill and Francie meant a great deal to Helen during the final years of her life. Reciprocally, Helen, as Francie comments, got them caught up in her world. 'Jill and I once built a fourteen foot crocodile out of concrete in the garden of my rented house in Claremont. My landlord had put up the rent twice. I left the house in good condition, but he had to deal with a fourteen foot crocodile, with china teeth and toenails in the yard.'
(Photograph: Johann Potgieter)

To Jill Miss Helen had once described the importance of her work:

> *Now, darling, as you get older, you realize that dying isn't the problem ... living is the problem. That is why you have got to live it well and to the full. My agony would be to 'live dying' without being able to work.*

How was she perceived in her lifetime, this woman who devoted the last quarter century of her life to the task of transforming her home into a bittersweet world of concrete and glass, a world filled with both enchantment and Angst, with consummate delight and with much pain and deep yearning? An acquaintance, Johann Potgieter, describes her:

> *She smelt of ginger and had a slight stubbly moustache. She was strange but not intolerably so, a somewhat dotty, eccentric aunt. A not unfamiliar type.*

Matie Cupido, who grew up in the house across the river from Miss Helen's Owl House, remembers that she was 'very much alive'. Matie recalled:

> *When she spoke to you she moved close, and when you moved back, she moved forward! She was a very affectionate woman. Very excitable. Miss Helen never said foolish things. There was no idle talk. When she spoke to us she never used Afrikaans. It was always English, although we were all bilingual.*

A neighbour, Cynthia Craig, whose father owned a shop next door to the Owl House, found her '... educated and beautifully spoken'.

She had a heart of gold. She was tiny, a sweet little thing; and she was a born romantic. But she had a terrible complex. She was so shy of people. She would rush out at five o'clock in the morning to collect water from the furrow for her garden. The furrow, which brought water to the village from up in the hills, ran past our house. If anyone was around when Miss Helen was out collecting water she would disappear indoors again. She was a lonely soul and only certain people were allowed to visit her. They had a particular knock for her front door which she was able to recognise before opening the door to admit them. Yes, she was certainly very shy of people. When the English minister came to Nieu Bethesda, as he did once a month, Tannie Hartzenberg would try to persuade Miss Helen to come along to the service, which was always held in one of the houses of the English-speaking people in the town. 'Now get yourself tidied up, put on that nice white dress of yours and come along,' Tannie Hartzenberg would say to Miss Helen. But Miss Helen never came. I once saw her all dressed up, a nice white bow in her hair, on her way to the service. But she was halfway down the road when she turned back. Perhaps she didn't like people looking at her. She was a frightened little thing.

How would I describe Miss Helen? I picture her wearing her frilly little dark dress with no shoes, or else just slip-slops. Her hair was always untidy. It was thick and frizzy, not unlike the perms some young people spend so much money on these days. She was not quite witch and not quite fairy. She was unique. There will never be another Miss Helen.

Jill Wenman was perhaps closer to the elderly Miss Helen than anyone else. She describes her as having

... a rare zest for living, a sharp wit and a burning enthusiasm for her glitter, wise men, owls, 'meccas' and suns — to mention but a few of the characters that made up her world. Most people in the village thought she was a crazy old misfit who wasted her money and time. Not that that seemed to bother her — it allowed her to get on with her work without being disturbed. 'I think they think it is a waste of time to argue with a mad person,' she once remarked, her eyes twinkling with mirth. Yet she was not unaffected by the remoteness, especially towards the end when she began to get tired and became frail. Then I think she missed some warm companionship and love.

John Moyle, who was with Jill when she first met Miss Helen, remembers:

She was tiny, thin and bird-like, in a faded cotton, little-girl dress, which was seemingly all she was wearing in the heat. She was shy and exaggeratedly self-deprecating. But when she spoke of and demonstrated her work, her diffidence was completely eclipsed by her enthusiasm — enthusiasm in the original meaning of the word: 'possessed by a god'.

She was brimful with excitement and energy, as another acquaintance, Peggy Delport, who owns a holiday house in Nieu Bethesda, comments:

She came across with excitement all the time. She just buzzed. Her mind was going and she had this self-generating energy. There was so much that was just bursting to come out on every kind of level. There was so much curiosity and excitement. And it wasn't only that she was single-minded about a certain vision and the work that she was formulat-

> *ing. Every aspect of the world around her was touching on her and making some connection with some other kind of world. Maybe it was a spiritual excitement. She was very imaginative, very romantic as well, very passionate, one felt; and she loved fine things, beautiful clothes, glitter. She was very sensual. In fact she was almost disturbing in that way. One felt all the time she wanted to open up her whole life and past. She was almost fuller than one imagined could be possible for someone who was so little and so circumscribed by the circumstances of her life.*

Miss Helen's intensity and her desire to live life to the full are reflected in a verse from the *Rubáiyát* which she chose to copy out in wire lettering. Together with the words 'A Camel Yard' (her title for the sculpture garden), it is the only writing that has been attached to the outside of the fence. It reads like a personal credo:

> *Ah, fill the Cup: — what boots it to repeat*
> *How time is slipping underneath our Feet:*
> *Unborn TO-MORROW, and dead YESTERDAY,*
> *Why fret about them if TODAY be sweet.*

And in the garden a bottle-skirted lady, as if in fulfilment of this credo, serves alcoholic refreshment to a seated gentleman. Other bottle-skirted ladies, tall, graceful and bejewelled, seem to be pointing the way, greeting and directing visitors along a path that leads to a pool of water. Above the pool a relief sculpture on the side of a water tank depicts an image that once appeared on the packaging of a well-known brand of headache powders. A woman clasps her head in her hands. A healing effigy on the opposite side of the tank confirms that this pool is to be understood as a place of healing — an allusion, perhaps, to the biblical Bethesda.

The graceful bottle-skirted ladies are the hostesses of

the garden. Their gestures guide the visitor and are a clear indication that one of the intended ways into the sculpture garden was from the galvanised gate at the side of the stoep. This gate, however, is now always kept locked. It has been locked since the death of Helen Martins.

Miss Helen was most selective as to whom she would permit to enter through the gate. It was a privilege to be admitted. Peggy Delport tells the story of how the artist Walter Battis, having heard of Miss Helen's Owl House, once made a special trip to Nieu Bethesda to visit the place. He knocked and knocked on the galvanised gate. Miss Helen doubtless heard him but, always suspicious of strangers, would not open up; and so missed the rare opportunity of meeting a kindred artist who might have been able to give her the encouragement and admiration that this lonely and misunderstood woman needed so much.

It appears to have been even more of a privilege to be one of the select few allowed to enter via the front door. Friends had their own special knock and, to double-check, Miss Helen would peer through the glass spy-hole in the door before opening up. It was only on Christmas Eve, Cynthia Craig, who was then a child, recollects, that Miss Helen's front door would be opened wide. Then all the lamps and candles in the house would be burning and everyone was welcome.

The Owl House is now a museum and can be freely visited. There is a visitors' book inside the house. It was started by Miss Helen to record the visits of friends and is still in use today. It is an old hardcover exercise book that has been covered in gift-wrap paper and decorated with kitsch sticky-backed flower posies. The comments record a spectrum of reactions:

'Astonishing and very moving.'
'It's overwhelming.'
'This is a very special place.'
'Disturbing work.'

'Strange and beautiful.'
'The real gem of the Karoo.'

Many visitors sense a certain melancholy in the work:

'Speechless and very sad.'
'Soulful but sad.'
'Wonderful and sad. Please repair before it is all lost.'

The plea to preserve is often voiced:

'Must be conserved at all costs.'
'Odd — but fascinating. Should be maintained and preserved.'
'This place should be preserved for future generations as a symbol of man's hunger for the divine and the mystery of his dreams.'

The book now lies on an old desk-top in the main living-room of the house. The walls and the ceiling of this room, and every other room in the house, are coated in crushed glass in multifaceted hues that have been worked into intricate geometric patterns. The glass coating even spreads to some of the furniture. There is the bizarre spectacle of chairs with glass dust glued to their seats. Like the walls with their sharp shards of glass, these chairs glitter and twinkle enticingly, at the same time alluring and hazardous.

There are numerous mirrors hanging on the walls of the interior. Many of these have been cut into special shapes — hearts, suns, stars and moons. A number are fashioned to look like giant hand-mirrors, so that the viewer is left with an Alice in Wonderland sensation of having shrunk to Lilliputian size.

The mirrors do more than distort the viewer's sense of size. They also distort the space, opening up unexpected vistas: odd glimpses of patterned ceilings, slices of adjacent rooms, fragments of the outside sculpture garden, views into other mirrors which ripple into infinity, multiplying and enlarging the interior. And the mirrors have another interesting effect. For the visitor, caught in a tangle of multitudinous reflections, the threshold between the real and the unreal begins to dissolve. There is a sense of ambiguity. There is also the enchantment: the walls glitter, the mirrors reflect and the interior could be some vast magic glitter-box of kaleidoscopic lighting effects.

That Miss Helen should have chosen to put up so many mirrors when, as Jill Wenman once observed, she disliked encountering her own reflection is a measure of their symbolic importance to her. Because she found her own appearance distressing, many of the mirrors were deliberately placed above her eye-level.

It is not only the mirrors that open up the interior spaces. Walls have been knocked out and large sheets of glass inserted in their place. Some of the picture windows look out towards the exterior, linking the interior of the house with the sculpture garden beyond. Other sheets of glass have been inserted into inside walls. Much of the glass, being tinted, transmits filtered rays of coloured light so that the interior becomes bathed in soft washes of shifting colour that add to the sense of an enchanted space.

Helen Martins played a magician's game with light; by day with sunlight, at night with lamp and candlelight. The vast array of lamps and candles in the house testify to this. As a museum, the house is never open at night and consequently the candles and the lamps are never lit. Jill Wenman remembers the house with the lamps and the candles glowing: 'It looked like bloody fairyland,' she said. But it is at night that the house comes alive. Much of the tattiness and shabbiness become shrouded and shadowed. The walls glitter and sparkle as they catch the light. It becomes easier to enter into a spirit of make-believe. New and intriguing facets of the house come into focus.

There is, for instance, the sun's face on the kitchen ceiling. Although both day and night it beams down with benign goodwill, it is only at night, when the lamplight is caught and reflected by the ground glass mosaic patterning from which it is created, that the sun actually appears to be shining. That the sun should be made to shine at night is typical of the paradox and reversal that Helen Martins loved to create. This is a space of complex gameplay and bewildering trickery.

Focusing on the array of pictures, oddments and ornaments that decorate every wall, line every windowsill and are clustered on every shelf and surface, certain linking themes begin to emerge. There is no doubt that Helen Martins was enamoured with the idea of bringing the imagery of the sea and the seashore into this world of her creation. Shells abound. There are even a number of fanciful little sailing boats delicately constructed out of miniature shells glued together; not to mention a vase of artificial flowers, the petals of which, on closer inspection, are made of tiny shells. Then there are the rows of miniature plaster mermaids, which appear to be maquettes for the larger mermaids to be found in the garden. There is also a seashore picture on the wall of the main living-room. In this space, claustrophobically cluttered and haphazard as it may seem, everything has been deliberately and carefully chosen and positioned for effect and for meaning. It is this conscious positioning of objects and deliberate choreographing of effects that makes this no ordinary domestic interior, but a space resonant with symbolic meaning.

The seaside imagery is but one strand of a thick web of interconnecting ideas. It is an important one, however, and its importance becomes clear to the perceptive visitor even before entering the Owl House. On the cement floor of the front veranda, which one must cross in order to arrive at the front door, is a liberally scattered sprinkling of white paint flecks. This is not all. Against the wall of the house, seasand has been glued to the floor to create a

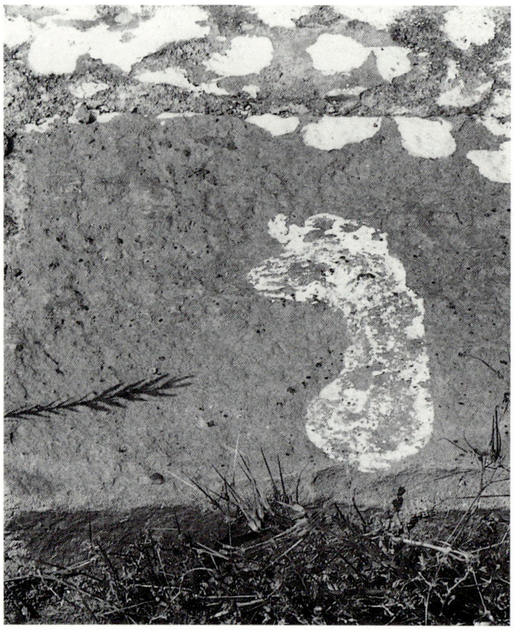

White footprints, as if someone had been walking in the snow, used to be visible on the steps leading up to the stoep. The white paint has long since worn away. The footprints showed only four toes and must have been Miss Helen's.
(Photograph: Johann Potgieter)

wave-like pattern. The white flecks take on the appearance of surf. The sand denotes the seashore with the waves tumbling in. Arriving at the front door, or even the galvanised stoep door that leads to the garden, yes, one has arrived at the Owl House, but one has also crossed an unknown ocean and arrived at an unknown shore.

Miss Helen delighted in double meanings. The spatterings of white paint on the veranda floor are not only flecks of ocean surf. They are also snowflakes that have drifted to the ground. Further snow, laboriously created from cement mixed with glass dust, has gathered thickly on the shutters and the two doors at the front of the house. It must be understood that it is very bleak and very cold out here.

The Owl House appears welcoming and warm, a wonderful refuge from the cruel cold. A smiling sun-mirror above the front door beams down a welcome. There are other suns that shine out from the windows. The idea that the Owl House is to be understood as a refuge and a haven, a respite from the cold, a place of sustenance and refreshment that will harbour the weary and feed the hungry makes perfect sense when details of the interior are examined.

The number of beds, the number of chairs, tables, teapots, cups and saucers in the house declare that numerous visitors are expected. The larder is well stocked with preserves. The house could be an inn with things laid ready for an important festive occasion. It is Christmas all year round at the Owl House. Tinsel festoons the walls and is wrapped around tall candle-holders. Shiny glass baubles hang from the ceiling. The house has been decorated and decked out in appropriate splendour.

Miss Helen had names for some of the rooms in the house. The bedroom off the entrance hall was named the Honeymoon Room. On the window a red sun with green eyes peers in. It is 'the sun with jealous eyes'. The room contains two single beds separated by a wardrobe. Single beds in a honeymoon room do not seem appropriate and when once asked about this, Miss Helen replied enigmatically, 'Ah! But love is always kept apart.'

The creation of the Owl House was the fulcrum of Miss Helen's life around which her thoughts and energies rotated.

Singlemindedly, and with passionate intensity, she devoted her time and money to transforming her domestic environment into a richly symbolic space. It is difficult to imagine that anyone could have lived comfortably in the Owl House, in an environment where, for instance, glass dust would perpetually drift down from the ceilings and the walls were razor sharp. It is clear that Miss Helen became utterly engrossed in, and totally obsessive about, the fantasy world she was making. Her work became a mission of enormous importance that crowded out all considerations of creature comfort.

What was it that caused her to devote herself, with such intensity, to this task? Where did her ideas come from? Was it perhaps the same inspiration as has caused other individuals, in other parts of the world, to do similar things?

In France a postman named Ferdinand Cheval spent thirty-four years creating an extraordinary fantasy palace, built on his home plot. It was a laborious procedure. He built the palace from carefully selected stones which he picked up on his rounds when delivering letters. He claimed that the idea for his whimsical, symbol-laden architecture came to him in his dreams.

> *... to distract my thoughts, I constructed in my dreams a faery palace, surpassing all imagination, everything the genius of a humble man could imagine (with grottoes, gardens, towers, castles, museums and sculptures), trying to bring to a new birth all the ancient architecture of primitive times; the whole thing so beautiful and picturesque that the image of it remained alive in my brain for ten years at least.*[1]

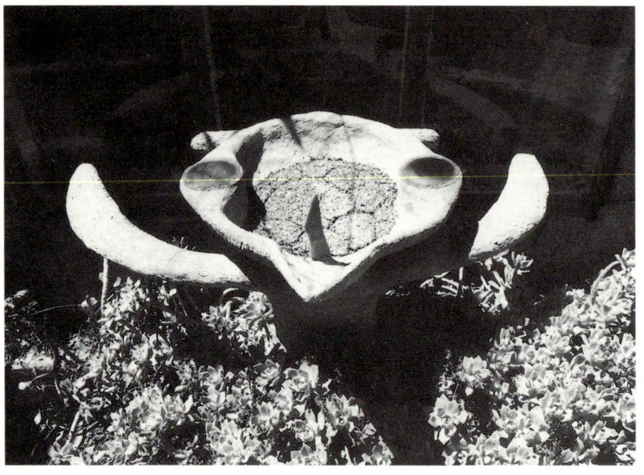

A half-faced owl stands in the sculpture garden. The concave-faced cavity of this owl was once kept filled with water, and served as a birdbath. Elsewhere, concave owl-faces were used as planters or as seats. The form of these owls came to Helen Martins in a dream. It was a dream that filled her with a tremendous sense of excitement and an urgent desire to create these multi-purpose owls in concrete.

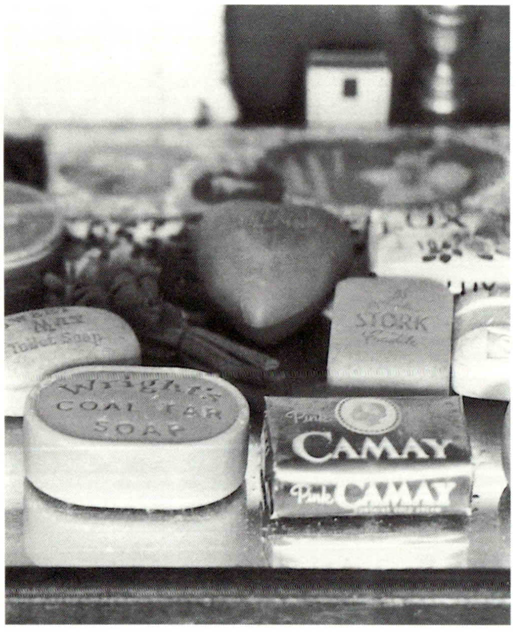

Taken when Miss Helen still lived at the Owl House, this display of beauty soaps and cosmetics was laid out on the mirrored surface on one of her numerous dressing-tables. It is indicative of her abiding interest in the theme of feminine allure, as well as her wish to indicate that the Owl House was a hospitable abode, amply stocked in readiness for guests. (Photograph: Johann Potgieter)

Like Ferdinand Cheval, Helen Martins found inspiration in her dreams. The idea, for instance, of creating the half-faced owls and the double-faced owls came to her in a dream. It was a dream that greatly excited her and she set to work with vigour to realise the creatures in concrete. It excited her that the form of these owls meant that they could be multi-functional. Some of the concave-faced owls were used as bird-baths. Others became planters and were filled with succulents. Inside the house, the concave owl-face was used as a seat. 'Imagine,' she was fond of saying, referring to her owl-faced seats, 'just imagine being able to sit on so much wisdom!'

Dreams might have been the source of inspiration for some of the work, but it was more the compelling nature of the imagery, welling up from her unconsciousness in dreams, that led her to devote at least twenty-five years to the task of creating her own unique and mysterious world. Perhaps, like Cheval the postman, she was bored with, as he expresses it, 'walking forever in the same decor'.

In the splendid and extravagant palace built by Cheval there is a clear element of wish-projection and compensation for a life of limited opportunities and status. In a journal entry he reveals his desire for fame and acknowledgement: '... My life should prove that even among people of my kind there are men of genius and accomplishment.'

In the space created by Miss Helen an element of wish-projection is, similarly, very evident. This reveals itself in her desire to evoke splendour and wealth and the glamour of exotic and far-off places. The front hall is an attempted replication of an Oriental bazaar that is to be seen in a picture on the wall in the main living-room. The fine satin coverlets and the beautifully wrought lace on the beds suggest opulence and extravagance. Jewellery is carefully laid out on the numerous dressing-tables, and splendidly bedecks the arms and hands of the bottle-skirted ladies in the garden. Miss Helen had the unusual habit of heaping piles of money onto surfaces and into containers throughout the house, as if to suggest that this was a place of wealth and plenty, whereas in reality she continually faced poverty and, living off a meagre pension, struggled to make ends meet. Through the world of her creation, Miss Helen managed to sublimate much of the harshness of her real world.

The bottle-skirted ladies in the garden who, like polite hostesses, point out the way and offer a hand in greeting, suggest that Miss Helen wanted visitors to experience this space, and in her will she recorded her desire that the Owl House should become a museum. She was concerned about preserving the space just as it was. It worried her that she had promised certain items to various people. To her nephew's wife, Barbara, she had promised her lamps. Jill Wenman recalls her saying:

> *I promised her my lamps and I can't break my promise. But the Owl House will not be the same without the lamps. Have you noticed how they glitter!*

She found an eccentric and delightful solution to her dilemma:

> *Barbara can have the lamps. They can be her lamps ... as long as she doesn't remove them from the Owl House.*

Implicit in these gestures is the hope for some sort of recognition, that what she had created might be seen by many and might live on after her death. The idea that, in spite of her present anonymity, she was creating for posterity something that might be of value was in her thoughts and must have helped to sustain her creative efforts.

Miss Helen had a friend in Nieu Bethesda, a retired schoolteacher, Miss Frances. The two would visit each other daily, which was somewhat surprising in light of the fact that Miss Frances openly disapproved of the work being undertaken at the Owl House. She continually criticised and upset Miss Helen, accusing her of wasting time and money. Miss Helen liked to point out that it was actually the other way around for, unlike Miss Frances, who was frittering away her money on trivia she,Helen, was creating something of real value, something that would long outlive her. Again taken from the *Rubâiyât* are the cut-out words Jill Wenman once read by the light of the moon, that are attached to the fence of the Camel Yard:

Ah, Moon of my Delight that know'st no wane,
The Moon of Heav'n is rising once again
How oft hereafter rising shall she look
Through this same Garden after me — in vain.

Ferdinand Cheval's palace also carries an inscription that acknowledges the transience of this life, the consequent value of encapsulating ideas in concrete form. The inscription could belong to the Owl House:

FOR FORTY YEARS I DUG
TO MAKE THIS FAERY PALACE
RISE FROM THE EARTH.
FOR MY IDEAS' SAKE MY BODY HAS CONFRONTED ALL:
TIME, RIDICULE, THE YEARS.
LIFE IS A SWIFT CHARGER
BUT MY THOUGHT WILL LIVE ON IN THIS ROCK.[2]

The Owl House, situated in the isolated Karoo village of Nieu Bethesda, and the palace built by Ferdinand Cheval in the small French village of Hauterives are comparable accomplishments. Similar conditions encourage the emergence of such work. There are common threads, as if a particular set of circumstances sparks off the spontaneous and compulsive drive of certain individuals, untrained as artists, to devote themselves with astonishing vigour to the task of totally transforming their home ground into the most fantastical world. They often begin their work only in the latter half of their lives. They can be described as reclusive personalities living in relatively isolated communities. They may be socially ostracised, the victims of unfounded rumour and vicious suspicion. Their work is often vandalised. They are outsiders and indeed 'Outsider Art' is one of the terms that has been coined to describe their output. It is a term used for creative artwork which does not fit the easy definitions of establishment art. It challenges the definition of art as it is normally understood. Many of the 'artists' are untutored. They often do not consider themselves to be artists and for many, the compulsive calling to create has a religious origin. The terms 'naive', 'folk' and 'visionary' are all labels that art historians use to describe the group to which Cheval and Helen Martins belong. 'Art Brut', a phrase coined by the French artist Jean Dubuffet, is also frequently used to categorise the work of these individuals, who are largely uncontaminated by cultural influences. As with 'Outsider Art', the makers and creative products of 'Art Brut' are found in places other than those usually assigned to the 'fine arts'. The 'art' displays an uncommon degree of originality and individuality.

One of the better known so-called 'Outsider' or 'Art Brut' artists, working in a similar manner to Helen Martins, is Simon Rodia. He created the extraordinary Watts Towers in Los Angeles, a veritable forest of lofty fantasy structures. When building his towers he came up against a considerable amount of suspicion and hostility. He reports: 'Some of the people say "What was he doing?" ... some of the people think I was crazy, and some people said I was going to do something.'[3] In the thirties, a hermit-like man, Clarence Schmidt, began the construction of a marvellous environment known as Toward Journey's End. On the slopes of the Ohayo mountains in New York State, he built a single log cabin, and over the years he kept adding to it, moving on up the mountain, room after room. It became a seven storey hillside house, partly gouged out of the cliff, interconnected by a labyrinth of passageways and filled with a strange assortment of kitsch and junk, much of it carefully wrapped in aluminum foil. Schmidt shared Helen Martins' fascination for lighting effects, creating a form of stained glass by coating windows with a translucent paint mixture, and rigging up a multitude of coloured lights. As at the Owl House, the changing lights and seasons alter the quality of light in the space. 'I love to see the light on it,' Schmidt remarks. 'The pieces are wonderful in the moonlight, and the sunset, and after a snowfall.'[4] Schmidt's garden, with its multi-level paths, junk sculpture, numerous old mirrors and tar-covered trees, completes the space. Like Rodia, this visionary and nonconformist man has been harassed and misunderstood. Maligned by neighbours, one of whom even tried to claim his land, he was also the victim of a suspected arson attempt, which partially destroyed the world he had so painstakingly created. Schmidt's motives for building his version of an 'ideal palace', that is, a palace that 'lives in the mind', were similar to Miss Helen's and the postman Cheval's. Schmidt says of his work:

> *I guess I did it to help humanity — to bring some comfort and pleasure to people. All my life I have dreamed of creating something that would live forever in the minds of men.*[5]

A South African artist, working in a similar environmental way to Helen Martins, is Jackson Hlunwani. He is a Shangaan, and lives in the isolated village of Mbhokoto in Gazankulu. Considered to be a spiritual leader by the community, he was ordained as a priest in the African Zionist Church in 1944. Hlunwani has for more than two decades been building from stone his Palace to God, and carving from wood the many sculptures that are placed within the stone-walled boundary of his New Jerusalem. He has no formal vocational art training. In fact he never went to school. While a migrant worker in Johannesburg, however, he lost a finger in an industrial accident, an

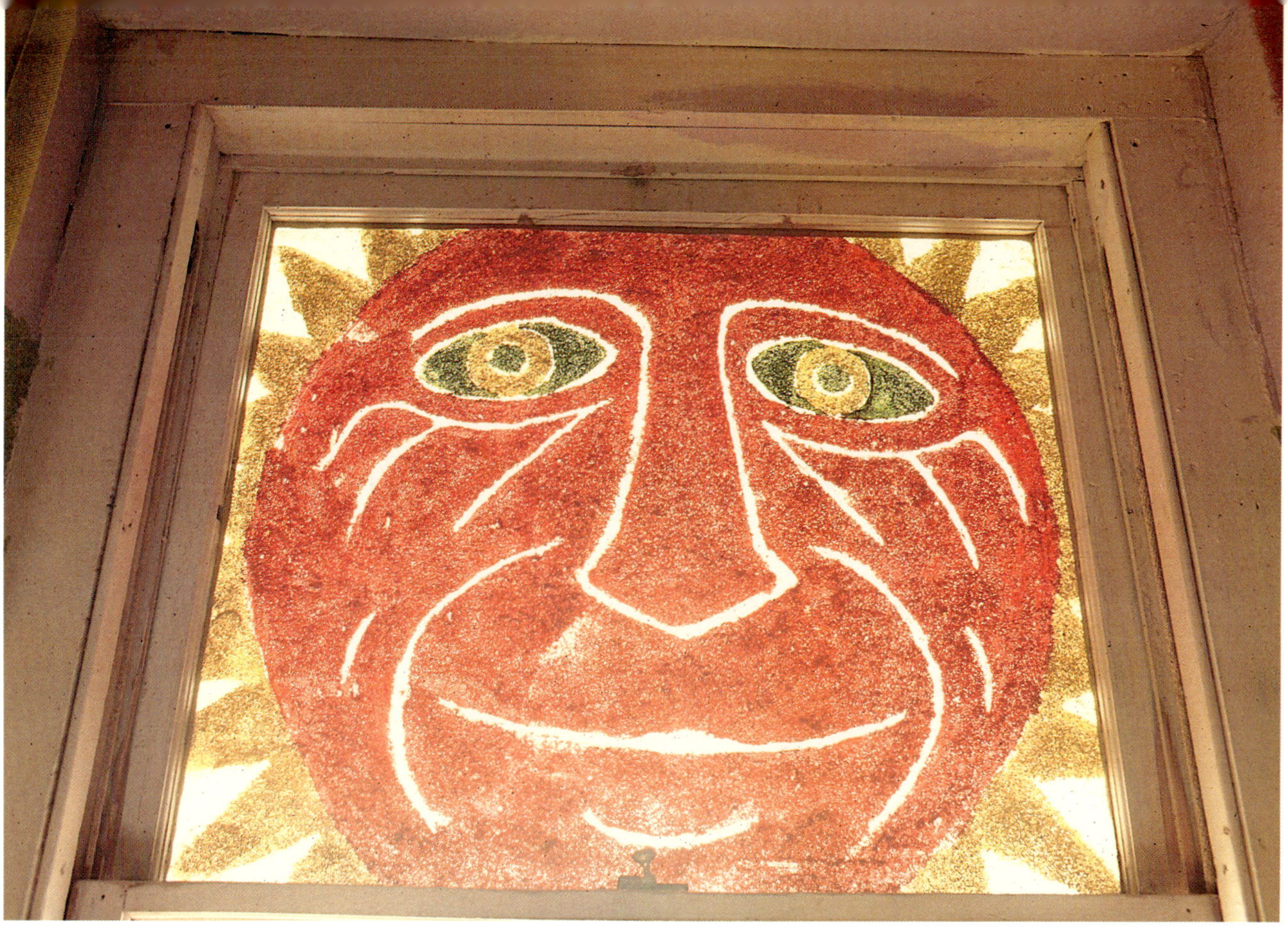

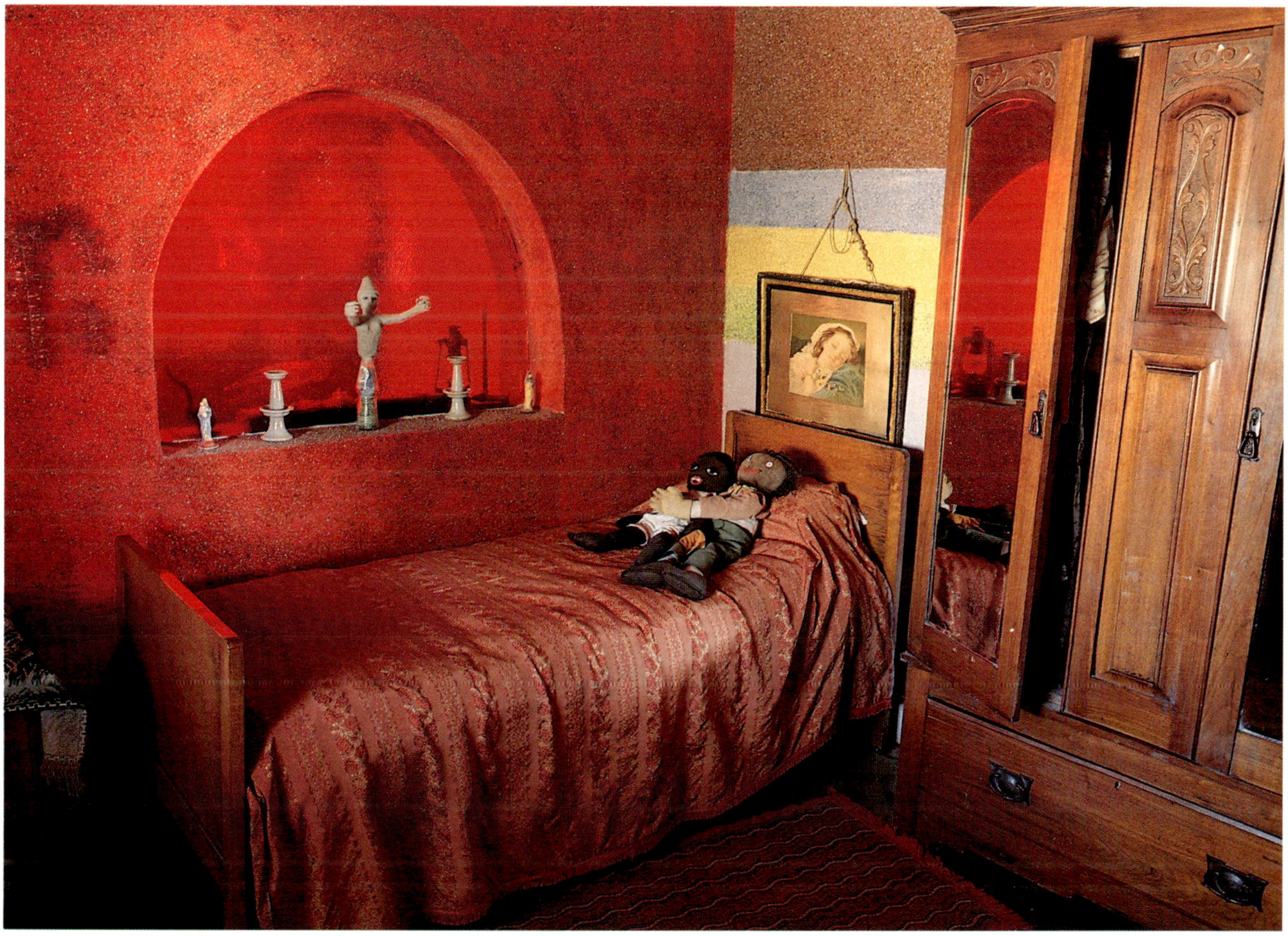

Top: A red sun, created from crushed glass glued to the window, beams into the Honeymoon Room. Miss Helen always referred to it as 'the sun with the jealous eyes'.

Above: The Honeymoon Room is suffused in an unearthly red light. It comes, partly, from the half-moon window with its red-tinted glass. For Miss Helen, red was a colour of passion.

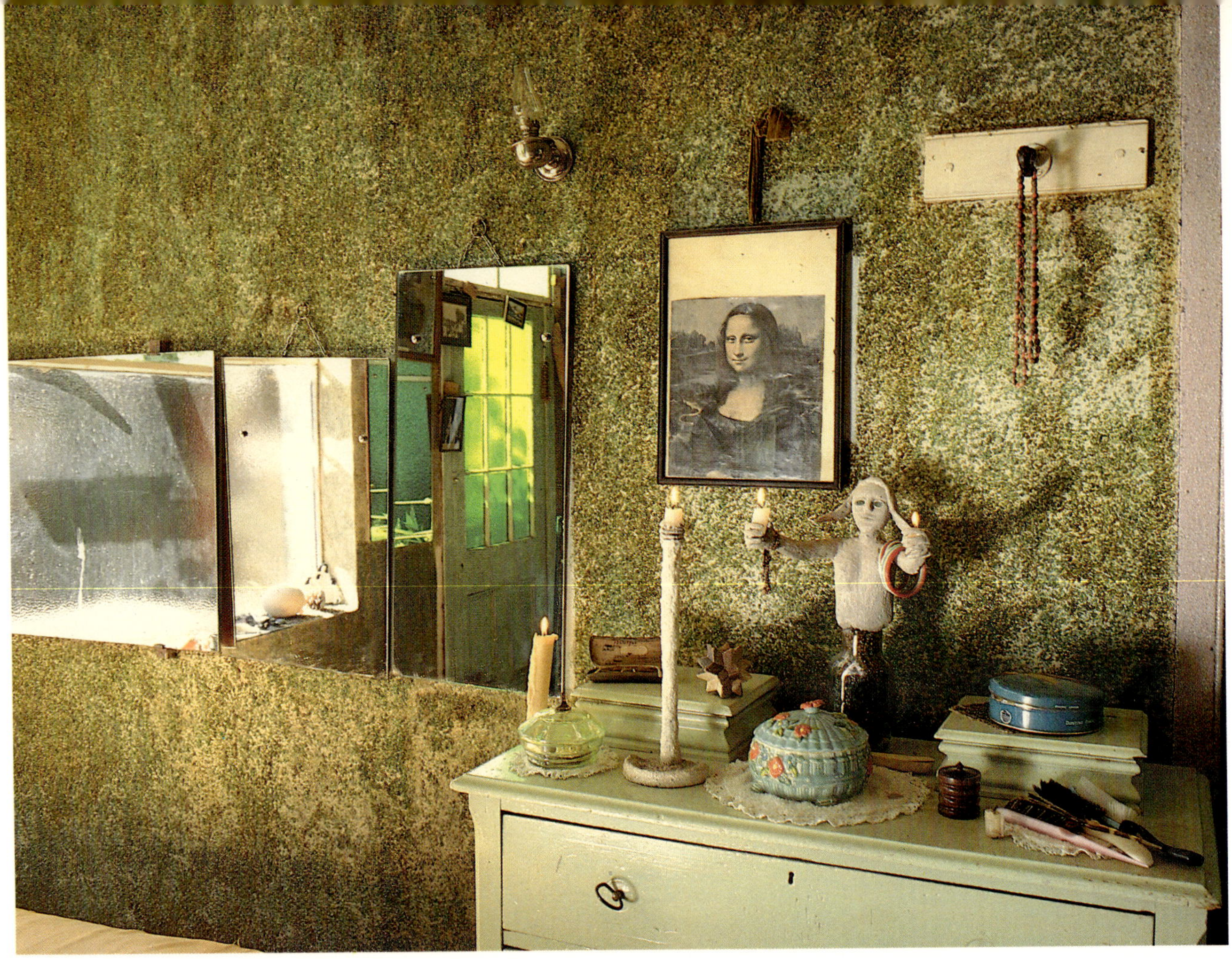

The Owl **HOUSE** has numerous dressing tables, all of them shrines to the idea of self-adornment and seductive female charm. They are strewn with beads, bangles, precious boxes and beauty aids. Some have a sprinkling of fine glass particles that glitter in lamp and candle light. The figurine, wearing a Dutch cap and with a candle in each hand, is one of the many such candle-holders in the house. Miss Helen thought of them as servers and dressing attendants, providing light while also holding bracelets and other articles of adornment. These figurines are the house equivalent of the larger bottle-skirted meisies which grace the garden. On the wall of the Green Bedroom, hanging above this dressing-table, is a print of the Mona Lisa. The image of the Mona Lisa, with her elusive smile and aura of mystery and all-knowingness, fascinated Helen.

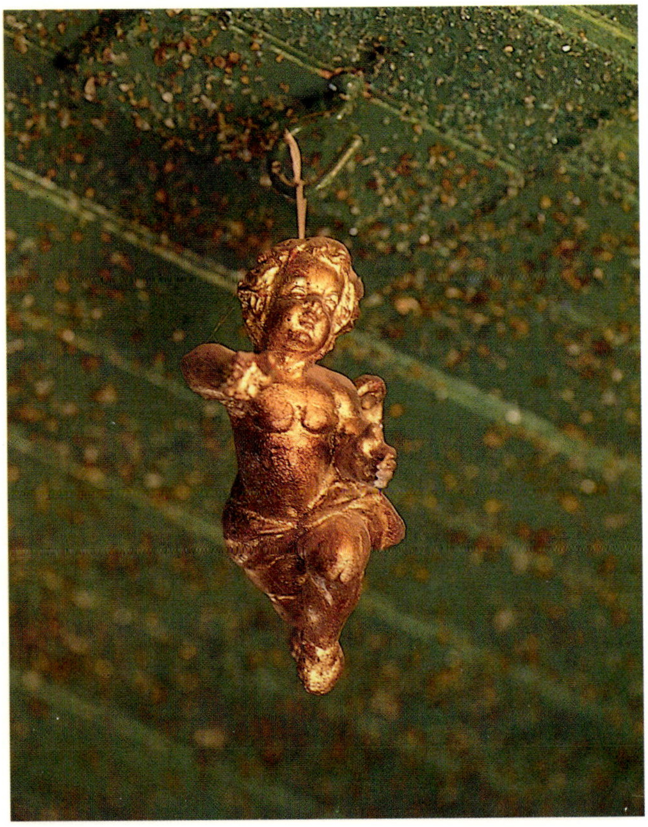

A golden cherub is one of the decorations that dangles from the glittering ceiling of the main living-room, lending an air of giddy festivity to a room in which it appears to be Christmas all year round.

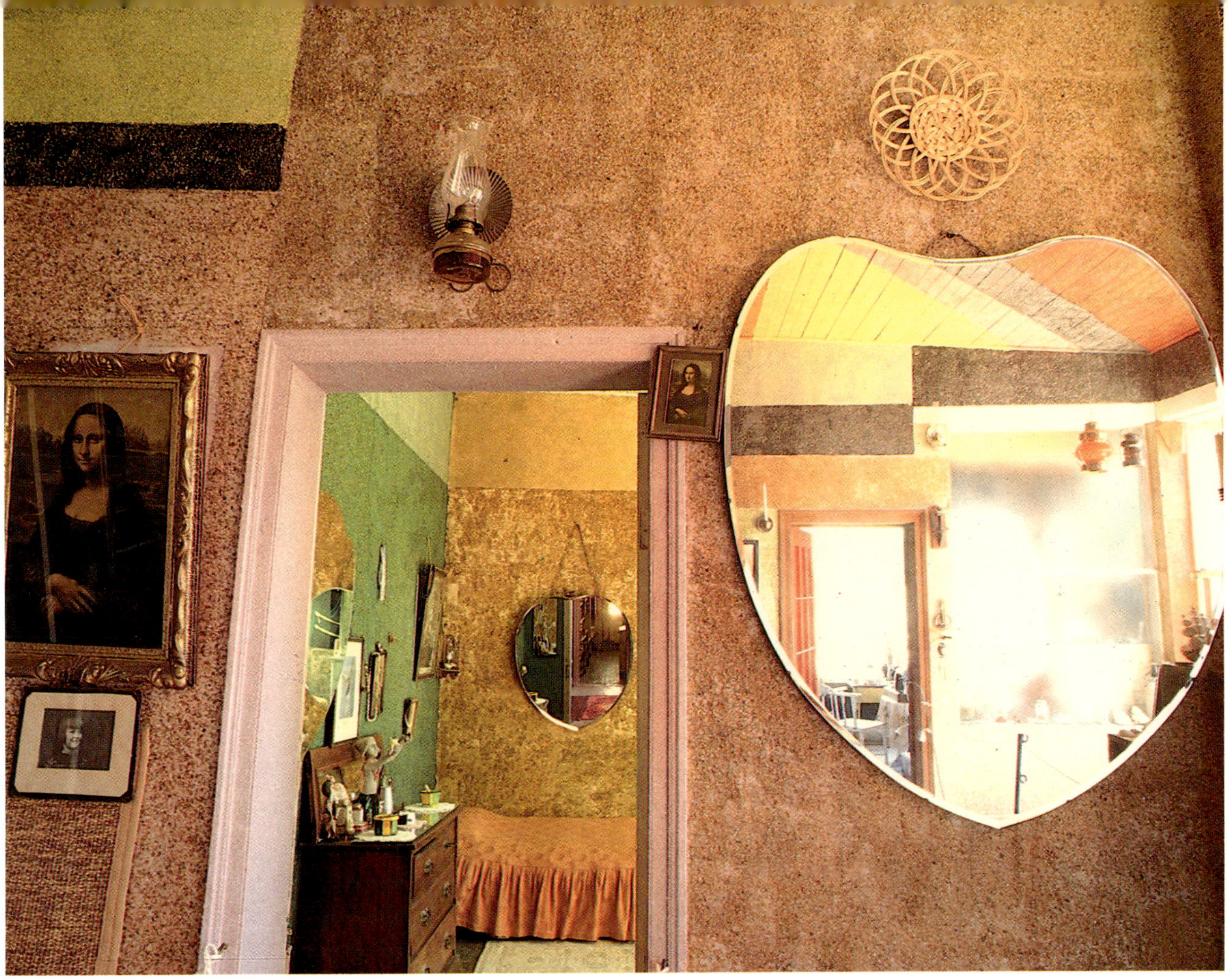

One of Miss Helen's heart-shaped mirrors hangs beside the doorway leading to the Green Bedroom. Exploring the theme of love was one of Helen's preoccupations at *the Owl* **HOUSE**, and the heart became an important recurring symbol.

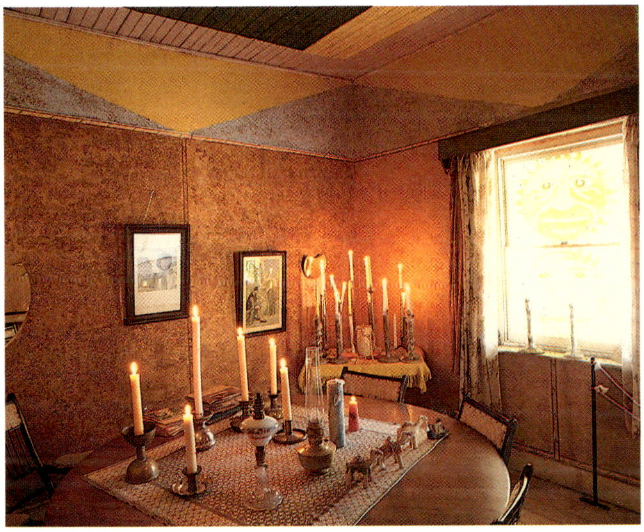

The dining-room table and sideboard are laden with candles. Miss Helen loved their flickering light which sparkled off walls and ceiling. Many of the ornaments, scattered throughout the house, are the prototypes for larger sculptural pieces in the garden. The miniature leather camel caravan that is displayed on the table, was a source of inspiration for camels in the Camel Yard.

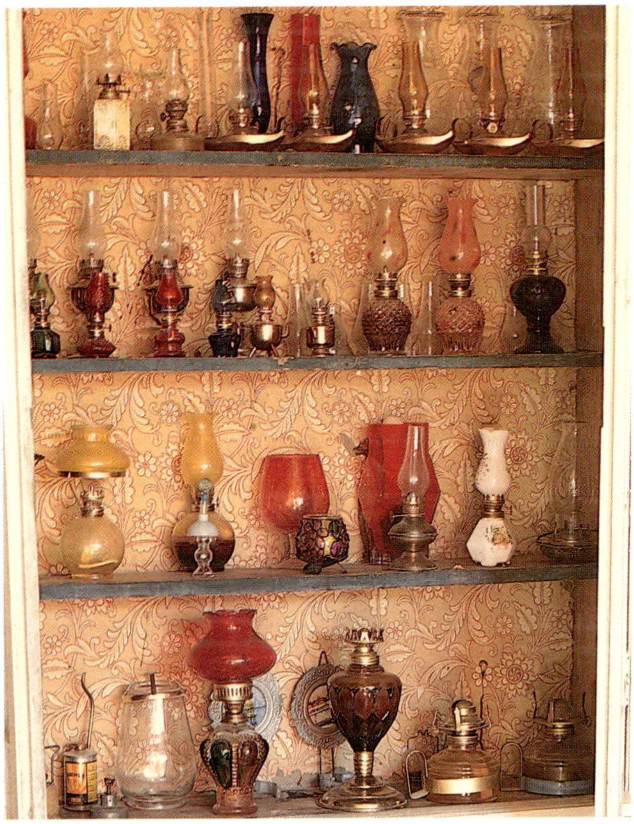

A display cabinet holds part of Miss Helen's vast collection of lamps.

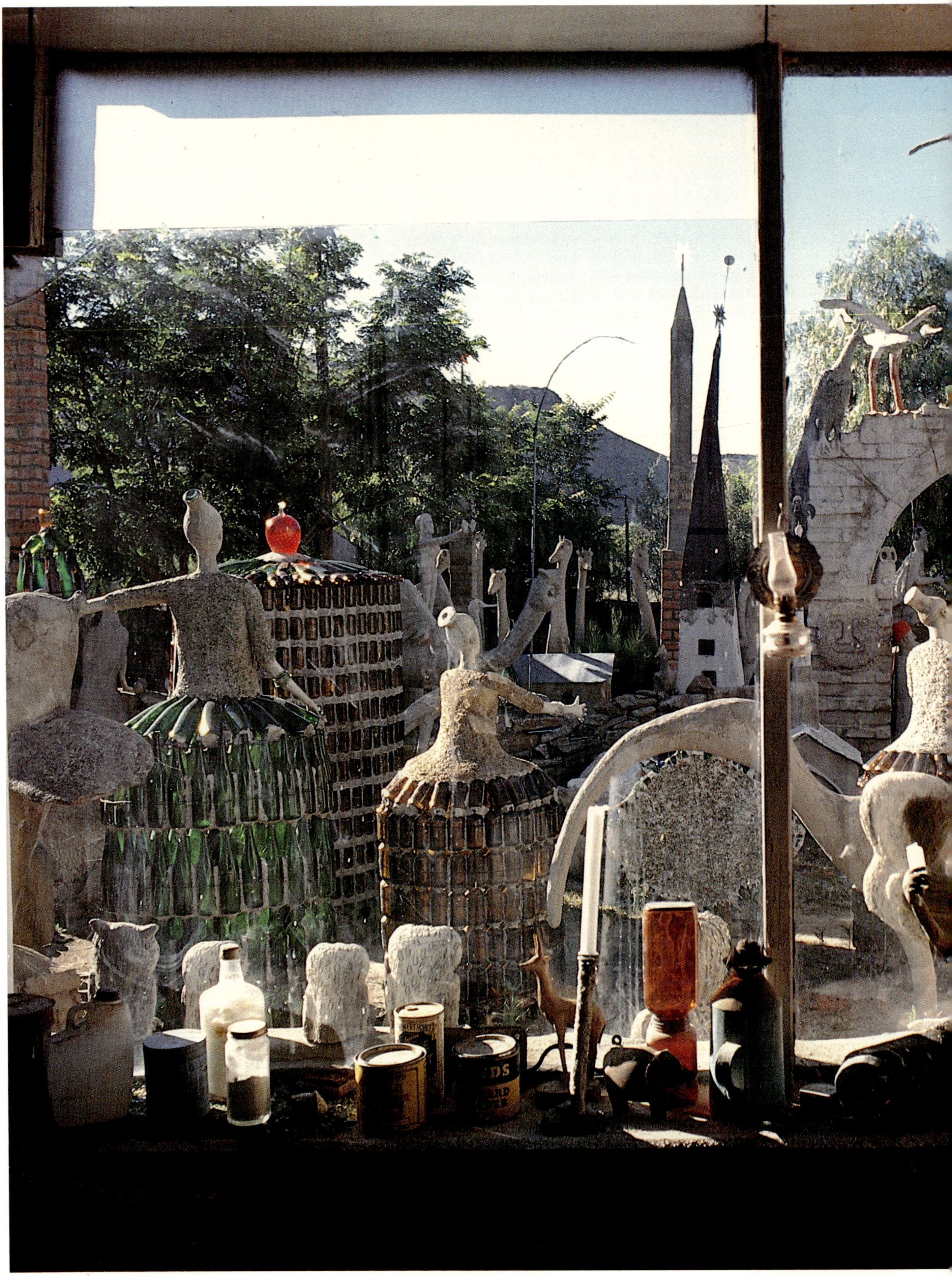

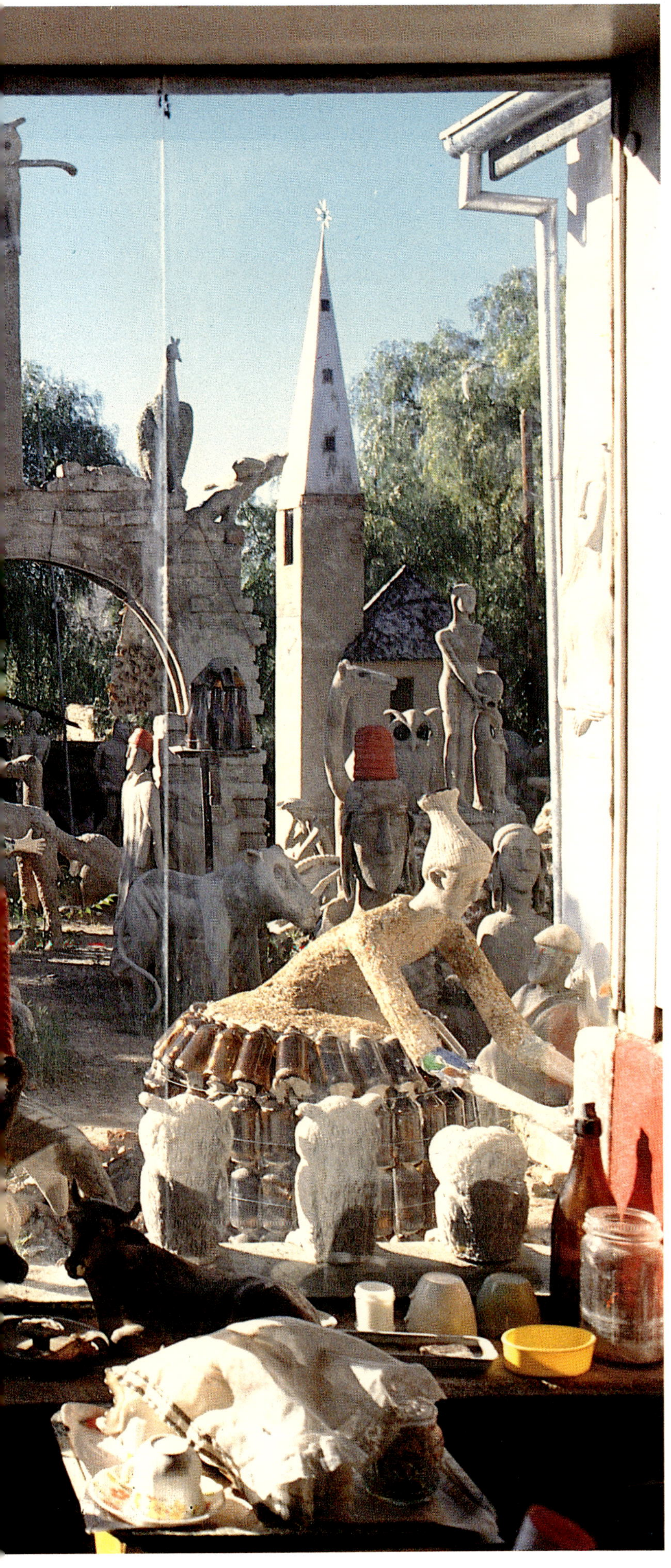

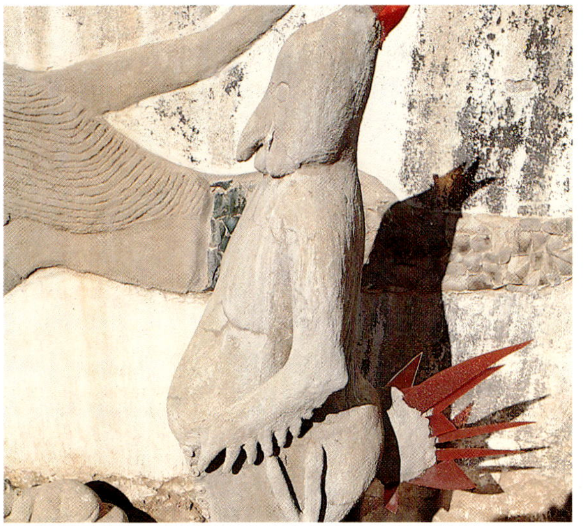

A comic cock-man, in the portion of the sculpture yard that Helen liked to refer to as the Corner of Debauchery, is an image of gluttony. He attempts to fasten his trouser buttons. The sculpture was inspired by a picture postcard. The cock-man was built at a time when Helen herself was experiencing difficulty fastening her own buttons, and is therefore partly autobiographical, built to turn pain into laughter. It was not gluttony, but arthritis in the hands that was the cause of her trouble. Koos had to help her to fasten clothing until Helen became distressed about what neighbours were saying about this practice. She believed it was perceived as scandalous, and confided in Jill Wenman, who managed to obviate the problem by procuring easy clothes for the elderly woman, such as elasticated track-suit pants.

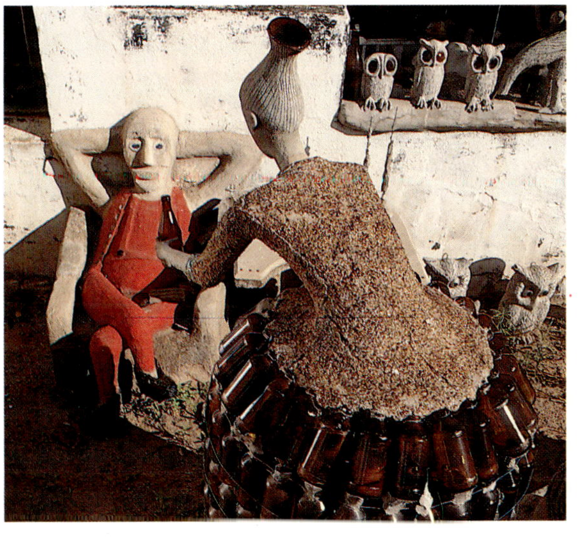

Occupying a portion of the sculpture yard that Helen referred to as the Corner of Debauchery, a bottle-skirted garden hostess offers alcoholic refreshment to a rotund reclining fellow, a weary traveller. He used to sport a real sheepskin beard, but this has disintegrated. John Moyle remembers how, one morning after some rain, the fat fellow's lap had filled with a puddle of water. Helen was delighted and amused, lewdly chuckling about his incontinence.

Left: The wide picture-window in the kitchen frames a panoramic view of the sculpture garden. Churches, the bird encrusted Gates of Paradise, a bottle shrine and a number of meisies, Helen's garden hostesses, are all visible.

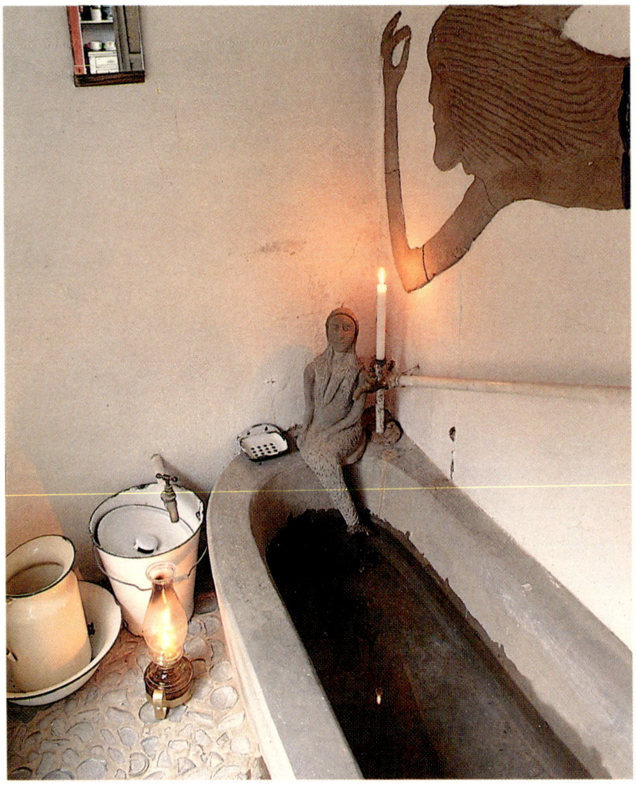

The bathroom at the Owl House has a mermaid on the side of the bathtub, while a relief, modelled by Koos Malgas, from a picture of an underwater swimmer wearing flippers, spans the length of one wall.

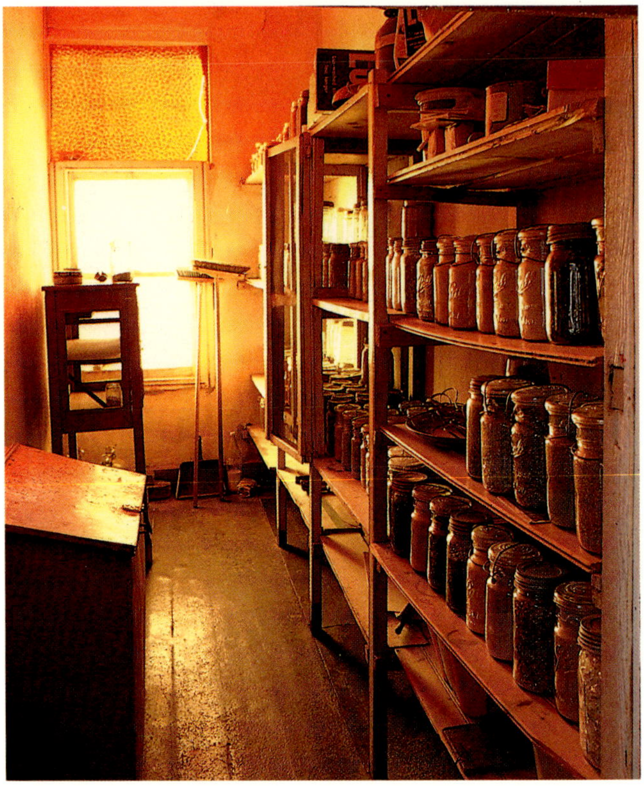

The shelves of the Owl House pantry hold rows and rows of preserve jars. Some are filled with bottled fruit, while others contain Miss Helen's carefully washed and graded assortments of coloured crushed glass.

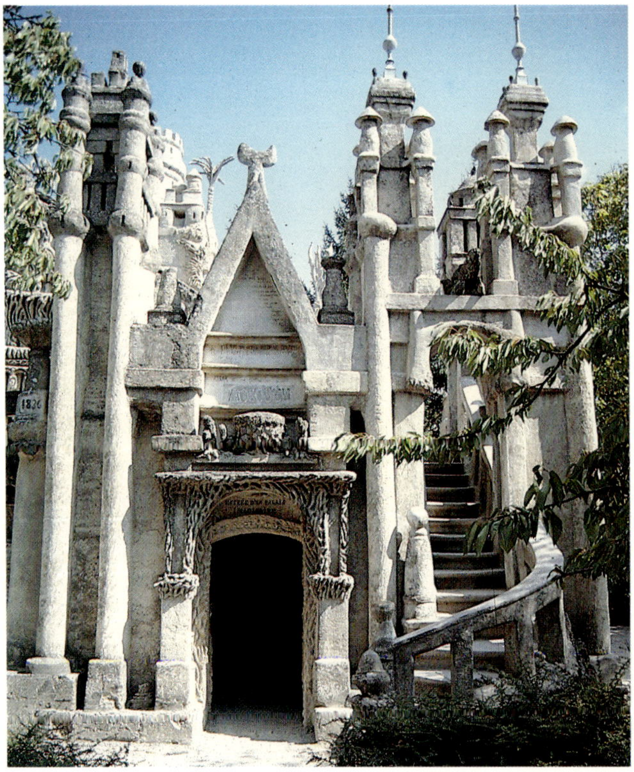

The *Palais Ideal* is a fantasy palace created by the French postman, Ferdinand Cheval. Like Helen Martins, Cheval was untrained as an artist, and only started his monumental undertaking during the second half of his life.

(*Photograph*: **ANNE EMSLIE**)

Top right: A white heron, known in mythology as the phoenix bird, flies above the sun. It is an image of transcendence.

Right: A cock, like the traditional weather cock, sits atop the spire of a church. For Miss Helen the cock was a creature who heralded the dawn, and thus symbolised the start of a new day, as well as the relentless march of time. A verse from the *Rubáiyát*, which Helen loved to quote, identifies the cock with the urgency of the moment:

And as the cock crew, those who stood before
The Tavern shouted — 'Open then the door!
You know how little while we have to stay,
And once departed, may return no more'
(Quatrain 3, Fitzgerald translation)

Far right: An owl, embellished with mosaic work of glass tesserae and fine glass dust.

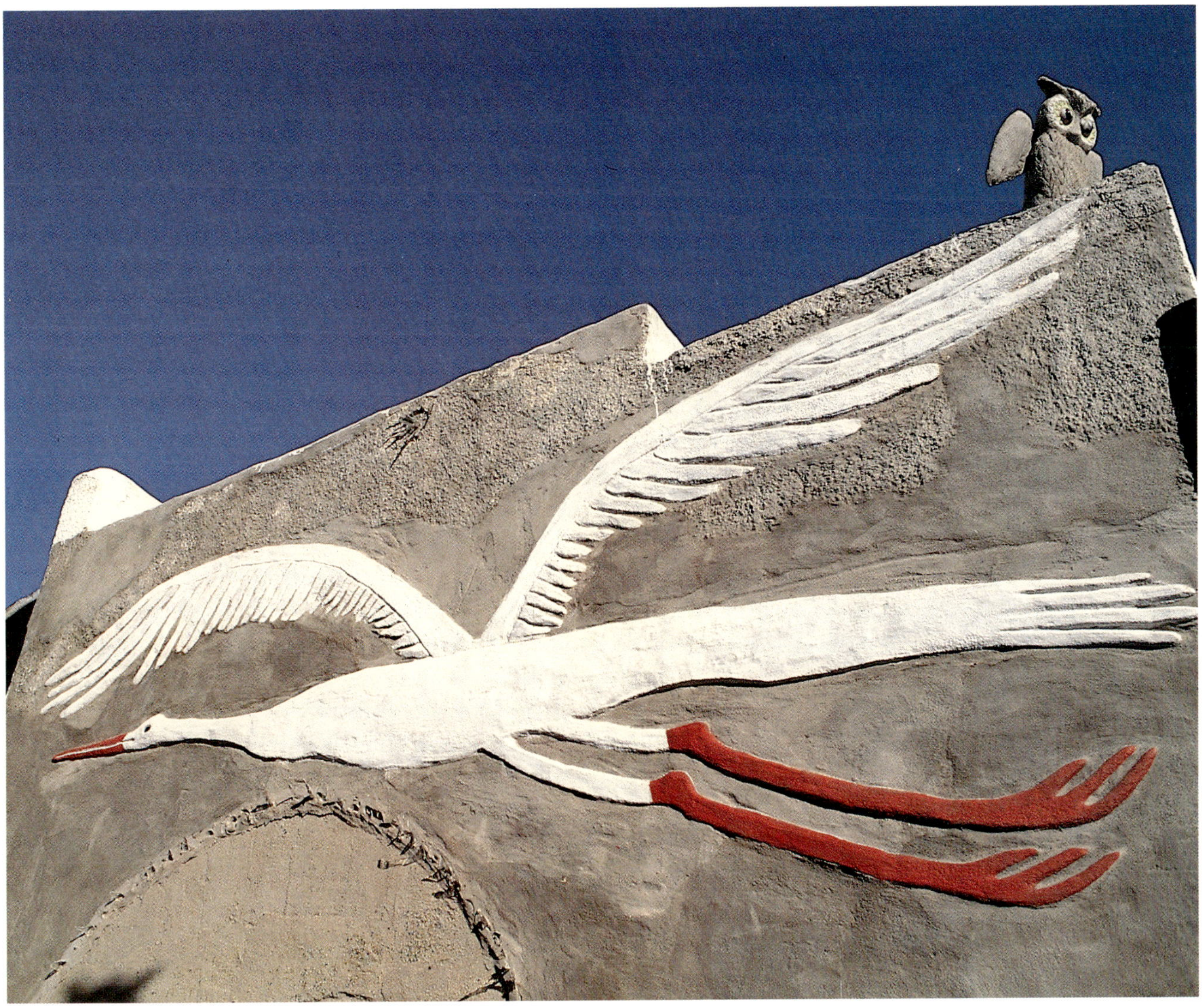

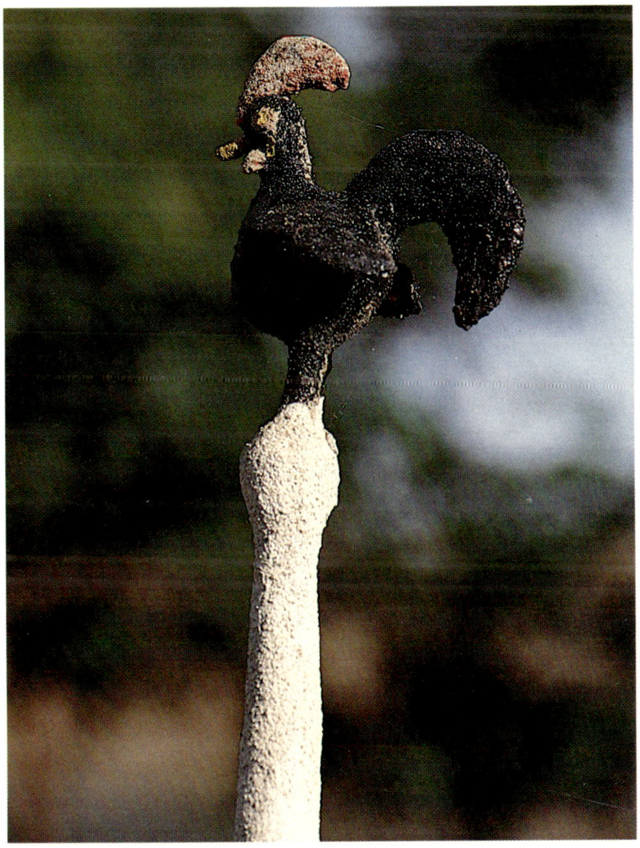

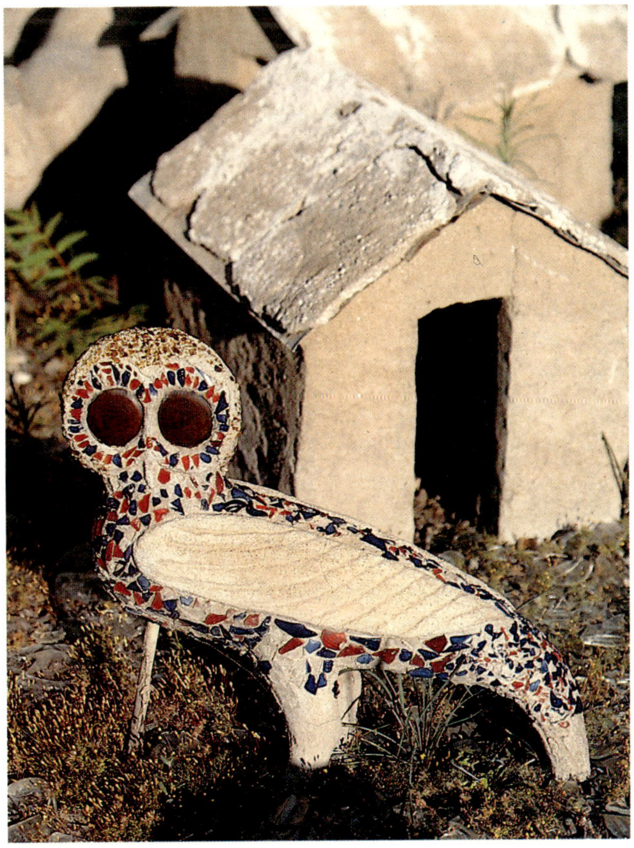

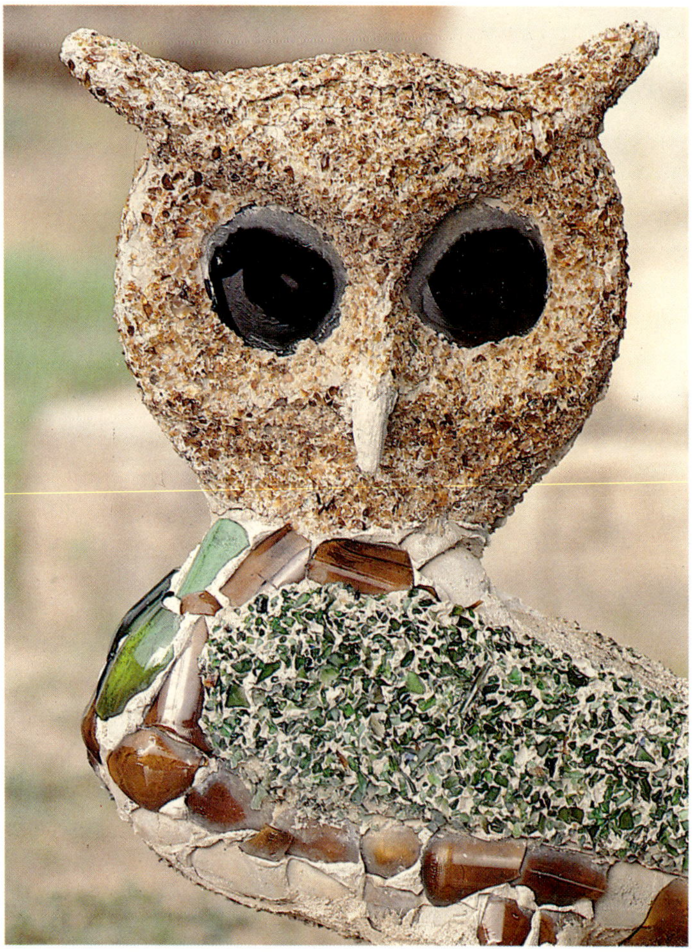

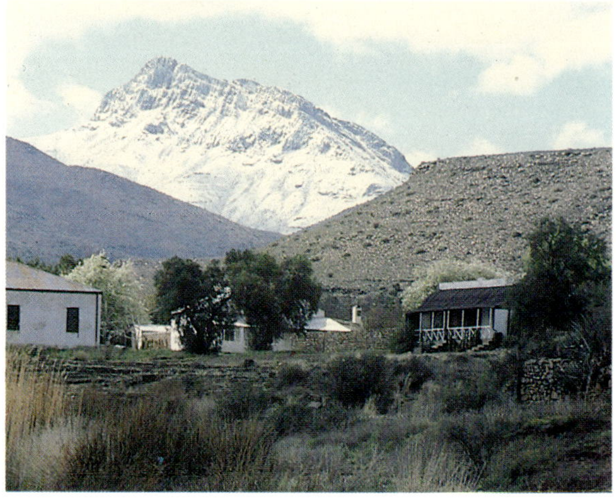

A view across the dry river bed to where *the Owl* **HOUSE** is situated on the bank. The lofty Spitzkop mountain, which Helen replicated in miniature in her garden, can be seen in the distance. Helen was most sensitive to her immediate environment. The piercing quality of the Karoo light, the winter cold, the heat in summer and the wide open spaces all influenced her work.

(*Photograph:* **IAN BALLANTYNE**)

One of Miss Helen's owls stares out from eyes which have been created from the bottoms of bottles.

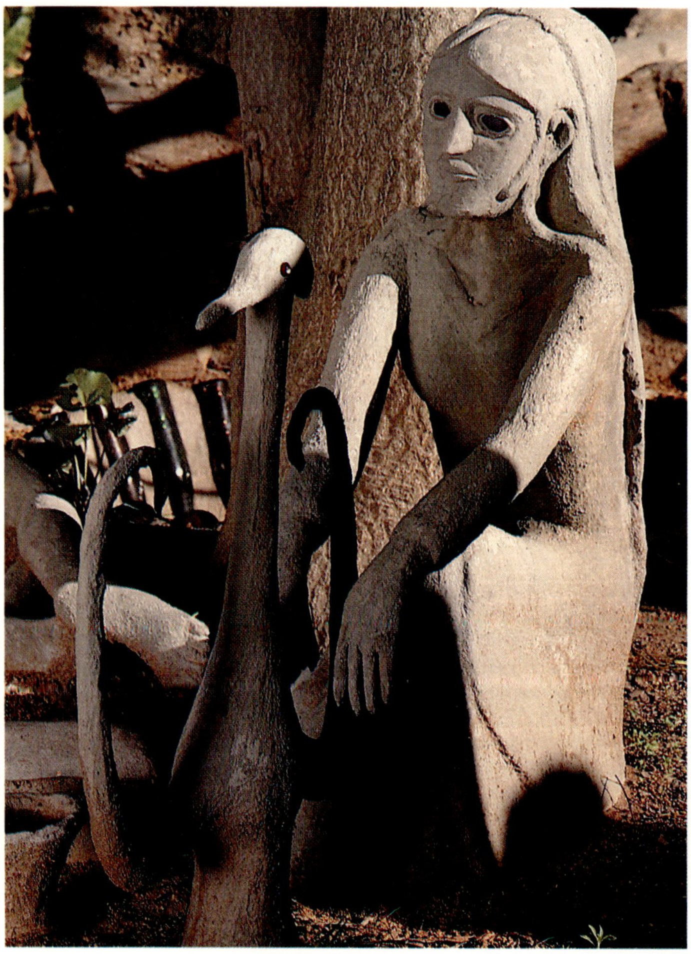

Beneath a tree in the garden is a girl who holds a bird-jug. She, too, is derived from a Sherriffs illustration in Helen's copy of the *Rubáiyát*. A cement nightingale, in the tree above her, completes the scenario that illustrates quatrain 12:

A Book of Verses underneath the Bough,
A jug of Wine, a Loaf of Bread — and Thou
Beside me singing in the Wilderness —
Oh, Wilderness were Paradise enow!

There are many indications that Helen wished the sculpture yard, at *the Owl* **HOUSE**, to convey connotations of being a paradise garden.

incident which caused him to take serious stock of his life. He decided to return home and embark upon the work that now occupies him. 'I must come home, work for myself and make my soul better,' was the decision he made at that turning point. His inspiration is religious. ' ... It comes from God Himself, and from the Lord, and from the Holy Spirit.' He says simply:

> *Well, this work of mine, what I am doing now, is not an image; it is not an idea, it is not a fairy-tale. It is truth itself ... The reason is that this work of mine does not originate in me.*[6]

Helen Martins has much in common with the other artists of her breed. She had received no formal art training. There is a strong religious dimension to her work, which is characterised by a quality of spiritual searching. It was only in the later years of her life that her intense and personal vision began to manifest itself, both in her innovative interior decor and in the homemade statuary that fills her half-acre plot. The same holds for the postman, Cheval, who only started his building when he was forty-three years of age.

Then, again like others, Helen was a 'misfit' who encountered a degree of victimisation and social ostracisation. The Nieu Bethesda locals remember how Miss Helen was teased. The children thought she was queer and would knock on her door and then run away. They also threw stones into her yard and this was one of the reasons she chose to erect the high fence that surrounds her property and grow the thorny cactus plants. Her obsession with the fortification, in so many ways, of the Owl House environment relates to her experience of being victimised.

Like Schmidt and others, Miss Helen was known as a loner, someone who wished to cut herself off from the world. After the death of her parents, when she was about fifty years old, she lived alone at the Owl House and kept, increasingly, to herself. She had dutifully returned to Nieu

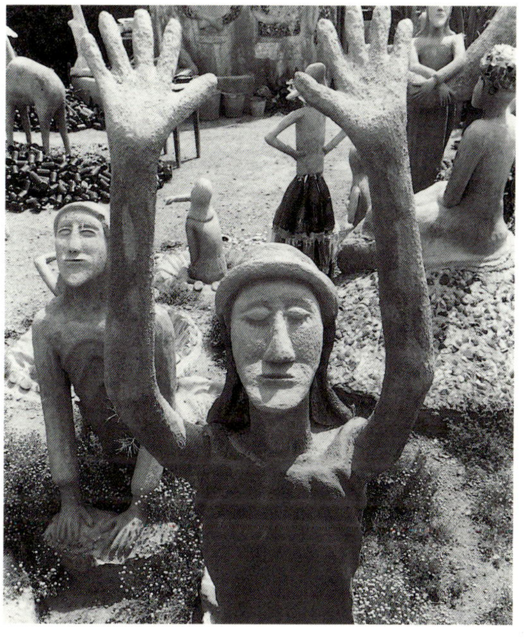

There is a quality of spiritual searching that imbues the work at the Owl House. It is evident in the multitude of worshipping figures, such as this pilgrim who raises his hands heavenwards.
(Photograph: Johann Potgieter)

Bethesda, still a young woman in her thirties, to care for her parents through the infirmities of their old age. Finally, after the death of her father, she married a local furniture restorer named Niemand. Like her first marriage, years earlier, when at the age of seventeen she had married a farmer, Johannes Pienaar, this marriage did not work out. In fact it lasted only a couple of months.

She became known, increasingly, as a recluse. She seldom mixed with the local community. She stopped attending church. She preferred to send one or other of the local children, who might happen to pass her house, on errands to shop or post-office rather than go herself. She paid them for their services with tammeletjie, a type of sweet she made from local fruit.

Matie Cupido, while a young girl, remembers running errands for Miss Helen. She describes how this came about, remembering with amusement how suspicious she was of Miss Helen's tammeletjie:

> *I had to pass Miss Helen's house on my way home. She used to call me: 'Little girl, little girl!' At first I ran away. I was frightened of Miss Helen. Then one day she shouted, 'Little girl, are you Piet Meyer's daughter? Don't be scared of me. I want to send you to collect my mail for me.' After that I often collected her mail. She would give me what we call 'tammeletjie'. It's like a sweet. We used to make our 'tammeletjie', at home, from boiled quince. The quince had to be put through a mincer and sugar was added. Then it would be dried in the sun, on a piece of wood smeared with butter. Our tammeletjie was creamy, and a lovely golden colour. Miss Helen's was so black to me! I took it but I never ate it.*

Perhaps one of the reasons for Miss Helen's shyness, reclusiveness and increasingly eccentric behaviour as she grew older was the acute embarrassment she suffered over her physical appearance. At some stage she had found it necessary to have the baby toes of both her feet amputated as a result of painful bunions; and there is no doubt that, mentally, she was severely affected by what she must have regarded as a deformity. One of the locals tells the story of how as a child she had observed Miss Helen walking to the post office when some visitors to Nieu Bethesda turned into the street. Rather than be seen to have deformed feet, Miss Helen sat down exactly where she was in the middle of the road and covered her feet with her skirt until the strangers had passed. Such an extreme response must be borne of deep and painful personal embarrassment.

The extent of Miss Helen's isolation was exacerbated by the fact that she never owned a car and so, except for the occasional trip by bus to the nearby town of Graaff-Reinet, she almost never left the vicinity of Nieu Bethesda. She lived a constricted and solitary life within a conservative small-town community. Perhaps it was a pressing desire to transcend the limitations of her life that led her to travel in her imagination where no travel in real life was possible. Francie Lund recollects her once having said: 'I haven't the money to travel. And even if I did, I'd be afraid. So I must make it [the world] myself.'

And in her imagination she travelled to the four corners of the world of her own making. But the direction, it appears, to which she was particularly drawn, was East.

'East' is signposted on one of the fences in the sculpture garden. It is not true east, for in her private world Miss Helen chose the directions of her own cardinal points herself. It is towards the 'East', spelt out in wire on the fence, that a seething mass of devout pilgrims are travelling. Some are riding cement camels. Some are proceeding on foot. They appear to be surging forward with urgent religious fervour. Seated on the ground near the fence and pointing upwards towards a sign, is an interesting and exquisite little statue of a woman. It is one of the few in the garden encrusted with glass, and it shimmers

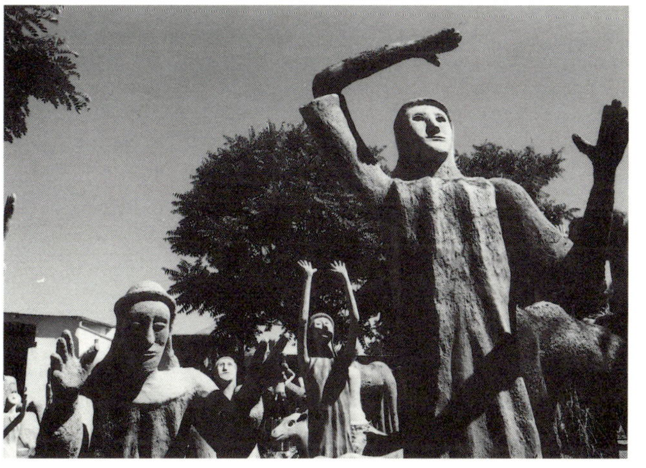

A vast procession of pilgrims travel through the land of the pyramids on their way to the East. They are not travelling true East, but towards a bilingual sign on the fence which proclaims 'East/Oos'. In this world of Helen Martins' own making, she chose to re-direct the cardinal points according to her own whim.

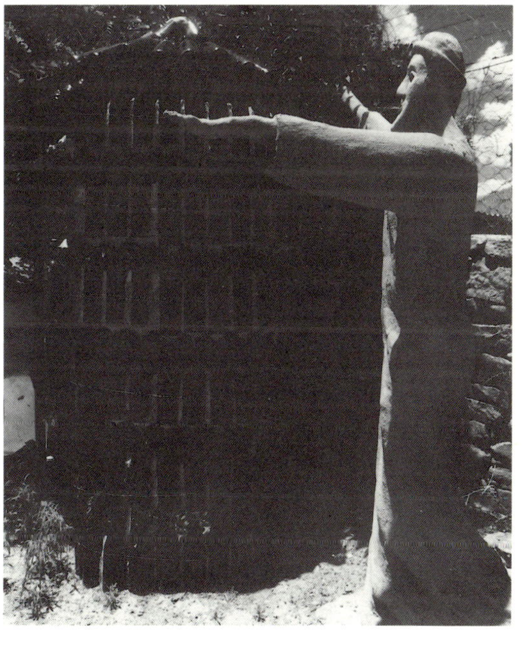

A robed pilgrim points the way to the East.

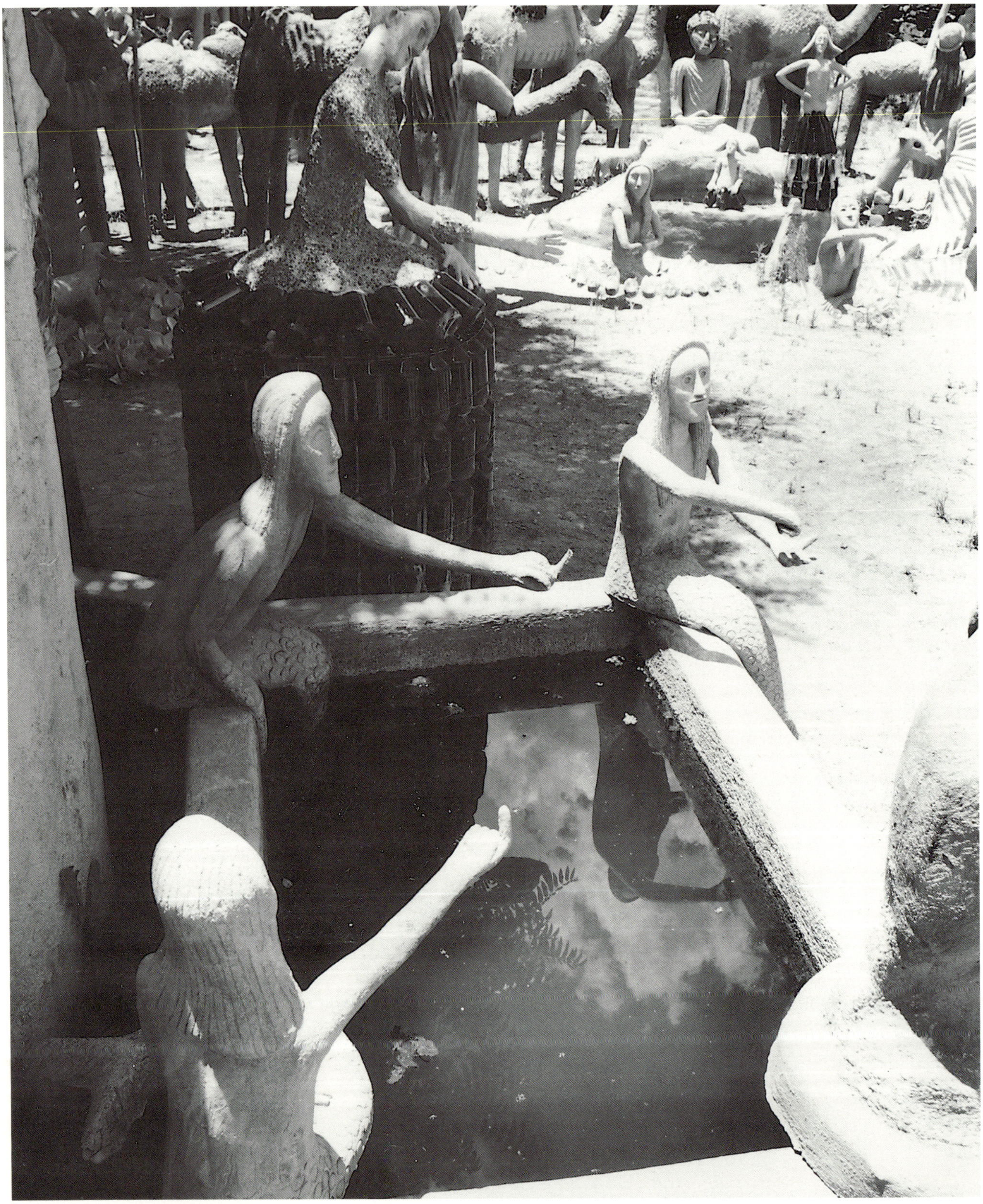

The pool of healing is flanked by mermaids. A garden hostess in the background guides visitors to the water.

and gleams as the light catches it. A startling detail is that each foot has been modelled with only four toes. This is clearly a self-portrait piece. Helen Martins had chosen to place herself in the garden and she had chosen to position herself in the 'Eastern' corner, amongst the pilgrims, the shepherds and the wise men who have travelled great distances in order to pay their tribute at the birth of the Holy Child. Below the 'Eastern' star, right up against the fence, is a shelter, with a car headlamp over the entrance. 'The Stable of Bethlehem' is what Miss Helen called this hut. The headlamp is Miss Helen's modern-day equivalent of the Star of Bethlehem. It lights the way for the travellers and indicates the whereabouts of the humble shed in which the Divine Child is to be found.

But perhaps more than towards any imaginary geographic destination, Helen Martins was travelling inwards. It was a spiritual journey and it was a journey that led her to explore the cavernous inner realm of the psyche. In so doing, she chanced upon the rich vein of archetypal imagery that gives her work its remarkable depth. The themes of the images that abound reverberate with a universality which makes them singularly powerful.

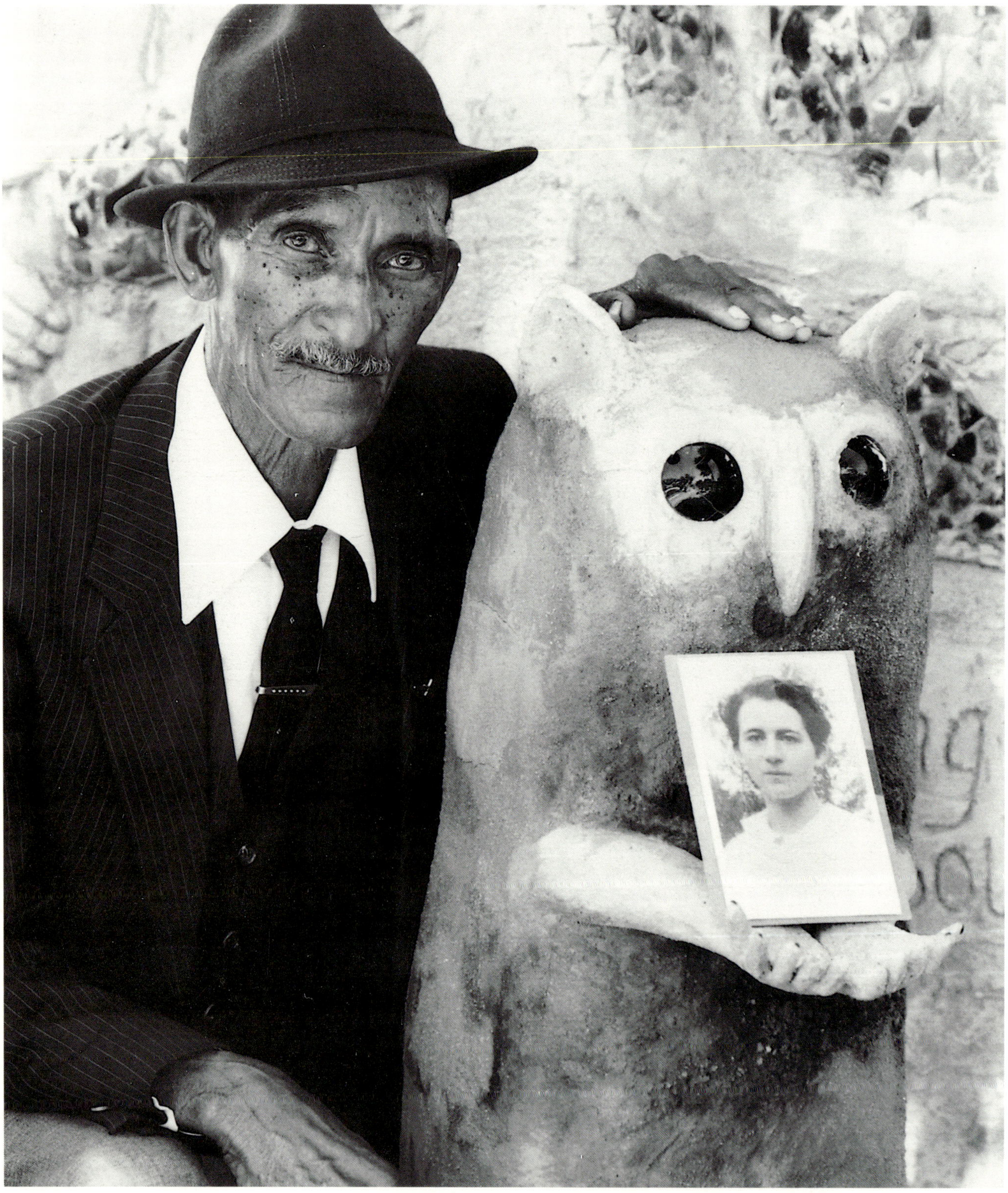

Piet van der Merwe did much of the early building work, and made some of the first sculptures at the Owl House. Here he sits beside one of the first owls he made. The owl's arms, a later addition, hold a photograph of Miss Helen as a young woman.

Part Two: THE ARTIST AND THE CREATOR

Not one of the sculptures in the garden was made by Helen Martins herself. Helen had an urgent vision and an immensely creative mind, but she never had any confidence in her own ability either to draw or to sculpt. This was compounded by the fact that she suffered from increasingly crippling arthritis in her hands as she grew older. Other people made the sculptures for her, and she made use of a variety of ornaments in her possession, as well as pictures from books and cards, to help indicate and explain what she wished to be built.

Helen sometimes made use of sketches done for her by friends. Johan van Meyeren was one. As a teenager he remembered 'Miss Helen' requesting him to make sketches to her specifications of statues she was planning for the garden. Most of Johan's drawings for Miss Helen were of owls. It was he who made the sketch for the very first owl to be built at the Owl House. He drew it with chalk on the stone floor of the stoep. This owl was made in cement by Piet van der Merwe. Piet, a local 'Coloured' builder, was employed by Miss Helen to help with much of the early work undertaken at the Owl House. An old Nieu Bethesda resident, he remembers Miss Helen over the years. His memories go back to when she was a young girl: 'She was very pretty but, like the rest of us, I suppose, she quickly grew old.' He remembers her father, too, Oubaas Martins, who used to sit on the front stoep with his hat pulled well down over his eyes. As an elderly man Helen's father acquired a reputation for being ill-tempered. Piet recalls raising his hat to the old gentleman in greeting, only to be shouted at: 'Don't bother me! Can't you see I'm sick!'

In fact Oubaas Martins' anti-social behaviour was legendary. Another local story told how some visitors arrived at the house one day to find Helen's father prostrate on the ground with an orange box over his head. When addressed, he lifted the box, said, 'Can't you see I'm busy?' and firmly replaced it, refusing to have anything more to do with his guests. Helen spent many years in the company of this difficult old man but the two of them did not get on and they quarrelled constantly. Eventually her father moved into an outside room, adjacent to the house, where, Piet remembers,'Oubaas made his own food and ate by himself.'

Oubaas Martins died in 1945 at the age of 89, four years after the death of Helen's mother. A neighbour of the Martins, Gertie Retief, recalls:

> *I think her mother died of cancer. In those days cancer patients used to be separated, you know. The Martins' side stoep was enclosed, and Helen's mother was put in there.*

Helen, the youngest of six children, had dutifully devoted herself to looking after her elderly parents. As a young woman she had left Nieu Bethesda and trained as a teacher in a Graaff-Reinet college. A testimonial from the college describes her as an exceptional student:

> *... she is enthusiastic and her work is singular for its thoroughness and sincerity. Her character is unimpeachable and I am convinced that her influence upon children will be beneficial She not only wishes to impart knowledge, but also the values of the spirit. I expect a great deal from her.*[7]

After graduating Helen married Johannes Pienaar, a Karoo farmer and later a diplomat. The marriage was, however, of short duration and ended in divorce. Afterwards Helen worked as an English teacher and undertook several other jobs. It was initially the deterioration in her mother's health that prompted Helen's homecoming. A letter, dated 20.1.32, from one of her older brothers, highlights this as a difficult time for her.

> *Dear Helen*
>
> *I am going over to Volksrust to see Piet — with the view of his relinquishing monies for mother and your support ... Helen, it would be sheer impertinence, on my part, to lay down the law to you in respect of the attitude you should adopt, under the trying circumstances you find yourself in.*
>
> *Permit me to thank you for your unselfish services to mother under the most trying and practically impossible conditions. Had I believed in God as the conceiver of the great majority — I would have relegated you his generosity as reward. Being utterly pagan and agnostic I feel the least we can do is to help ameliorate your trials and incidentally also mother's ...*

When she was eventually released from the burden of caring for her ill and elderly parents, Helen began to transform the house. One of the first projects upon which she embarked was the transformation of the outhouse her father had occupied. It was a very dark room, having no window, the only source of light when the door was closed coming from the skylight above it. Helen instructed Piet to paint the entire room black. The skylight was also to be covered with black paint, eliminating any light whatsoever. A second doorway was knocked through so that the room was accessible from the yard. Afterwards Piet coated the black walls with shards of crushed glass. Helen always referred to this space as 'The Black Room'. On the doorstep Piet engraved the words 'The Lion's Den'. 'The Lion' had been a nickname for Helen's father.

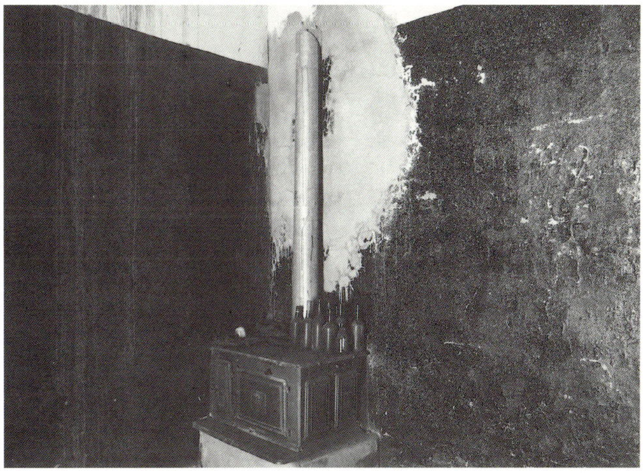

A stove stands in the corner of the out-room in which Piet Martins once slept. After the death of her father, Helen had the window bricked up, and the walls of the room painted black and covered in crushed glass. She called this room the Black Room.

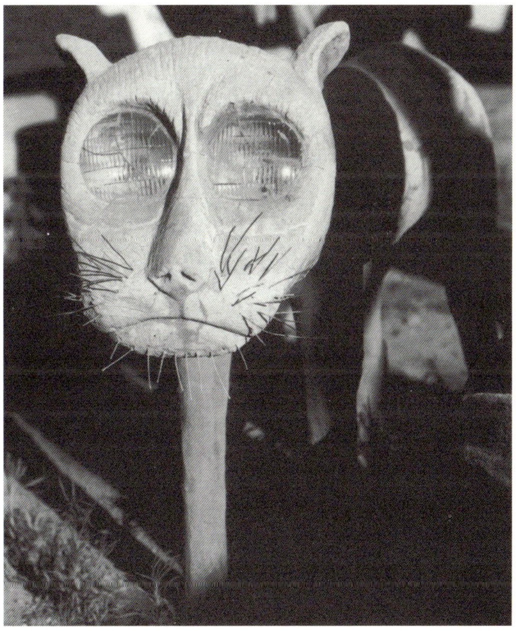

A wire-whiskered lion guards the Gates of Paradise. His headlamp eyes come from a Volkswagen that had crashed in the district. They provide him with piercing vision and, like the owls, he is able to see in the dark. The Black Room, also known as the Lion's Den, would come alive under his illuminating gaze.

Two small cement animals, a cat and a dog, were placed in protective positions, one on either side of the door.

Years later a lion was constructed in the garden by Koos Malgas. With wire whiskers bristling and a fearsome expression, it was placed close to the Lion's Den. Its large, headlamp eyes were lifted from a Volkswagen that had crashed somewhere in the district. Like the owls, everywhere, the lion is one of the guards of the garden, positioned to protect the entrance to the adjacent arched gateway. Koos Malgas comments about this piece:

> *The lion is moving towards the arch. He wants to go through the gate. He is a guard. He is on the look-out. If children come along, he can see that they don't take anything.*

The lion's searchlight eyes provide night-vision, too, and suggest that, of all the garden creatures, this lion would be most capable of penetrating the darkness of its den, The Black Room, and lighting up the myriad glass particles adhering to the walls. Perhaps, too, there is a connection with the biblical Daniel, who survived against all odds in the lions' den. This is a salvation story which prefigures the Christ story that so fascinated Helen Martins. It is as if the lion, with his headlamp eyes, provides the light of salvation, penetrating even the darkest and most desperate of places.

Piet van der Merwe's long acquaintance with Helen Martins and his involvement in the transforming early stages of the Owl House development, created between them a lasting bond of friendship. Piet and his family were among the privileged few who, over the years, were invited by Miss Helen to share her enjoyment of the world she had created. Piet reminisces:

> *About every two weeks she would come to fetch me. It would be about five o'clock in the afternoon. 'Tonight we are going to light up,' she would say.*

I lit the lamps and placed them around the garden, one here and one there, so that all her stars shone in the light. Inside, she lit the candles. Everything sparkled. Later, I came over again with my family. The 'Ouma' who worked for her, Bokkie's mother, would also be there. She had a large family, and she would bring the entire household along, the children too. All the lights were burning. We gazed at her stars that twinkled in the lamplight. Inside, we admired the glittering walls of glass. Miss Helen made tea for us. Then, at about nine o'clock, we left.

Gertie Retief remembers similar evenings, when Helen would invite her neighbours to the Owl House.

She would show you around. She was thrilled about every little thing. She had a way of taking you aside and talking intimately with you. She showed you all her little things. She was very excitable, talking all the time. She had a story for everything. She would take you by the arm and peer into your face, her nose only a few inches away.

Rosemary van der Merwe remembers visits too:

She had beautiful furniture, some of which was swiped when she died. But she didn't want you to admire that, only what she had done. She was very eager for praise. Almost childlike in her eagerness for praise for what she had done, and for your praise for the whole thing.

Piet believes that Helen always felt the garden was at its best at night, especially at the time of a full moon. The house, too, was at its best at night. It was as if, in the words of Peggy Delport, 'the place came alive at night because

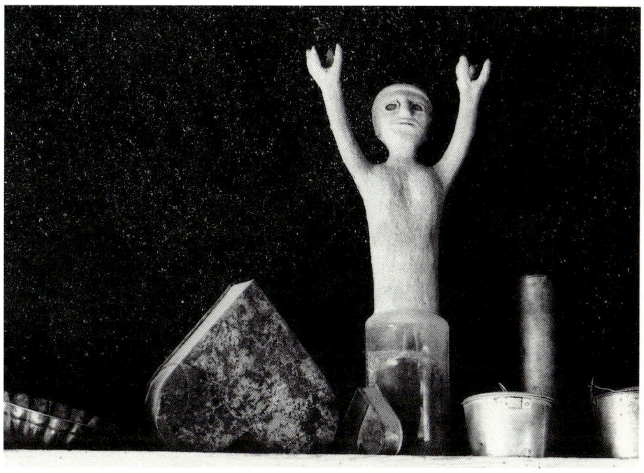

'She showed you all her little things,' recalls Gertie Retief about visits to the Owl House, where every shelf and every surface contained personal collections of objects. Here a shelf in the corner of the kitchen holds an array of carefully chosen items. The heart was a favourite motif of Helen's, one which she also used for a number of her mirrors. The figure, with arms upraised, was modelled by Koos Malgas onto a glass bottle. It is one of many similar figures in the house. Helen saw these figures as servers. They are all intended to hold candles in their hands, providing light. Some on dressing-tables also hold jewellery and accessories. They are dressing attendants, holding and passing things. These servers in the house are the forerunners of the garden hostesses. Resting on their bottle skirts, like their garden counterparts, they formally resemble them, only in miniature.

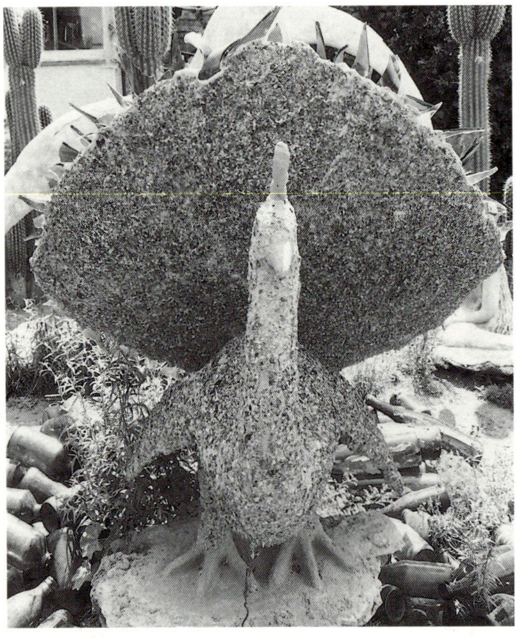

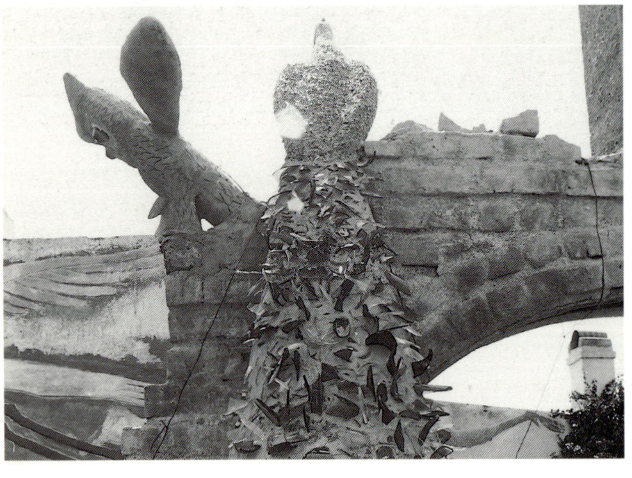

The exotic tails of the sculptured peacocks are studded with coloured shards of glass that glint in the sunlight. This is one of the innumerable inventive ways in which Helen employed the medium of glass. These pictures, taken by Johann Potgieter, show the peacock tails shortly after they were made and in pristine condition. Sadly, much of the glass has since come adrift.

she had all this glitter'.

Piet was of assistance to Helen in many small ways. She would often call upon him to do odd jobs for her. Cleaning the lamps was one of these. He would perform these chores early in the morning before he began his working day as a builder. 'Six o'clock she would come to fetch me. Miss Helen liked the walk early in the morning.'

While employed in the garden by Miss Helen, Piet made a second owl, identical to the first. These first two owls, he said, were made in remembrance of a pair of owls Miss Helen had kept as pets and which had died in captivity. These early owls, although far less sophisticated than much of the later work, set a precedent for the sculptural use of glass and cement. Over the years these humble materials were to be lavishly employed at the Owl House.

Cement and glass were materials that were readily available to Miss Helen. The glass came from empty bottles which the local 'Coloured' children collected for her. Unbroken empty bottles as well as the crushed glass made from the bottles were marvellously used in a multitude of imaginative and inventive ways. It is partly the awe-inspiring use of commonplace materials, such as this glass from discarded bottles, that infuses the Owl House with a considerable degree of formal fascination. Walking over a section of patio paving, one becomes aware, for instance, that the surface has been created using the bottoms of upturned bottles. The bottoms of bottles are again cleverly used to create the glinting eyes of the army of staring owls. Elsewhere, bottles have been filled with coloured shards of crushed glass and laid out on the ground so as to form a paving that gleams, in moonlight and sunshine, with innumerable sparkling hues. Then there are the shrine structures, which Miss Helen called her 'Meccas'. These were ingeniously built from tiers of beer bottles, as were the skirts of the stately garden hostesses. A number of ornate peacocks, as well as some beautiful wall murals that shimmer in the light, were created from cement embedded with jagged shards and finely ground glass particles. Miss Helen's use of glass is extensive, and truly innovative.

However, perhaps the most spectacular display of glass is the crushed glass on the walls and ceilings inside the Owl House.

Piet van der Merwe recalls their first attempt when, with Miss Helen's guidance, he created the very first patch of wall to be covered in this manner. The way this exterior glass mural twinkled and glittered in the moonlight absolutely delighted Miss Helen and it was then that the concept of using glass throughout the house occurred to her.

The first 'test-patch' for the glass experiment had been a small section of wall on the patio. Miss Helen had prepared the glass herself, crushing it and carefully washing it in water so as to get rid of all dust. She then spread the shining particles out on a mat to dry. Piet painted a clear adhesive onto the wall and then, using a plasterer's board, he flung the ground glass particles onto the wet, sticky surface. Those particles that fell to the ground were meticulously gathered up by Miss Helen, who washed them again and re-sorted them according to colour and size.

Preparing the glass was Miss Helen's self-appointed task and one which she always performed herself. She would grade the particles carefully and keep them in special preserve jars on the larder shelf. In the early days the task of 'plastering' the glass onto the walls was done by Piet and it was he who covered most of the walls in the house. The procedure never changed much from the first method tried, except when sometimes coloured paint was substituted for the clear adhesive and Miss Helen began to make use of old coffee grinders to grind the glass into fine particles. Miss Helen always supervised Piet closely, directing operations, making decisions as to when a change of colour was needed, and gathering up the fallen glass. Piet was always afraid of glass particles

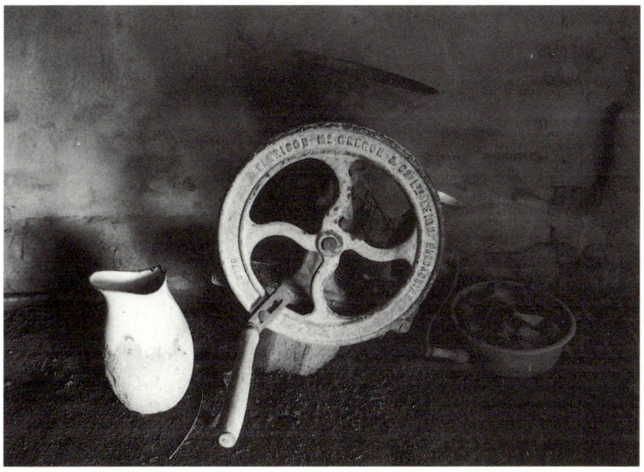

Helen used an old coffee grinder to crush glass into fine particles. She always carefully washed the crushed glass and graded it according to size. The graded glass was kept in preserve jars on the larder shelf, ready for use. Peggy Delport recalls Helen's obsession with glass-glitter, and the way she made it her self-appointed task to process the glass: 'Of course, all that glitter, that was her. Every surface, every chair was covered with crushed glass. She would pay all the children around here to go and collect all that glass, and she would grind it with her own hands in an old coffee grinder.'

falling in his eyes and Miss Helen would admonish him, saying that there was no reason to be scared. Then she would take a handful of glass, stretch her arm up into the air and open her hand so that the glass came showering down on her head like confetti. Piet was not convinced but he never wore goggles. When fragments of glass did get into his eyes, Miss Helen would dampen a handkerchief and dab gently at the glass. Nevertheless the work took its toll on Piet van der Merwe's eyesight:

> *This left eye of mine, a lot of glass got into it. It can't see very well. I got the glass out. I got the glass out easily, but the eye never came right. It has always remained dim. I've gone to the doctor time and again, but nothing has helped.*

Koos Malgas, who in later years took over the glass work from Piet, and who covered the ceilings of the house in the same manner as the walls had been covered, remembers that Miss Helen had devised a more effective remedy for glass that got into the eye. Instructing Koos on no account to rub his eye, she would fill a white basin with clean water and bring it to wherever he was. Then she would make him use his fingers to open and close his top and bottom eyelids, while bathing the eye in the water. According to Koos, the glass would then simply 'float out'.

Miss Helen was not satisfied until glass covered almost every available surface indoors — walls, ceilings, doors, window frames, chairs and chests. The Owl House became a house of glass. The shimmering glass interior was part of her obsession with surfaces and substances that caught the light and sparkled. It was her desire to create a world of glitter.

When Jill Wenman and Francie Lund travelled up to Nieu Bethesda from Cape Town to visit Helen one weekend, the gift they brought with them typified what Helen loved most. Francie recalls:

Miss Helen wrote asking for shiny things, so Jill went to the OK Bazaars and bought two kilos of tinsel and three yards of silver lamé.

The glittering substances with which Helen Martins chose to bedeck her house respond best to point sources of light. Her candles and her lamps were ideal in this respect. When seen in the daytime, the house seems peculiarly flat and rather lifeless, a little like a stage-set in broad daylight without the magic of theatrical lighting.

In pursuit of her world of glitter, however, both Piet and Koos remember Miss Helen as a tireless worker. She transmitted a sense of urgency, almost as if time were running out for her, and those who worked with her were driven to work equally hard. 'The work had to go on,' said Piet. 'She never grew tired.'

Piet van der Merwe was employed to undertake much of the early building work which began the radical transformation of the modest dorp house into an elaborate fantasy environment, a sort of Aladdin's cave packed with treasures. Helen's fascination with the effects of light and her desire to create the right degree of unearthly illumination for the interior spaces led her to devise the idea of knocking out large windows between rooms into which panes of coloured glass were inserted. Piet was also instructed to knock out a number of exterior walls and insert windows, some of which were coloured, which had the effect of flooding the interior with tinted light.

Piet remembers working on the windows alongside 'Baas Hattingh'. This Mr Hattingh was a builder, an exceptionally tall man, and it was believed that the long bed in the Green Bedroom was built especially for him. Local gossip had it that at one time, when the sun was setting in the evening, Mr Hattingh could regularly be seen walking down the road to the Owl House. In the early mornings he would be seen walking back.

Even the building work that Piet was employed to

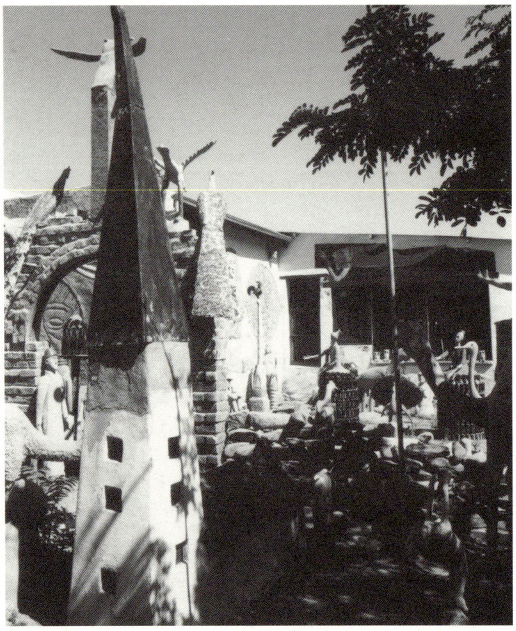

Piet van der Merwe helped build this church with its tall, pointed spire. At the top of the steeple is a shiny star. Miss Helen enjoyed observing the play of the sun and moonlight on the heavenly bodies of her making.

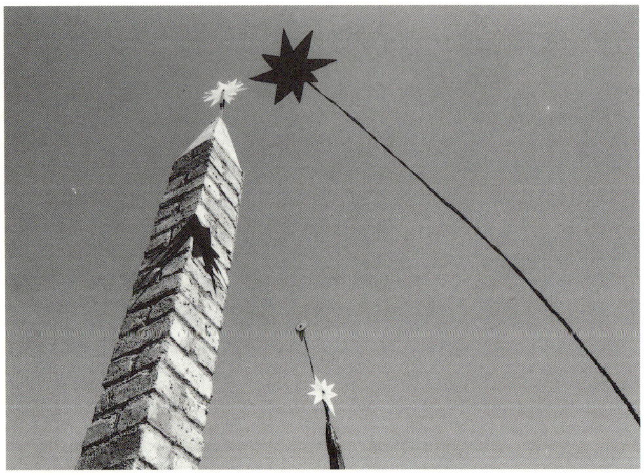

A multitude of stars, atop pillars, steeples and slender wire stalks, once hung over the yard. Many have fallen down. The few that remain give some indication of how Miss Helen's own heaven below heaven once appeared.

construct outside of the house embodied something of Miss Helen's abiding fascination with manipulating the play of light. Helped on this occasion by his young son, Piet built the two largest churches in the yard. In a rare interview, granted to a reporter, Miss Helen talked about one of the churches and explained the intricacy of her engineered light effects.

> *Look there, in my yard. There is my church, that I had built. On top of the steeple is a star, made from three different sorts of glass. And on that other steeple, there is also a star and a half-moon. At certain times of the day, those stars reflect the sunlight through my coloured windows. And at night my half-moon again reflects light through my windows.*

A woman leans from one of the windows of a church in the yard. She clutches a candle holder in her hand, lighting the way in the dark. Here, as elsewhere, Miss Helen's fascination with light takes on symbolic significance. The idea of the guiding light, as again manifested in her various representations of the Eastern star, contains a spiritual dimension, the suggestion being that the journey towards the light is a focal point of personal aspiration and fulfilment.

It was Miss Helen's desire to experiment with reflected light-effects that contributed to her love of mirrors. It was Piet who was instructed to hang the custom-made mirrors which Helen ordered from around the country on the walls of the house. Helen began collecting mirrors at the time when she first began to transform the interior of the house after the death of her parents. She went to great lengths to obtain her exact requirements. A letter, written in 1957, from a Johannesburg supplier of mirrors, reveals her attempt to acquire an anthropomorphised sun mirror of certain specifications, perhaps even the one that now hangs above the front door. (At the time, Miss Helen was

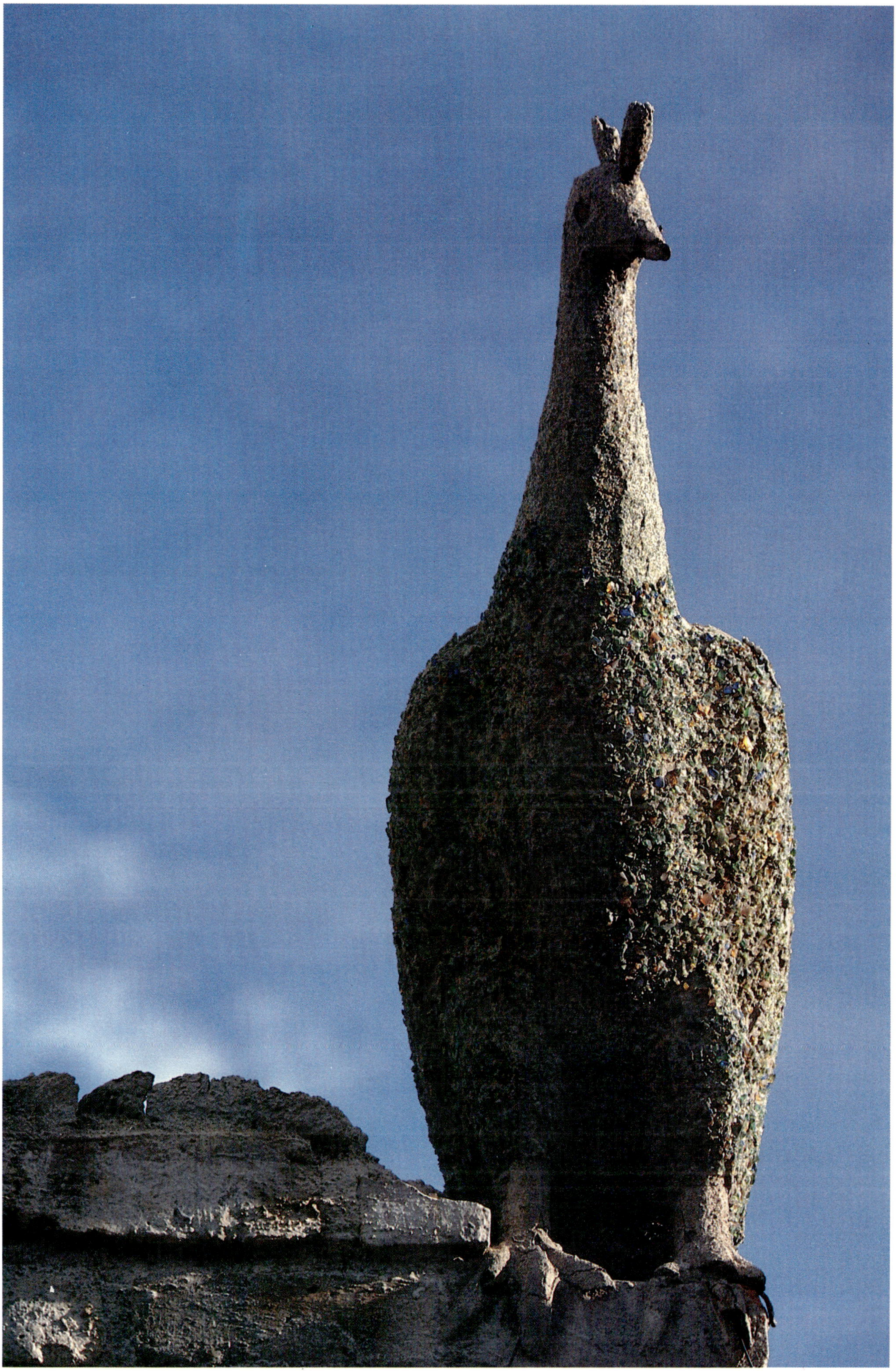

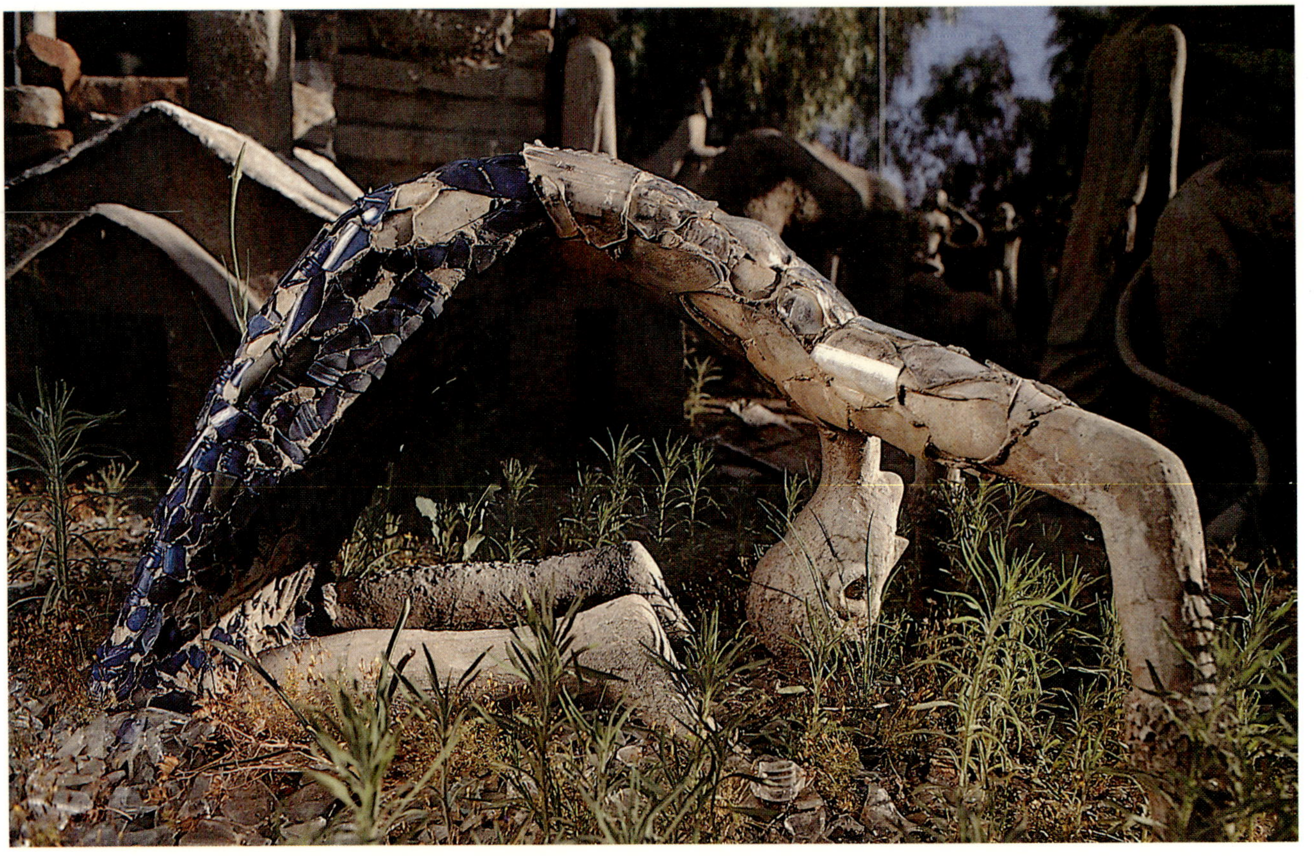

This tumbling-back figure is a sun-worshipper. The sun-worshippers are exultant, prayerful figures. However, rather than bending forward, with heads bowed down, as in traditional worship, Miss Helen's worshippers wish to face the source of the godhead and thus arch backwards.

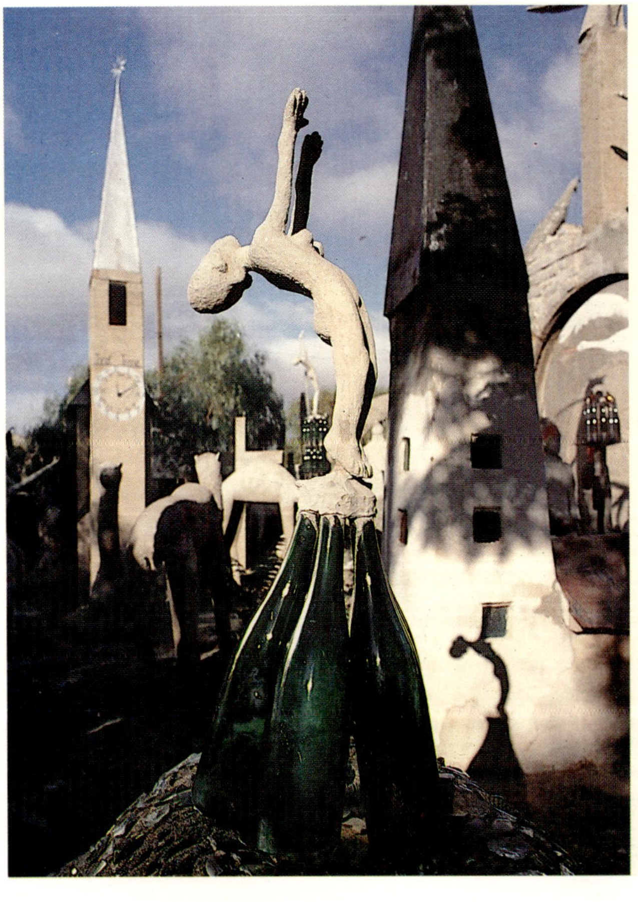

A miniature sun-worshipper, balanced on a pedestal of bottles, bends backwards in prayerful ecstasy.

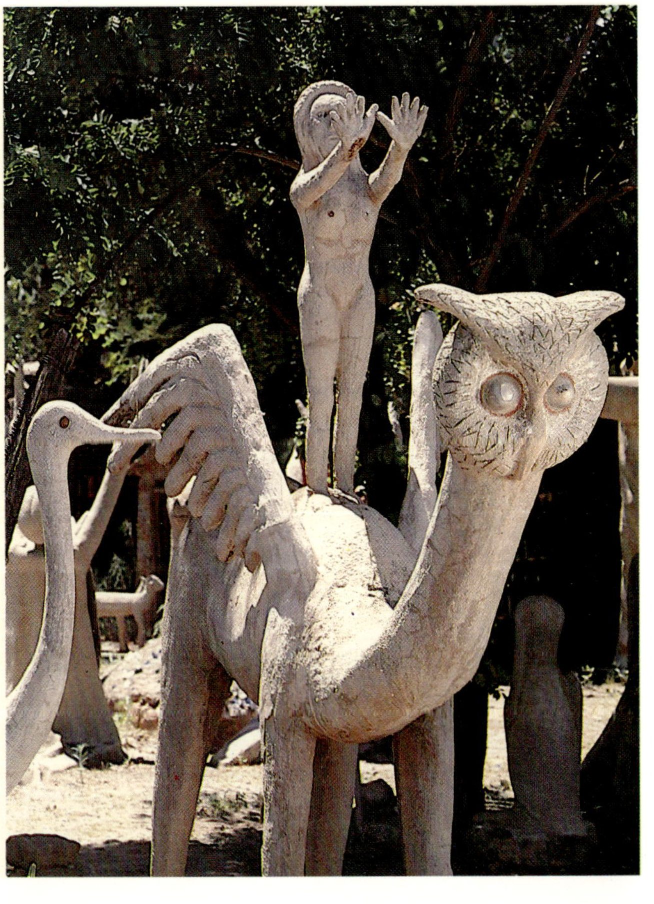

A lady upon a creature that is both camel and owl. She holds up her hands, 'to shield her eyes', Helen said, 'from the brightness of the light'.

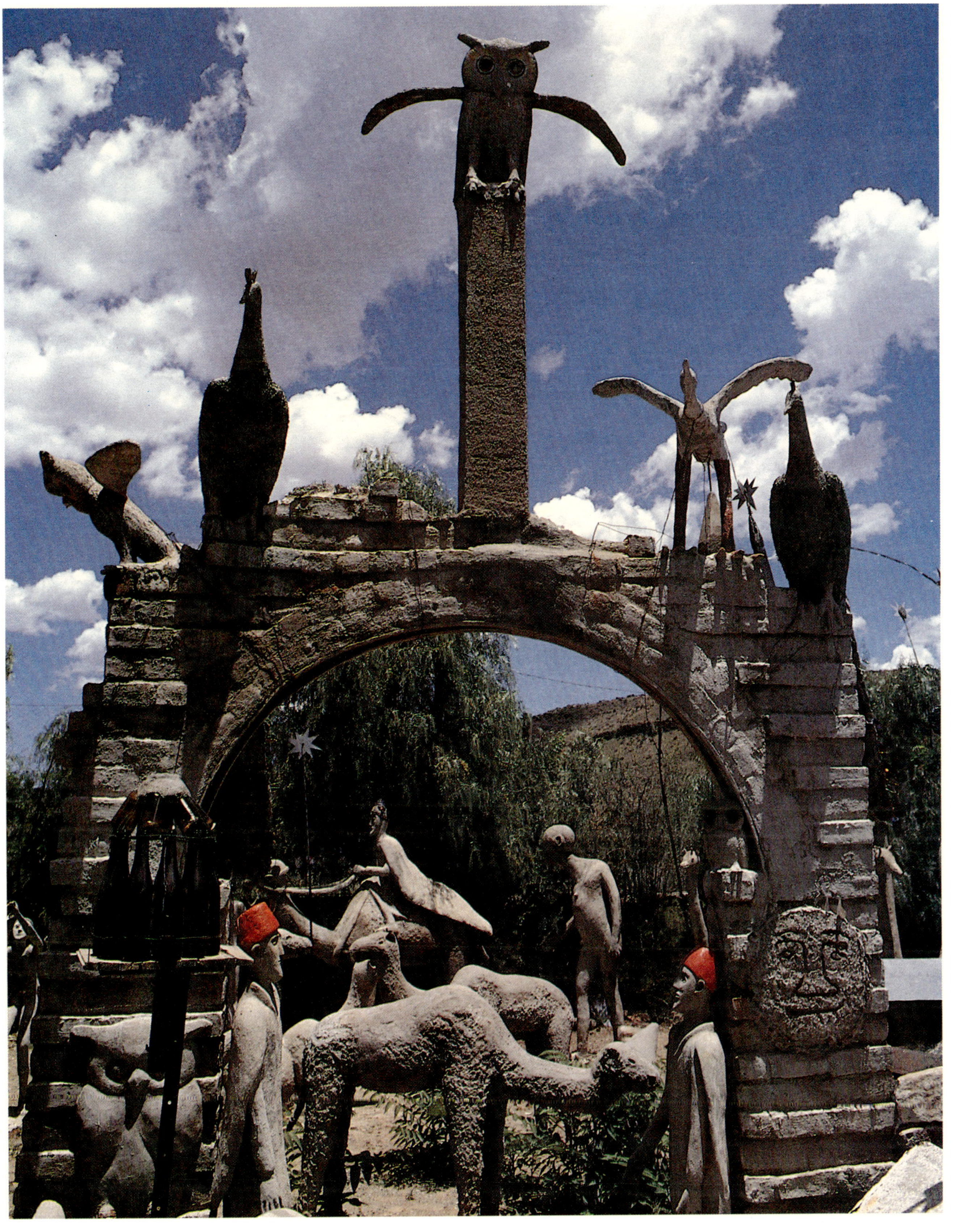

In 1971, when Dominee and Mrs Cloete took up residence in Nieu Bethesda, they were astonished to discover the existence of the Owl House behind the parsonage. 'I don't think she was really understood by the people of Nieu Bethesda,' Mrs Cloete said. 'We couldn't really get to know her. She was such an enigmatic person.'

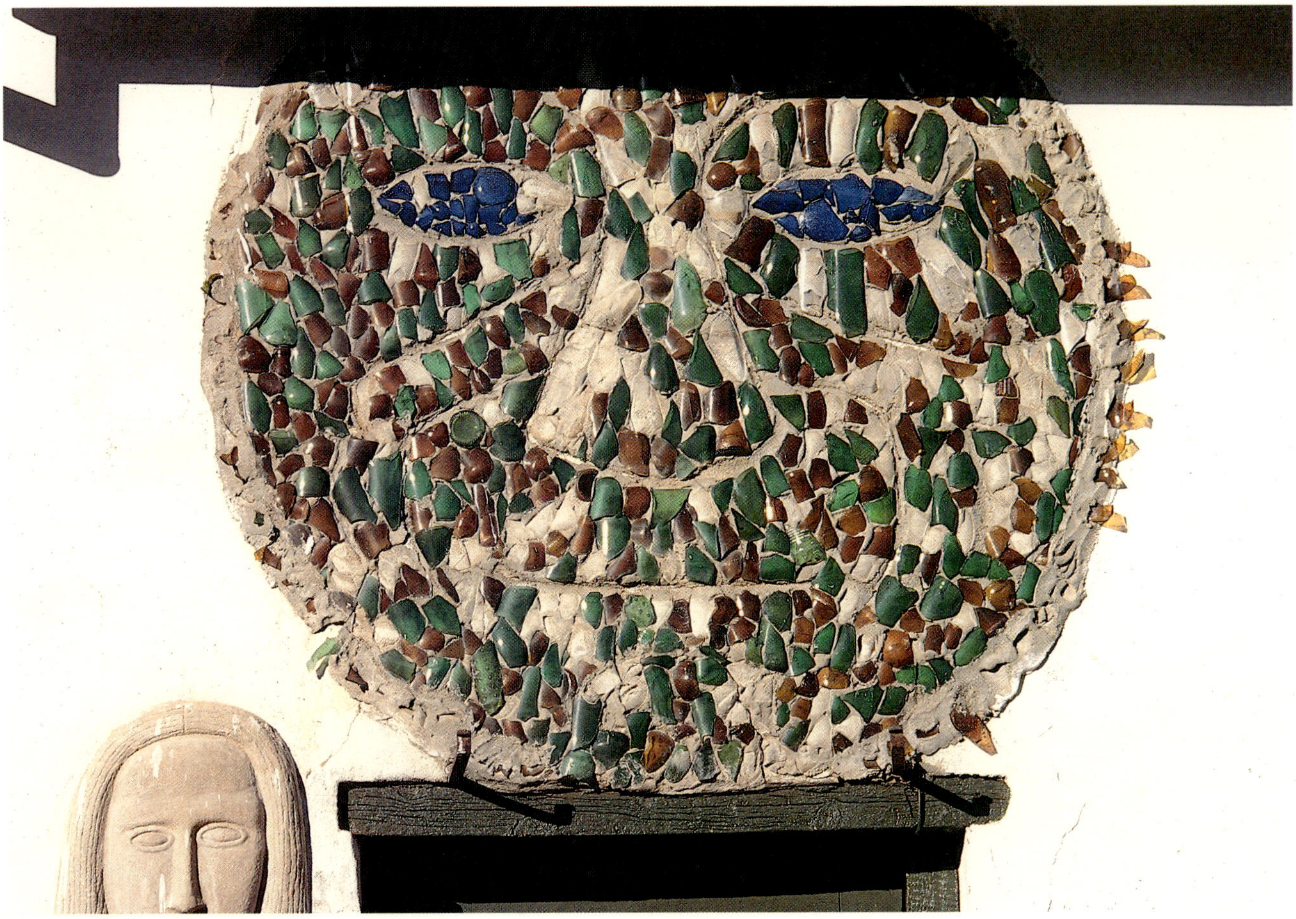

Jagged, broken shards were used in mosaic work to create rich and colourful surfaces, such as the large sun relief above the door of the Lion's Den. More finely crushed glass dust was flung onto wet cement and adhered to form a twinkling patina on many of the sculptural pieces. The breasts of peacocks have been coated in this manner, as have the upper torsos of the meisies, or the garden hostesses. The skirts of the hostesses, constructed from tiers of intact bottles, show another manner in which glass has been ingeniously used. Details of glass work, such as the exquisite clusters of gems on the wrists and hands of the hostesses, show Helen's inventiveness in using a commonplace material.

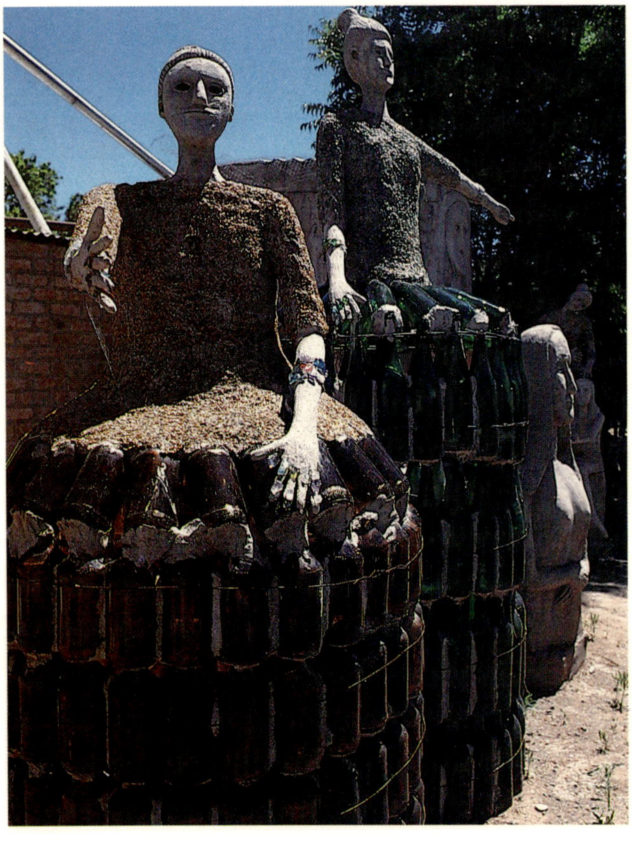

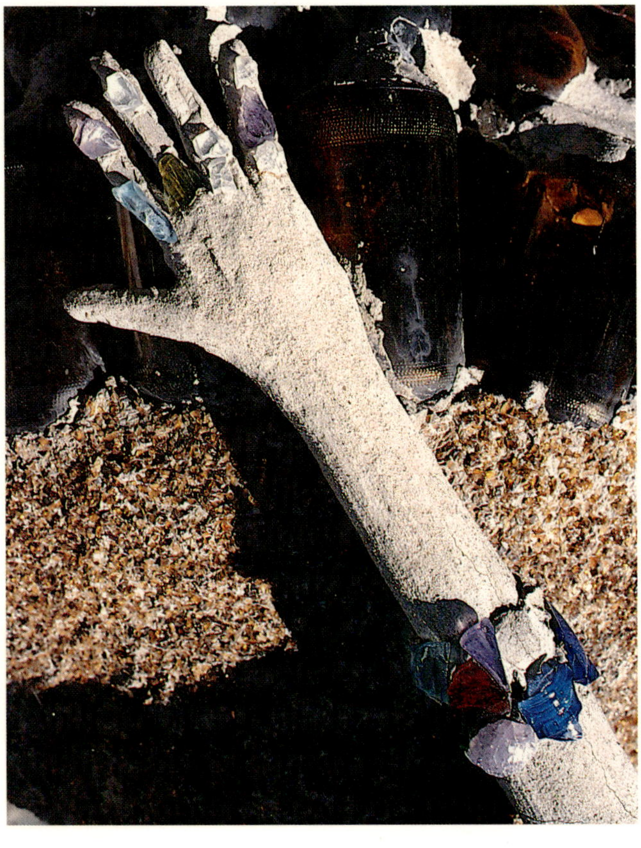

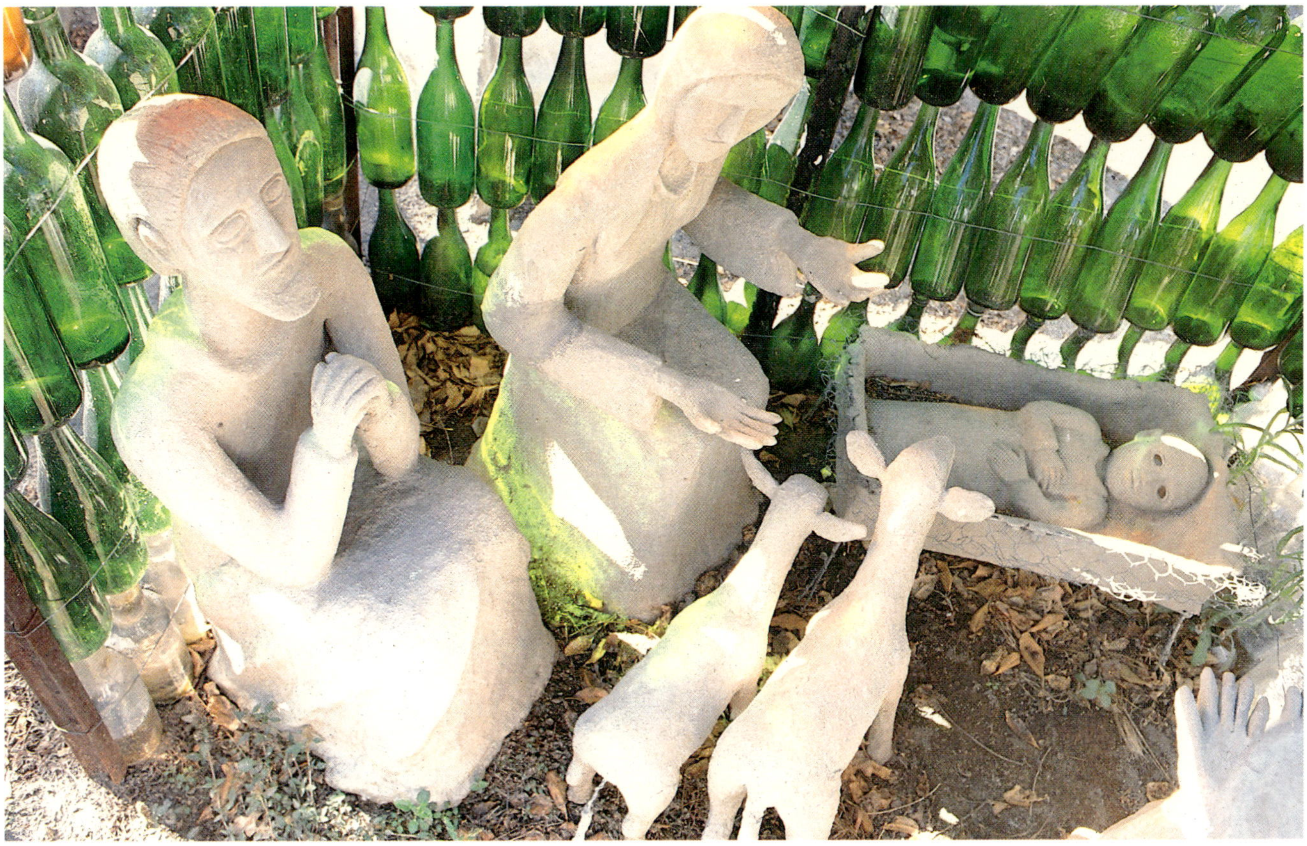

Sheltered in a shed built from bottles is a depiction of the Nativity. Sheep curiously nose up to the crib, while behind them come the shepherds and wise men. It is an important focal point in the garden, towards which worshippers are moving. It used to be surmounted by a star, the Star of Bethlehem. A second, more unorthodox, Stable of Bethlehem, as Helen called it, is situated beneath the sign on the fence proclaiming East/Oos. This hut is also the focus of a pilgrimage. A shepherd with his flock has arrived. The stable is marked, not by a star, but by a modern-day equivalent in the form of a powerful headlamp.

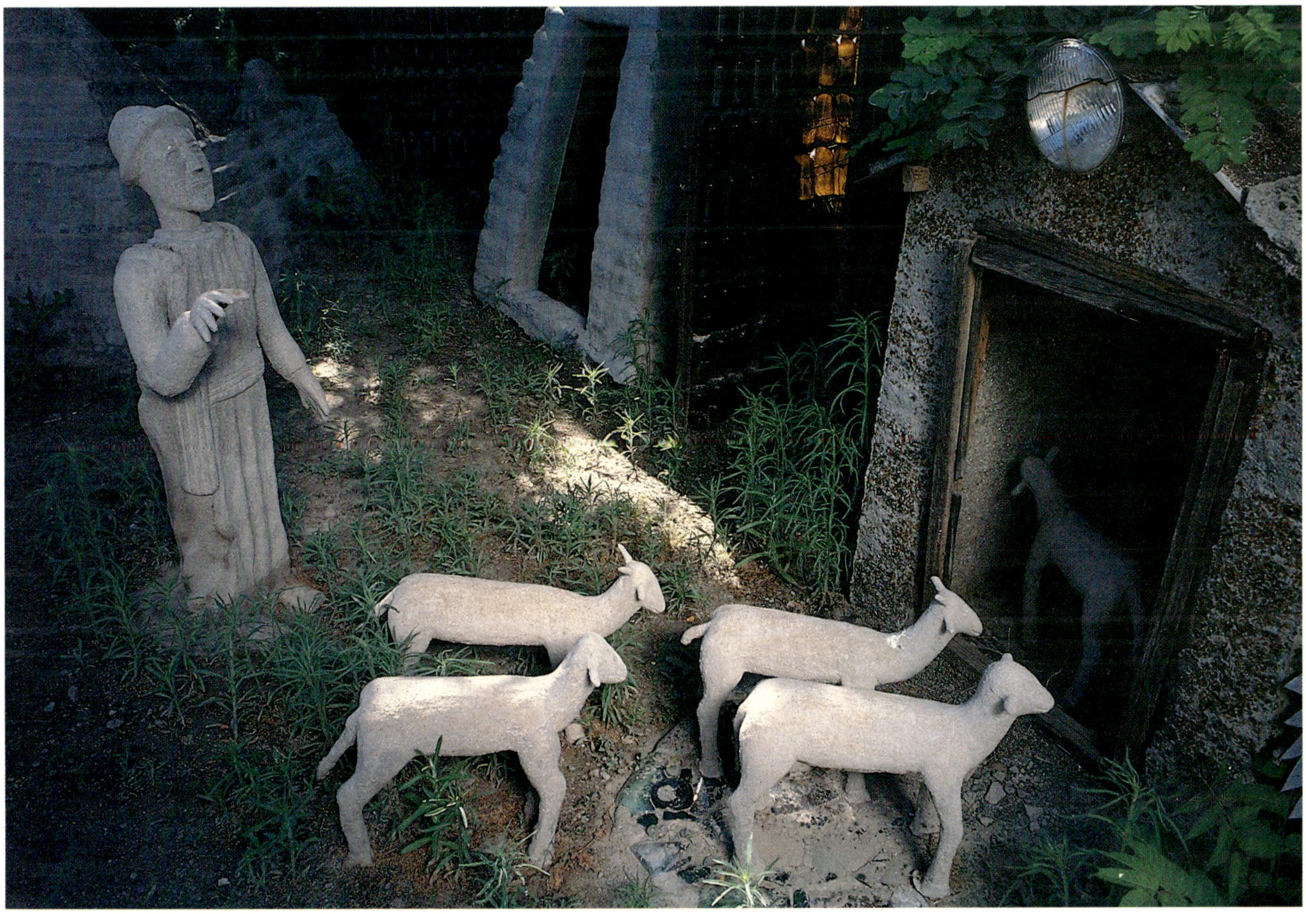

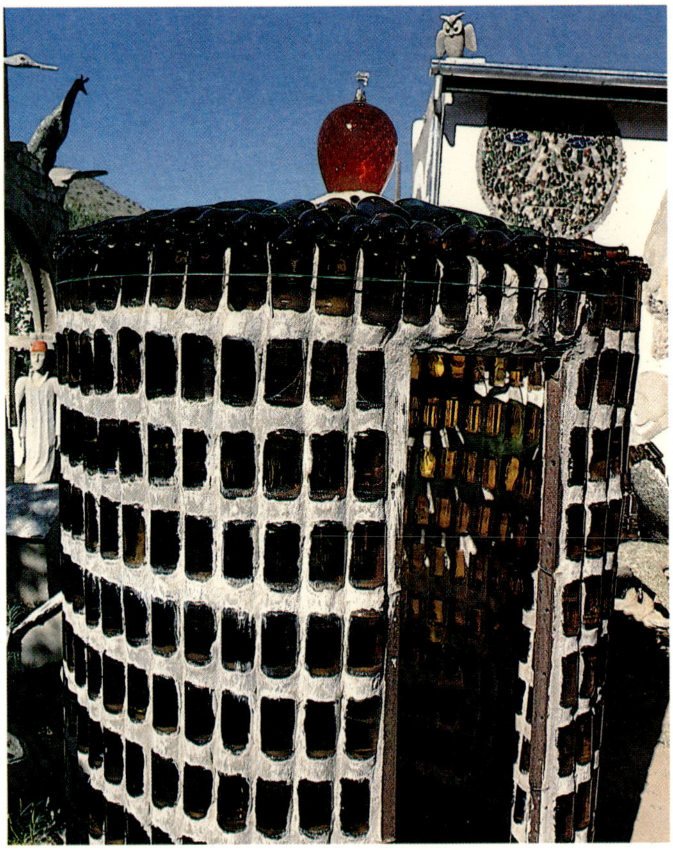

Top left and below: Helen called the bottle shrines her Meccas. Interested in Islam, she at one stage entered into a lengthy correspondence with an Islamic religious organisation. But although intrigued by aspects of the religion she was not a convert, and took a witty pleasure in undermining some of the fundamentalist tenets. Her Meccas, built from bottles which once contained alcohol, are a sly dig against Islamic law.

The Meccas are contemplation shrines. One even holds a seat where the meditator can sit and reflect, while gazing down at a half-moon dammetjie. The beehive-like structure of the shrines, and the honey coloured light that is filtered to the inside, are significant: the bee and its honey are symbolically associated with inspiration and the ability to discern the essence of life. The bee gathers its honey from many different blooms. Honey is an essence. It has been used as a symbol of the essence of life which lies beneath the surface of existence. Likewise, contemplation and self-reflection are bound up with an attempt to discern the essence of things and delve beneath the surface of experience. The structure of the shrines, with their beehive associations, provide most suitable contemplation spaces.

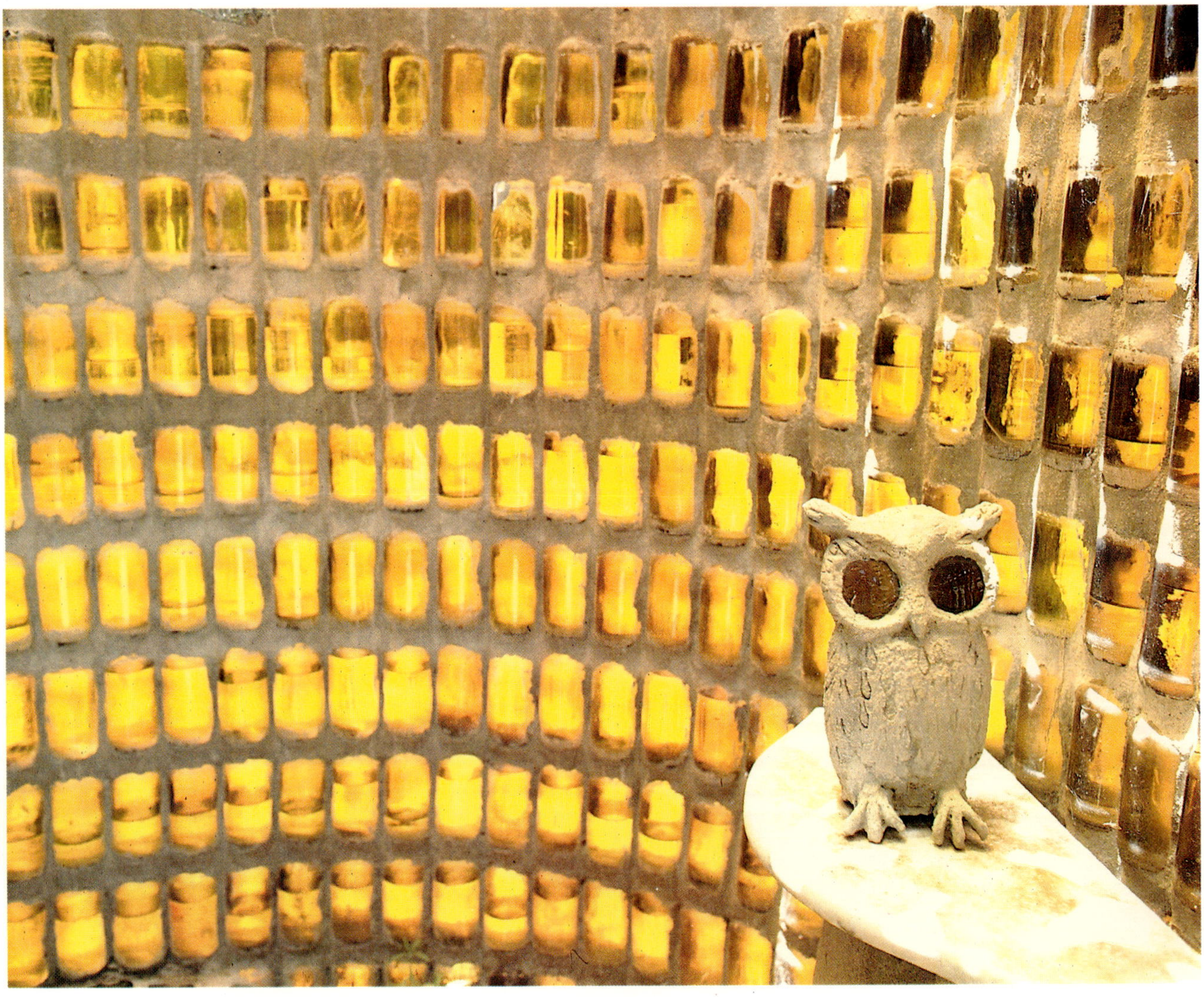

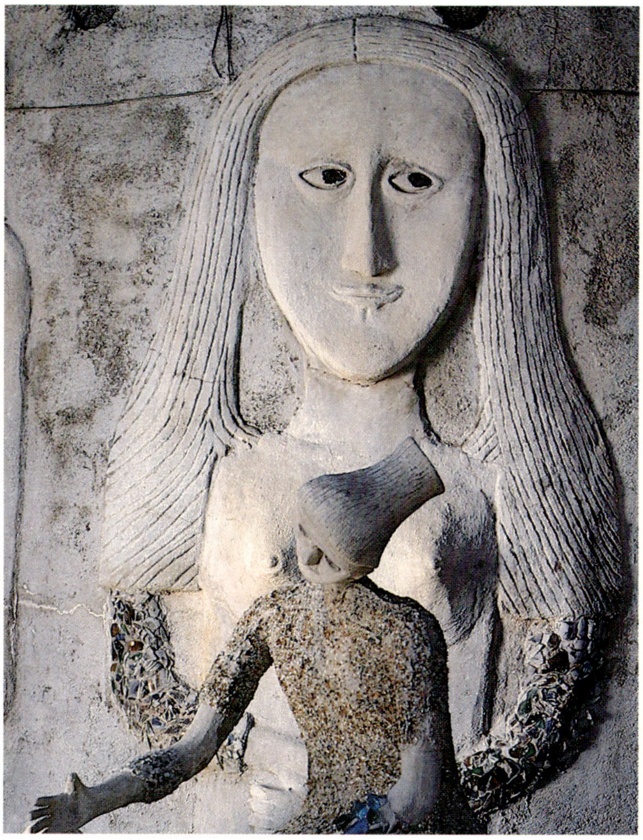

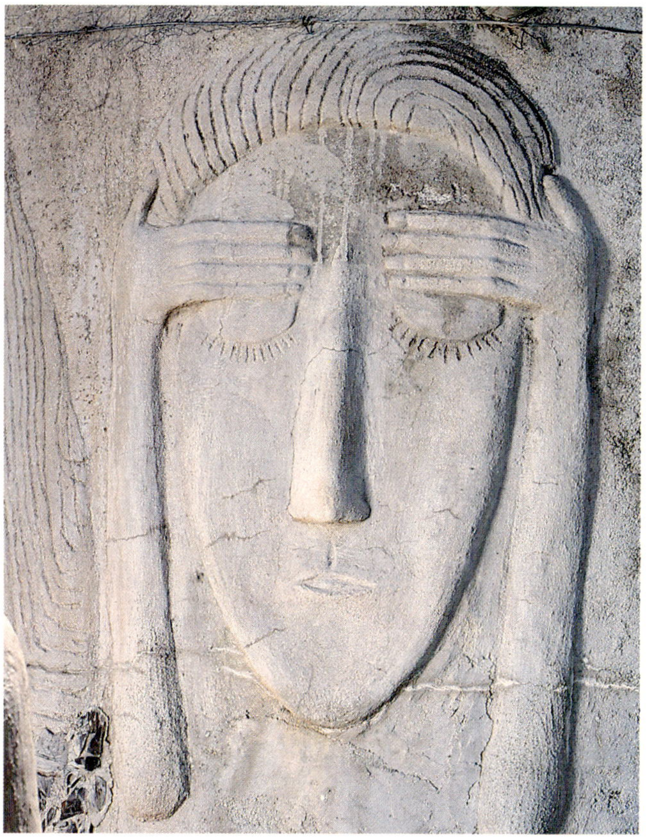

Two renditions of the Mona Lisa have been created on the exterior of the water tank. The Mona Lisa was an important icon for Helen Martins. Prints of the Mona Lisa hang in the house, while numerous cement renditions are scattered around the garden. It is believed Helen thought that, as a young woman, she looked like the Mona Lisa, and hence identified with it. But more importantly, in the context of *the Owl* **HOUSE**, the image of the Mona Lisa, the all-knowing, beautiful and enigmatic female is a 'wisdom anima'. The anima is a psychological term for the female element in the male unconscious. There are known to be four stages in the development of the anima, all of which Helen represented in her creative environment. The first and lowest stage represents instinctual and biological relations, such as are symbolised, at *the Owl* **HOUSE**, by the image of Eve. The second stage is personified, by Helen, in her use of images that convey the idea of courtly and romantic love. The Virgin Mary, visible in the sculpture garden as well as in the house, is a typical manifestation of the third level. She raises love to the heights of spiritual devotion. The highest level is the 'wisdom anima', of which the Mona Lisa is a manifestation. The Mona Lisa imagery at *the Owl* **HOUSE** is one of many indications of Helen's thematic interest in the development of the psyche.

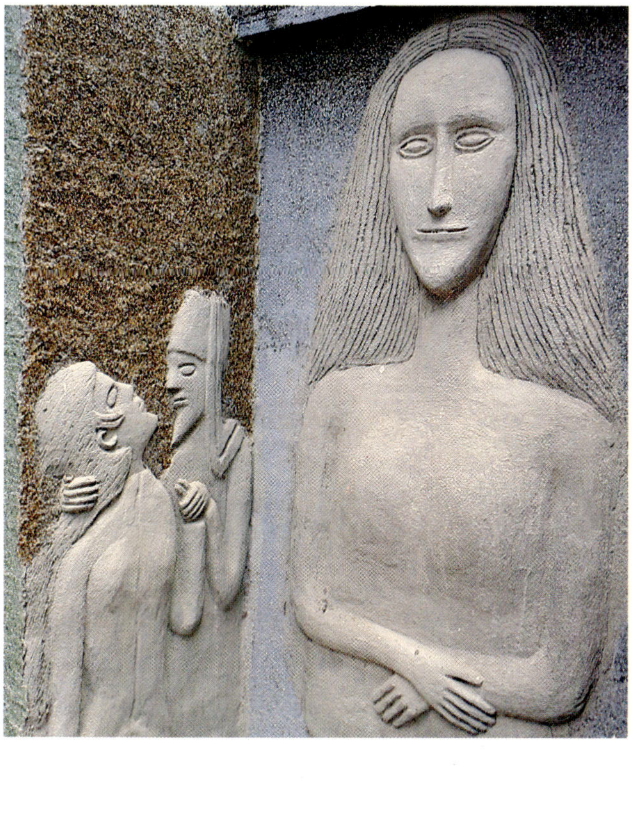

A Mona Lisa, arms folded and breasts exposed, as is typical of the Mona Lisas at the Owl House, has been modelled onto the wall of the patio. In the corner of the adjacent wall is an image of lovers. It has been copied from a Sherriffs illustration in one of the versions of the *Rubáiyát* that Helen had acquired.

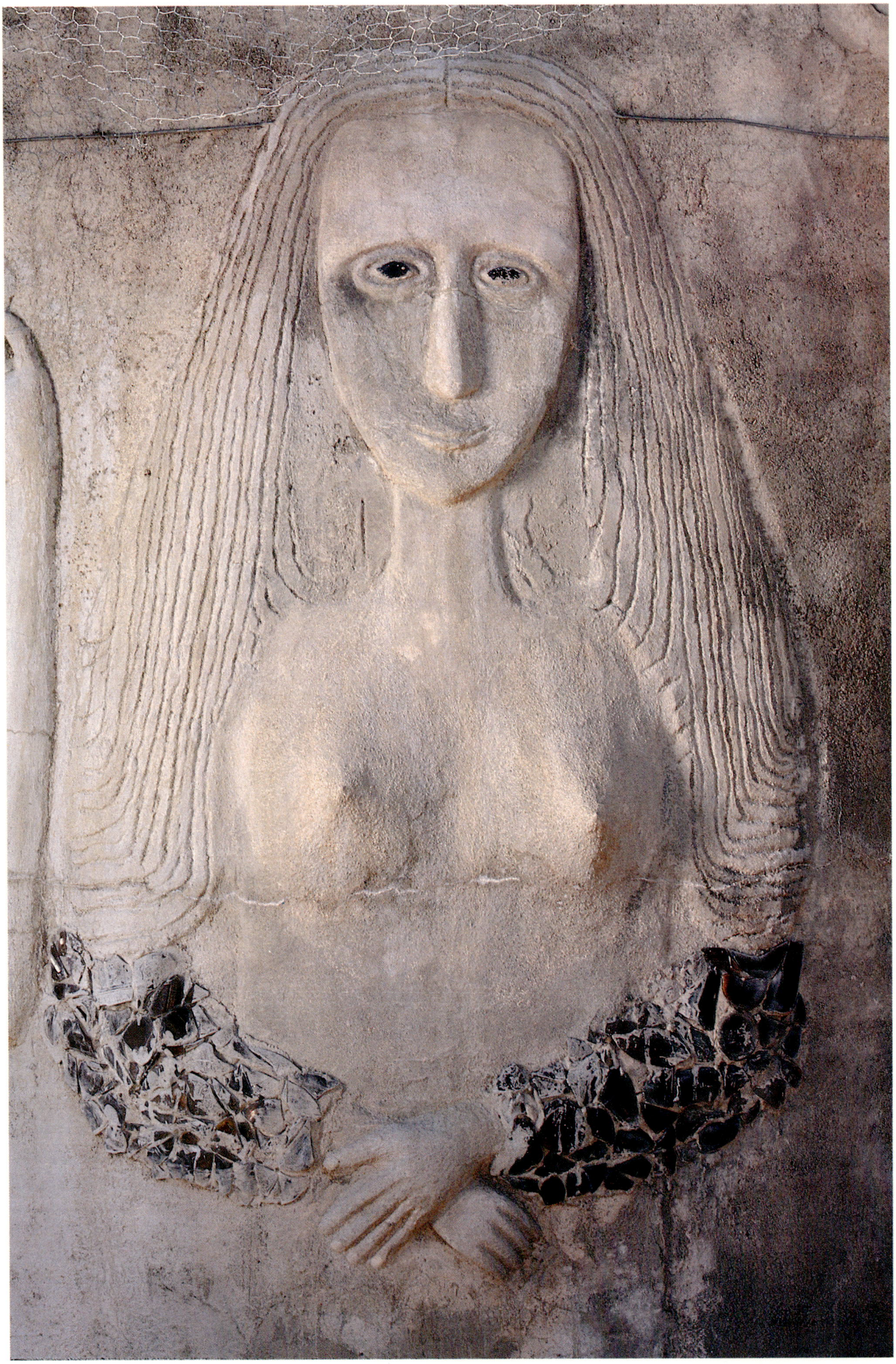

using her name from her first marriage, Pienaar.)

> *Dear Mrs Pienaar*
> *I have just been informed that as an alternative to the mirrored background, my agency can offer a background of Black Vitradite Glass. The effect of the face will be even more intense as it will be reflected in a whitish colour and will contrast to the black of the background.*

Not only mirrors, but her tinted glass, too, was ordered, often with great difficulty, from around the country. A letter from Richard and Barlow in Cape Town informed her, with regret, that they could not match 'any of the samples of tinted glass submitted'.

The purchase of glass, mirrors and other materials was a considerable expense. So was the large quantity of chicken meal Helen Martins needed to feed her birds, and she often complained of being in debt. Piet recalled with a laugh how she would nevertheless have heaps of coins scattered around the house, as if lack of money was not an issue. In order to make out on her meagre pension, she would economise on personal items such as clothing. 'Clothes,' she would say, 'are nothing. One must only be clean. I buy glass and mirrors instead.'

Miss Helen was known for her eccentric attire. Rosemary van der Merwe, a villager, remembers her being 'rather oddly dressed'. She wore 'the clothes her two sisters Alida and Annie sent her, and very haphazardly, old evening dresses as nightgowns and so on'.

Helen economised not only on clothes, but on food. She lived mainly on bread and tea, and would drink her tea to the dregs: 'It must not be wasted,' she explained once to a visitor.

Her health was a worry to her friends and neighbours, but, as Francie Lund recalls, Helen was fiercely independent and there was little anyone could do:

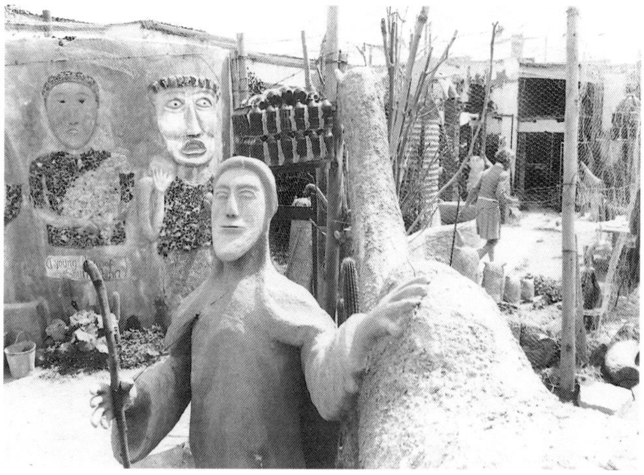

In the background, the small figure of Miss Helen can be seen walking through one of her bird-cages. The cost of feeding the many birds she once kept was a considerable drain on her small income. (Photograph: Johann Potgieter)

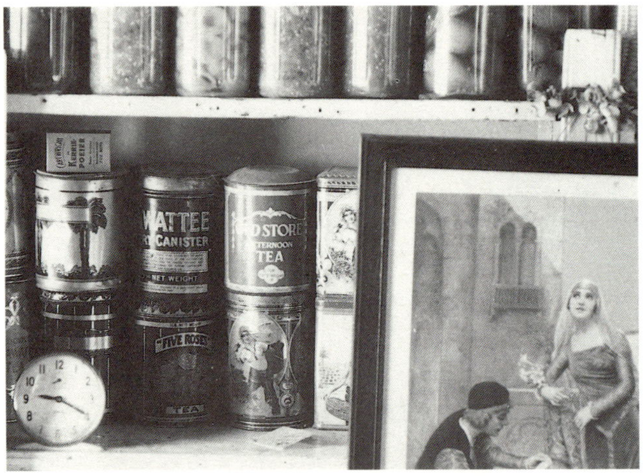

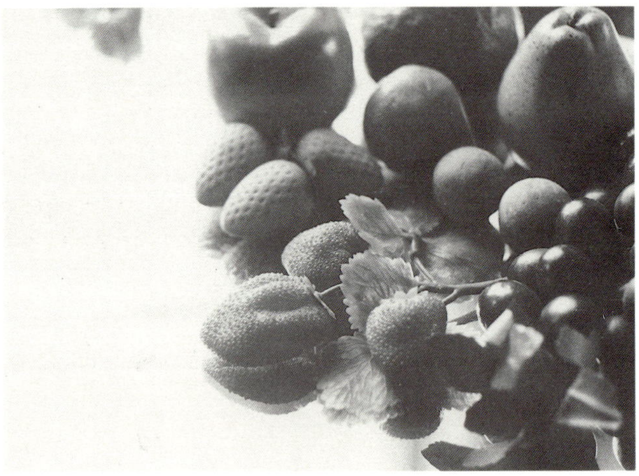

Jars, with colourful bottled preserves, and arrangements of plastic fruit, are liberally displayed at the Owl House, suggesting a haven of plenty. Yet Helen was often a worry to her neighbours, who felt that she was not feeding herself properly. Peggy Delport recalls seeing the rows of preserves which were never eaten: 'There were jars of old preserves. Some were thirty years old, which she hadn't even touched. They were just there.' John Moyle remembers that Helen kept the preserves on display because she enjoyed looking at the colours — 'but she kept pinching the lids for the eyes of her owls', and much of the bottled fruit went bad.

(Photographs: Johann Potgieter)

A friend (Jill Wenman) *and I drove Miss Helen up to Winkelspruit in Natal to see her sister Annie, combining it with a family holiday for ourselves. The return trip was shared with my brother, a doctor, who met Miss Helen for the first time when we fetched her from Annie's. There had been a general concern over Miss Helen's health — she was skinny and wasn't eating properly. I asked my brother to pull a bit of medical rank and talk to her about this. He did this in the car on the way down, pointing out that even though she felt strong, black tea and bread was not the best way to keep her bones strong. There would be weakening that was not visible, he told her. He said he would send her vitamin pills and iron tablets, and that she should supplement her diet with these. She listened attentively and said, 'Thank you very much.'*

We arrived at Nieu Bethesda after dark, and after the kettle had boiled, she said she had something to show me. Holding me by the hand, she led me to a bedroom by the light of a paraffin lamp — I think it was the Honeymoon Room. She opened a vast, dark cupboard, and asked me to open a cardboard box at the bottom of it. There were boxes and boxes of vitamin pills, iron tablets and so on — sent to her over the months by family and friends. She said, 'My darling, I know you and your brother mean well, but I promise you will only be wasting your money if you send me these things, because I will not take them. I will not be like one of these old people who go on and on and finally you have to beat them over the head with a hammer to make them die. I know what I'm doing.'

I collapsed in a heap of laughter on the bed. Touché, Miss Helen, touché. I promise to try never to patronise you again.

In addition to the cost of her raw materials, Miss Helen had another expense to consider: payment to the men she employed. She paid them well, by local standards. Piet was paid by the week. 'In those days,' he said, 'it was ten pounds. That was a good wage. Most people were paid three shillings a day.'

Koos Malgas remembered an incentive system whereby Miss Helen would pay him according to how pleased she was with his work.

> *She would wait until a piece was finished. If it was not one hundred per cent she would not pay so much. I remember that a camel would take me about a week to make, and for that I could expect to be paid about R60, but it would vary.*

In the early years, before Koos Malgas began to work for Helen Martins, she relied on the labour of Jonas Adams, Piet van der Merwe and a number of other temporary workers. Of these, Piet seems to have done the most work. In addition to the owls, the churches and his work inside the house, Piet also built the Moon Gate and the large free-standing arch, although it was only later that these became embellished with birds. Another local man, known as 'Oupa Frans', helped with the construction of the arch. 'Oupa Frans' has become immortalised in the garden in the large figure of an old man, made by Piet. Piet said that Miss Helen had wanted a figure that looked very old, and when the piece was completed they named him after the old man in the village.

According to Piet van der Merwe the source of inspiration for much of the building work he did at the Owl House in these early years was a large, well-illustrated book belonging to Miss Helen. The book has since vanished from the house and, as Piet cannot read, he was unable to identify it. However, it was more than likely the large family Bible which Rosemary van der Merwe remembers seeing around the house. Piet confirmed that

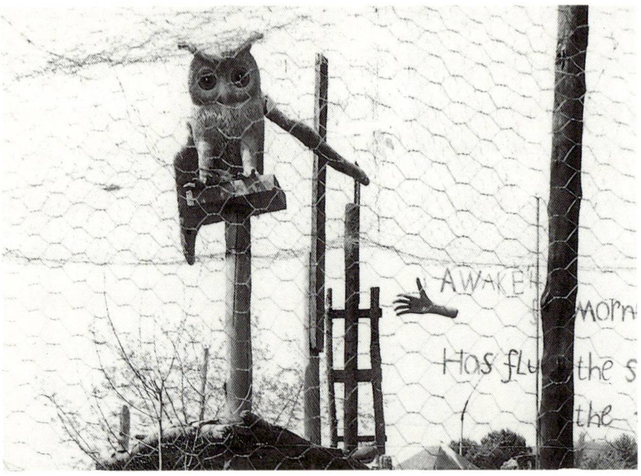

An owl perched atop a high pole in this portion of the wire caging. Today neither the owl on his platform, nor the wire caging, remain. The words on the fence are part of a quatrain from the *Rubáiyát*. (Photograph: Johann Potgieter)

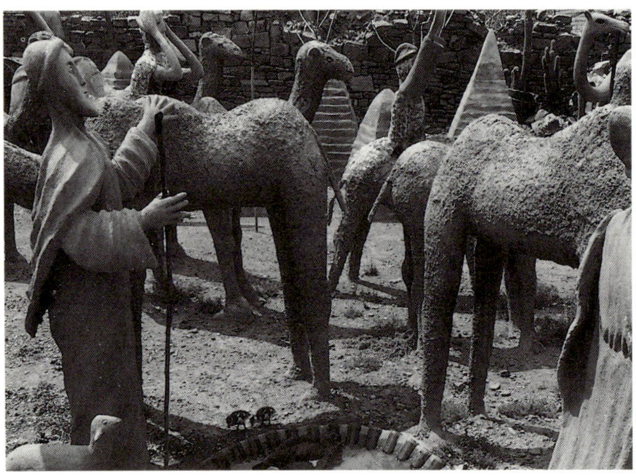

Egyptian geese used to swim in the dammetjies at the Owl House, as seen in Johann Potgieter's photograph of the garden as it was during the early seventies.

the church as well as the arch came from pictures out of the book. Miss Helen always kept the book beside her, he said, and the birds and the birdbath and many of the other things, also came out of it.

At Miss Helen's request, Piet, this time working with 'Baas Hattingh', enclosed the yard with chicken wire and created a series of interconnecting cages, and cages within cages, for Miss Helen's birds. At one time she kept numerous birds of many species. She even had peacocks confined in the cages. The local children would catch birds for her in the veld, which they would then bring to the Owl House. Her interest in birds was well known and people would bring birds to Nieu Bethesda from far and wide. At the time of Miss Helen's death, although the bird population had dwindled, there were still a large number of white pigeons and Egyptian geese on the property. The pigeons were released, and Jill Wenman took responsibility for the geese. She loaded them into her Volkswagen and drove with them to Knysna, where her father had a farm. A year later, on the anniversary of Miss Helen's death, dogs broke into the enclosure where the geese were kept, and they were all killed.

Peggy Delport visited the Owl House when the wire caging still existed and the cages were full.

> *You know, it was a very trapped feeling with all these birds. The whole place was covered with wire mesh, and then under that there was still other caging. There was an apricot tree just as you came out from the back door, that maybe had just come up by itself. There was wire mesh around that too, and there were doves in there. There were lots of those. And there was water, because of the birds, dammetjies of water.*

The dammetjies were sunken cement circles, edged with wine or beer bottles. Miss Helen always kept them filled with water for the birds. The task of keeping these pools filled with water was onerous. The water had to be collected in buckets from the furrow or the river. The dammetjies, however, were not the only birdbaths. Many of the concave-faced owls were birdbaths, too. There were other sculptures, within the once caged area, that were meant to be understood in relation to the birds that lived there. Tall, totem-like columns of owls, one on top of another, with outstretched wings, once stood in the caged area. The long wings served as cement branches upon which the birds could roost. The topmost owl was concave-faced, and it served as a birdbath. There were also the two female figures, hands cupped to create nests for the birds to lay eggs in. Other nests, now deserted, woven from wire, were hung from the roof of a beer-bottle shrine. Peggy Delport remembers being guided through the Owl House by Miss Helen, and she stressed that the live birds had to be seen as part of the total environment.

> *Everything was interacting and inter-leading: the live things and the people and the statues and what was said. I still remember the sound of her (Helen's) voice, the pace of it. And the glitter and the glass — there was tremendous excitement. Everything inter-led from one thing to another and from one space to another. And the cactus flowers and the aprtcot tree coming out and the white doves. I suppose my early memories of it, with all those birds, were that it was very dense, but it definitely ended at a certain point. There was a sense of totality to it.*

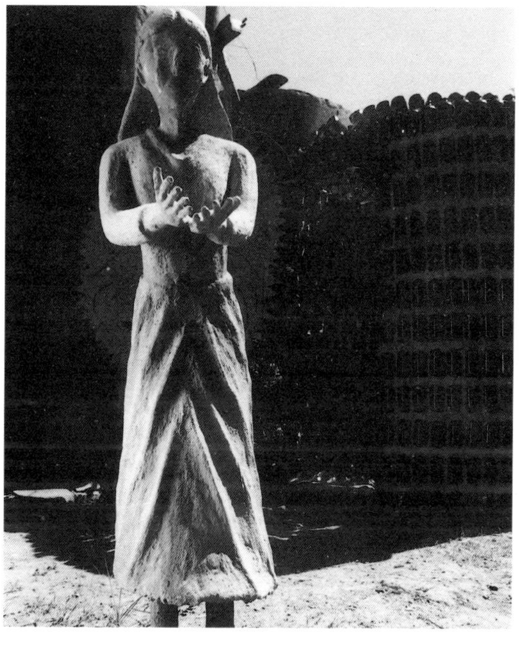

A female figure cups her hands to form a nest. Here the birds could lay their eggs, in the days when this portion of the yard was a bird-cage.

Enclosing the entire yard beneath wire mesh proved to be an impractical undertaking. The mesh roof eventually collapsed, and Miss Helen decided to remove much of the caging, retaining only a small area adjacent to the patio and the work-shed. From then onwards she kept only white pigeons and Egyptian geese and it was then that she began to fill the garden with more and more cement birds,

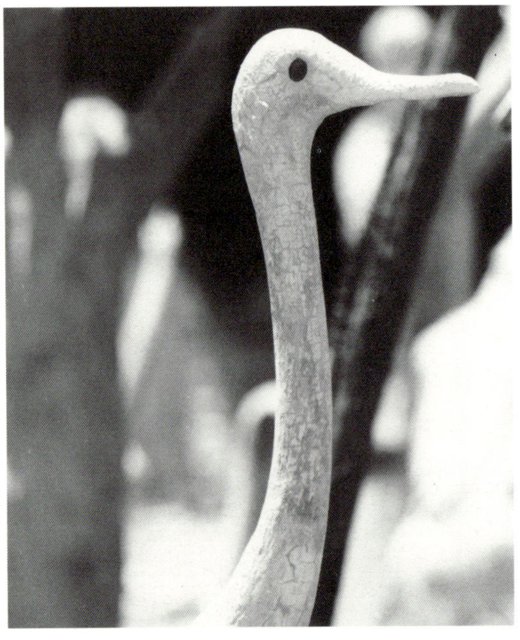

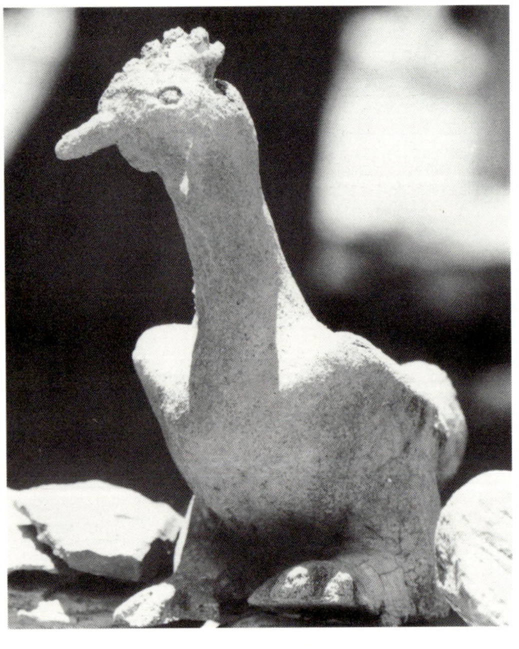

Helen Martins once kept many live birds. When this proved to be impractical, she began to substitute with cement birds.

as if these were a substitute for the real birds that once occupied the space.

Beneath the extensive roof of wire netting that once existed, Piet van der Merwe built many tall pillars out of which arose slender wire stalks, supporting heavy-foil stars. Other stars he supported on wooden poles and all of them quivered in the air on their wire stems just above the roof of chicken wire. They created a heaven below heaven, a world within a world. Piet explained why Miss Helen wanted the stars:

> *Look, when the stars at night come out above, then you think that these are them. The moon is also here. She wished to have her very own heaven. It was very beautiful at night.*

Many of the stars have now fallen down and only a few remain to provide a shadow of what it must once have looked like. The notion of macro and microcosm was one of the early themes Helen Martins developed.

Another of the sculptural pieces that was constructed in the early days was the miniature version of the Spitzkop mountain. Also known as Kompasberg, Spitzkop is the tallest peak in the area and is visible from Helen Martins' back garden. This replication of the world beyond within the world of her own making, is a marked characteristic of the Owl House environment. It can be seen again in her placing of her own 'East' in the opposite direction to true East. 'We simply made the "East" on that side,' said Koos. 'It was the direction in which the camels were walking.'

It is indicative of Helen Martins' urge to create her own self-sufficient universe in which she could dictate her own terms and live out her fantasies. Francie Lund comments on this, as well as on Helen's replication of Spitzkop and the East:

> *She was about the right to make decisions in the world ... to create ... make your own conditions for*

being alive ... she was always ready to change her reality, make it work for her. She decided after she had made some of the camels that they should face East. They didn't. So she made a wire sign saying 'East', pointing in the direction in which her camels were pointing.

She also wanted to watch the sun rise and set above the Spitzkop. She made a Spitzkop on the opposite side to the real one so she could have it both ways.

The garden Spitzkop was built by Jonas Adams. Jonas was of the same generation as Miss Helen, being born in Nieu Bethesda in 1900. Initially, he farmed his own land until, as he explains it, 'the law took it from me'. This was a land law that prevented black men, like Jonas, from owning land in certain areas. He found employment as an odd-job man in the village, and for some years he worked on a part-time basis for Helen Martins. He built a great many of the camels, a number of which have since collapsed. In these early days Miss Helen had not yet perfected the cement mix and the camels built by Jonas were far cruder and more roughly textured than those built by Koos Malgas in the latter years. A number of the camels originally built by Jonas now have wise men seated on their backs. These wise men, built by Koos, were later additions. Helen created her environment in an organic manner, adding to sculptural pieces, changing them, even moving them from one point in the garden to another as the urge took her. At one stage, for instance, she decided that one of the early owls made by Piet should be anthropomorphosed. She asked Koos to attach hands to the piece, and these hands the owl now extends, as if begging for money. 'The owl is asking for a donation,' Koos explained.

Another time Koos was working on one of the sphinxes. With his fingers he had hollowed out two cavernous holes into which he intended to insert eyes, as he had done with other sphinxes. Miss Helen, standing back to survey his

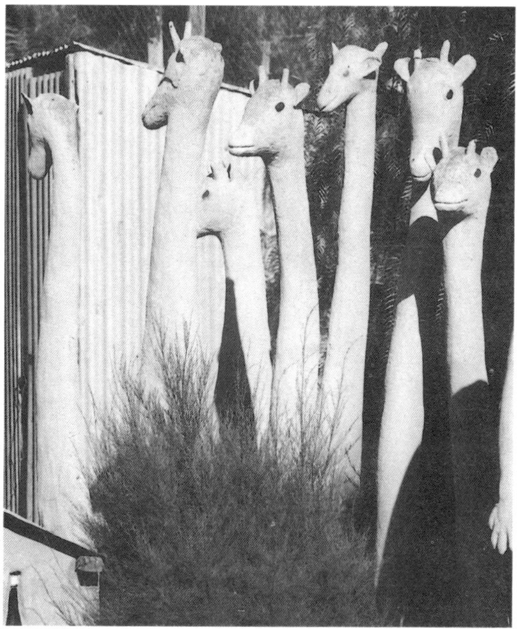

Jonas Adams made this forest of giraffes, whose necks rise from the ground like treetrunks. The giraffes, fashioned as images of transcendence, were deliberately made to a height at which they could be nibbling the tops of some bushes Miss Helen nurtured in this part of the garden.

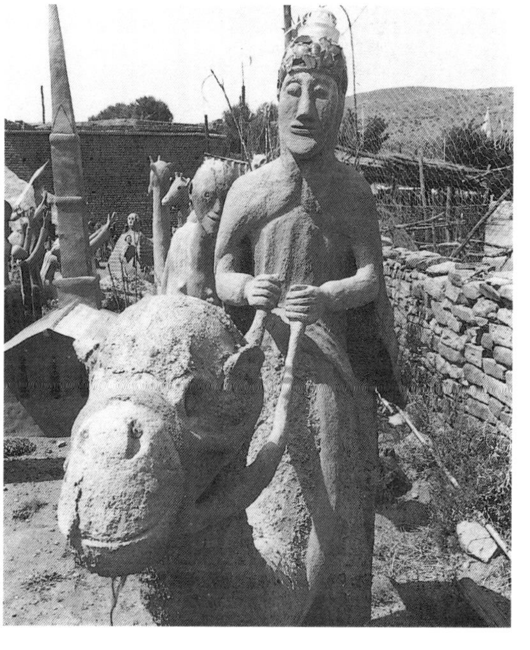

Some of the early roughly textured camels, like this one, were made by Jonas, but it was Koos who gave them riders. This picture, taken by Johann Potgieter, shows Miss Helen's favourite wise man on a camel's back.

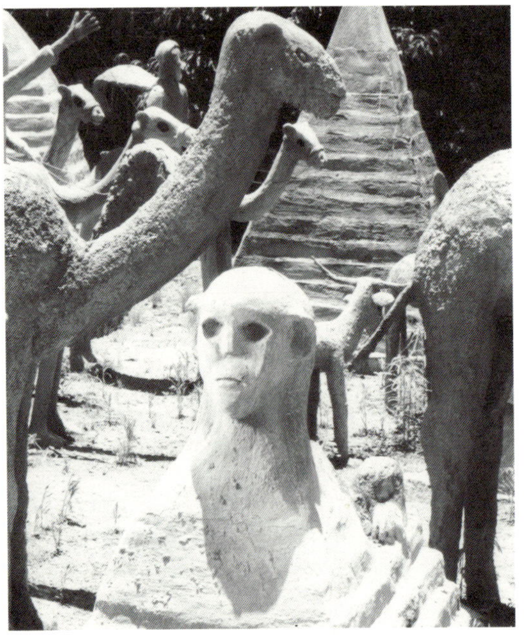

A blind sphinx broods over the garden. Before Koos could insert the eyes, Miss Helen stopped him. 'Let's leave him with those empty sockets,' she said.

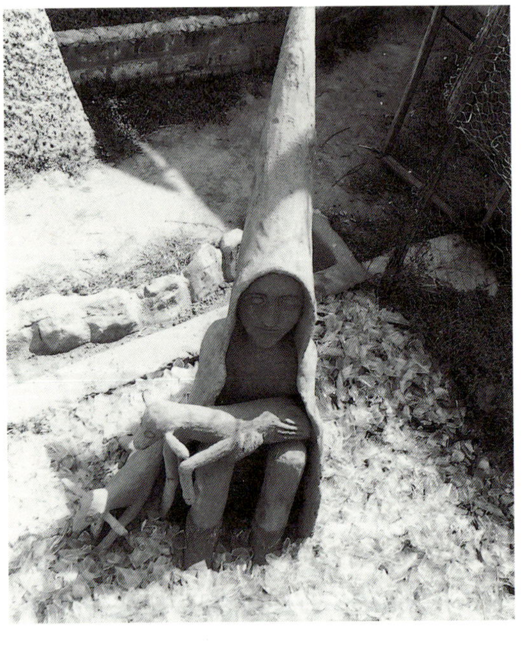

One of Miss Helen's crouched shepherds, a lamb on his lap and another beside him, sits huddled in the crushed glass. The glittering glass, sprinkled over the ground, was Miss Helen's metaphor for snow. Her 'snow', in the garden, is no longer as thick as it is shown here in the early 1970s. This is only one of the ways in which the passage of time has adversely affected the sculpture environment.
(Photograph: Johann Potgieter)

work, exclaimed, 'Koos, that is just perfect! Let's leave him with those empty sockets.' It had suddenly come to her that the sphinx should be blind.

Peggy Delport, for whom Nieu Bethesda was a holiday retreat, watched the Owl House develop over the years. Arriving in the village for the first time, Peggy and her family met Helen almost immediately.

> *She sidled up and down the road past our cottage and eyed us, and then an invitation came, very formally, you know — would we like to visit? We saw her very regularly ... I think she heard I was a painter, and this was the sort of thing she yearned for ... yes, I think she was eager to meet us because she felt very alienated from the local people, who she felt ridiculed her work. And she yearned for people who would be responsive and interested in creative things. She wanted an audience for her work and ideas, and welcomed all our visits over the years.*

Peggy commented on the manner in which Miss Helen worked, how one thing seemed to spark off another and how the surroundings were always a very important influence.

> *There were things on the go all the time. It was hectic. She would talk about what was happening — and I don't think it was a completely worked-out vision. You know, like this is how it will look when it is complete. But certainly all the time one thing generated another, and there was a very definite direction. She was visually so kind of* alive, *that in every corner of her environment she was seeing a further possibility all the time. It was not just as if distant or abstract sources stimulated her. The actual environment inspired her — the cold and the light and the village and the stars and the brilliant moonlight.*

The Karoo climate is extreme, very hot in summer and bitter in the winter. Helen Martins was sensitive to the nuances of change that the seasons brought to the Owl House. And she particularly loved it under snow. 'In the snow, my darling,' she wrote in a letter to Jill Wenman, 'the garden is like a paradise ... and the owls all stare at one from behind long, snow beards ...'

As it obviously couldn't snow throughout the year, Helen liberally sprinkled clear crushed glass between the statues to form a ground-cover of 'snow' that sparkled brilliantly in the light. It was her way of ensuring that, at least symbolically, the snow never left the garden. The significance of the glass snow relates, too, to her fascination with the Christmas story. The infant Jesus was born in the winter and it was a long, cold journey for the wise men who came to see the newborn baby. Their journey is re-enacted in the garden. One sculptured scenario depicts a group of travellers and their camels. The camels are weary. They lie down in the snow to rest. In another scenario, three wise men, cloaks flying in the wind, travel on their camels towards the star in the 'East'. A short distance from them is a nativity scene. In a structure built from wire and bottles is the manger in which the baby Jesus lies. Mary and Joseph are there. A wise man kneels in homage with hands outstretched. Near the entrance are a number of animals — an ox, a donkey and sheep. These animals have been modelled with a sensitive understanding of the beasts, as if from close familiarity, and their presence in the garden will strike a chord with anyone who has passed through Nieu Bethesda. Sheep grazing in the fields of lucerne that flank the road leading into the village are an everyday sight. So, too, are donkeys. More often than not, one encounters a donkey-drawn cart, trip-trapping along the dirt road into town. Amongst the local people this is the accepted manner of transport. These and other everyday details of local life seem to have found their way into the Owl House environment, intricately linking the space to the surroundings.

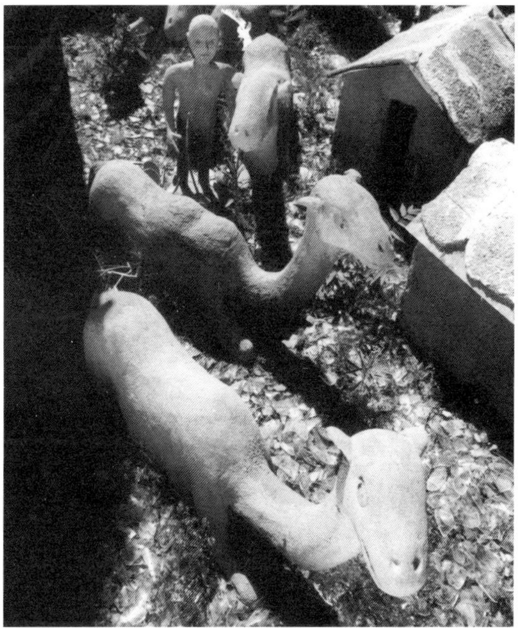

'And the camels galled, sore-footed, refractory, /Lying down in the melting snow'. The lines from T S Eliot's *Journey of the Magi* perfectly describe this scene with the camels and their attendant. The weary camels rest in the cold snow, created from a thick layer of clear, crushed glass.

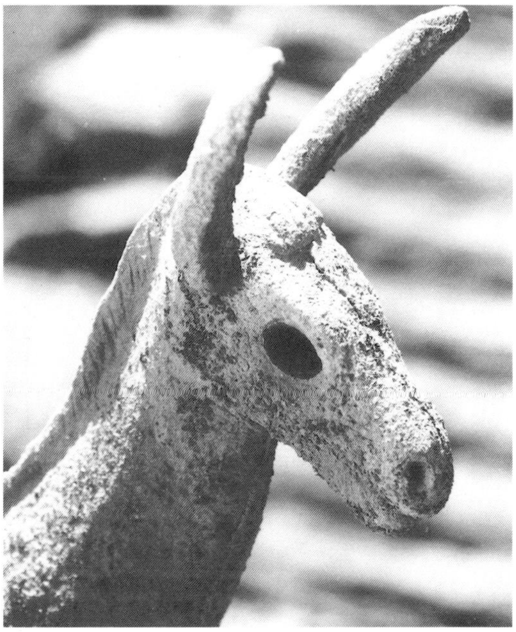

Miss Helen was much influenced by her surroundings. One manifestation of this is her inclusion, in the sculpture garden, of a donkey and many sheep. These animals are a common sight in the Nieu Bethesda landscape.

But it was not only her surroundings that inspired Miss Helen. Her sources were multiple; Peggy Delport said that she read poetry.

> *She loved and quoted Omar Kháyyám. Quite clearly she was intrigued by the East, and there were other books as well. There was the Bible. But she had many other sources. There were lots of postcards, and I think some little religious pictures, plus a diversity of other things. There were so many different sources, little tourist objects from England, from Egypt, funny bits of 'twenties tourist kitsch (little kneeling girls and so on). A little thing would spark off a kind of a significant fantasy and would be processed in some way.*

Poetry, quotes, pictures, sentimental ornaments — all found their way into her sculptural work. This gives the work a collage-like quality, being a juxtaposition of eclectically acquired bits and pieces from different sources that found their way into her garden and home because she became enraptured with them. A quote on the fence — ' Sy kom. Sy kom met die sukkelmaan' — is a case in point, as John Moyle observes:

> *It wasn't something she invented. It was a phrase that she picked up. A phrase that she loved so much that she had to use it. It was intoxication with the poetry of the phrase. Things got to her and she had to incorporate them. She simply picked them up.*

Yet it isn't the nature of her sources, which were often sentimental, trite or downright kitsch, but how she altered, contextualised and transformed them that is of prime interest.

Cards were a frequent source of inspiration. A comic cock-man, with glass tears on his cheeks, occupies the portion of the garden Miss Helen referred to as The Corner

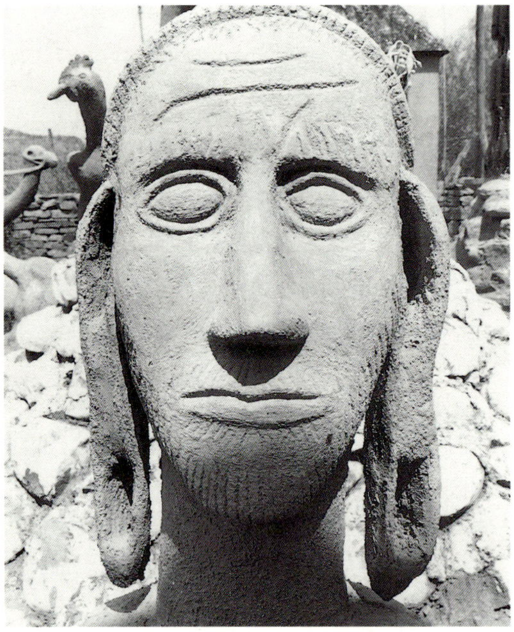

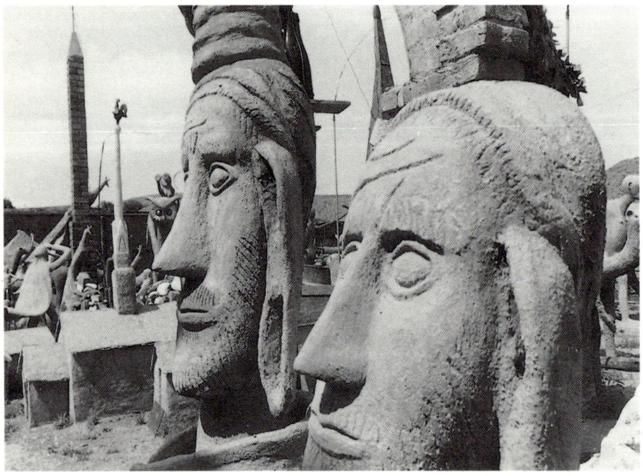

The presence of these Long Ears statues at the Owl House is indicative of Miss Helen's fascination with exotic and far-off cultures. (Photographs: Johann Potgieter)

of Debauchery. He came off a postcard which was sent to her from Durban. A quote accompanies the image on the card:

> *Now he knows the terrible fate that overcomes all gluttons. He will reform, it's not too late to do up all his buttons.*

The repeated image in the garden of a crouching shepherd with his sheep was taken from a Christmas card Helen received from Cynthia Craig.

The statues of Long Ears also come from a secondary source. On one visit to the Owl House, Jill Wenman's father had told Helen the story of the Easter Island figures and she had declared that she would love to have the Long Ears in her garden. Mr Wenman then found and sent her some diagrams from which Koos could work. As with the other images derived from secondary sources, her decision to place them in the garden was not random. The two Long Ears are part of a body of statues that relate to her interest in exotic cultures, as well as cultures from the remote past. This absorption and her desire to transcend the boundaries of time and space, perhaps had their source in a personal need to sublimate her own experience of cultural isolation. The positioning of the Easter Island figures opposite the anthropomorphised sun mural on the wall, is significant. It elaborates upon mythological ideas that exist elsewhere in her work.

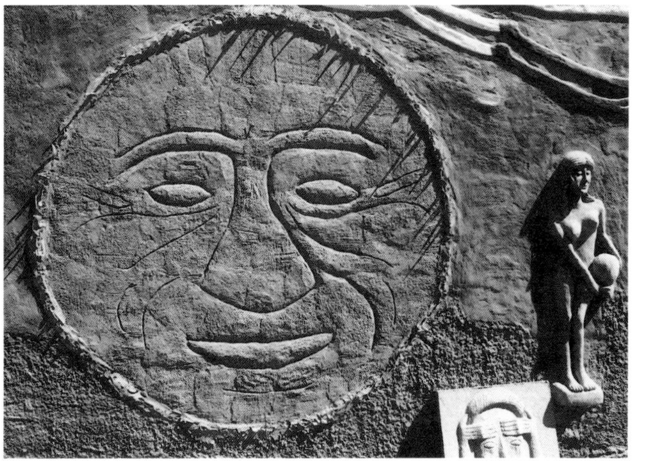

As on Easter Island, where Long Ears sculptures were placed so as to greet the rising or setting sun, so in Miss Helen's garden they face this large sun mural.

On Easter Island Long Ears sculptures were deliberately placed so as to greet the rising or the setting sun. The Easter Island figures in Helen Martins' garden suggest that the sun is to be seen as either rising or setting. The portion of the garden occupied by the Long Ears and the sun mural is the structured beginning and ending of the space. It is here that the visitor enters via the zinc gate and it is back at this point and the Moon Gate, having gone full circle, that the garden ends. The rising sun is a symbol of generation, of beginnings, while the setting sun symbolises

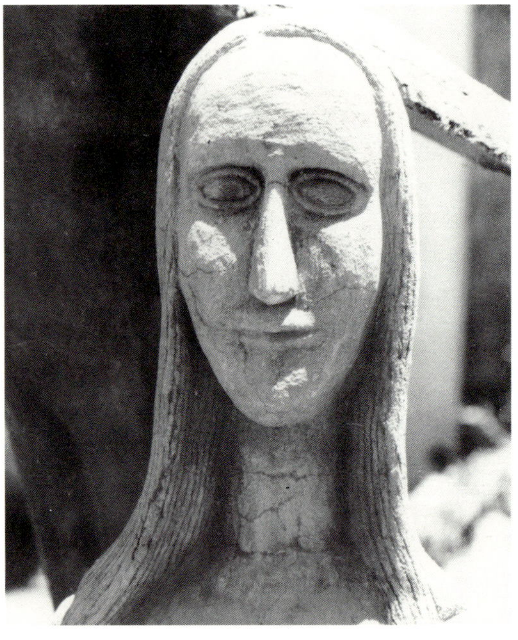

A free-standing sculpture of the Mona Lisa. The last of Koos's many attempts, Miss Helen felt that with this one he had finally achieved the secret smile.

an ending. The presence of the Long Ears statues and their affiliation with the cycle of the sun suggests, too, the notion of sun worship and of a *participation mystique* in the rhythms of nature. These ideas are inherent in the larger sculptural environment, finding expression in numerous sculptured scenarios.

A good deal of the inspiration for the sculpture garden came, too, from memorabilia and other objects that Helen collected. These still hang from walls or rest on table-tops and window-ledges inside the house. They create a sense of continuity between house and garden, for the house often contains miniature versions of what can be found in the yard outside. This replication of things links, very directly, the interior and exterior spaces.

The very first piece that Koos Malgas made for Miss Helen was in an empty sardine tin. It was the relief, modelled in clay, of a lady clasping her brow. This same image appears, as a much larger relief, on the wall of the water-tank. The Mona Lisa prints which hang on the walls of the interior were the source of inspiration for the numerous Mona Lisas in the yard. Koos remembers making the Mona Lisa twelve times. Many of these are wall-murals, but the one which he considered to be his best was a free-standing sculpture. Over and over again he had attempted to capture the enigmatic and mysterious smile of the Mona Lisa, as Miss Helen wanted him to do. However, it was only in this free-standing piece, his final Mona Lisa, that she told him he had finally achieved it. Koos had his own standards:

> *Miss Helen liked this Mona Lisa very much. But it is still not her. Look, here is the problem. The mouth is too flat. It is not as a person's mouth should be.*

There are seemingly endless links in the Owl House between interior and exterior. The plaster mermaids that appear as ornaments throughout the house, are obviously the prototype for the mermaids in the garden. Where it suited her intentions, Miss Helen would instruct Koos to make suitable adjustments, so that the mermaids do not all simply sit in the same poses as do their prototypes in the house. One mermaid holds a yellow plastic comb, others point the way or beckon alluringly.

Helen often used her sources very imaginatively. One tourist object, a small wooden carving of a coiled snake, was the inspiration for the unique snake tables that Koos built from cement, while a sepia studio portrait of a nude became, in the garden, the ecstatic, backwards bending sun-worshippers. When another studio-nude photograph hanging in the house was shown to Koos, he created the marvellous airborne statue of a delicately poised girl, defying the laws of gravity and stepping out into the atmosphere. He describes her as 'walking on air' and 'on the tips of her toes'.

These studio-nude photographs are some of the most interesting images in the house that have been used as inspirational material for sculptures. They might have come from some early photographic book of art nudes. However, Koos recalls Miss Helen telling him that the model in some of the photographs was her sister Alida. John Moyle also gained the impression that Helen and her sisters had been inspired by photographic books to attempt nude studies of each other with the equipment available to them. There is an erotic dimension to Helen's art, which is in keeping with the sisters taking artfully posed nude photographs of one another. There is, for example, the cement nude who balances on the back of a camel-owl creature. Flirting with erotica, Helen gave this nude glittering ruby-red nipples of glass. The fantastical beast upon which she stands is one illustration of how Helen juxtaposed and metamorphosed her varied imagery in order to create striking effects.

Another interesting metamorphosing creature is the reclining camel, whose back is also a dammetjie, where Helen paradoxically and suggestively combines the water motif with her animal of the desert.

Sometimes it is the positioning of two images together, or in proximity, which creates the meaning. A case in point is the figure who stands close to a dammetjie, hands behind her back, staring meditatively downwards. Koos modelled this figure from a photograph of a nude, but it is the positioning of the figure that is important. As in the Narcissus myth, the reflective surface of the water that once filled the pool suggested a mirror. The contemplative figure, staring down into the pool, finds her own reflection upon which to muse. As elsewhere in the garden, water is an aid to meditation and the attainment of self-knowledge.

There is another sculpture which makes use of the proximity of water to emphasise the idea that insight can be gained through contemplation. This is a figure with an ornate turban, created from a mosaic of glass fragments, sitting in a typical yoga posture, legs crossed over one another. He appears to be meditating. The negative shape between his legs forms a dammetjie or pool. Miss Helen used to ensure that the pool was cleaned every week and kept filled with water. The pool was not only a contemplative aid for the turbaned Eastern figure, it was also a birdbath. Birds, as creatures of flight, are symbolic of the urge towards transcendence in man. Their affiliation with the meditating figure signifies that Miss Helen understood meditation to be an important means of attaining transcendence.

Koos Malgas, who, following Miss Helen's instructions, made this sculptured piece, perceived it in an interesting way. Unfamiliar with Eastern dress and ways, he believes he was making, not an Eastern figure at all, but a 'Bantu *vrou*', a black woman in tribal dress with the traditional scarf wound around her head. Working according to Helen's ideas, he was sometimes baffled by what he was asked to make. Another of the sculptures he made but which perplexed him greatly was the fantastical beast that is both owl and camel. He asked Miss Helen more than once why she wanted him to make such a creature, and shook his head over it, thinking it was really a very odd idea, not at all his notion of good sculpture. He never could understand why Miss Helen wished him to make such a strange creature.

The wire-whiskered lion was another piece with which he was dissatisfied, but for different reasons. 'It is not right,' he said. 'It is not as a lion should be. Can you see — the body is much too thin and small for the head.' Correct proportion was one of the criteria with which he evaluated his own work. Another criterion was the sharp delineation and clarity of the modelling. For this reason he was very pleased with the figure of the shepherd who stands at the fence, pointing towards the Star of Bethlehem.

> *Look how well that shepherd, by the house with the light, directs the way. He has very clear features. Miss Helen was proud of him. Beautiful and clear face, hands and figure. Nice big eyes and everything.*

'The features in his face are clearly modelled and they stand out at a distance,' he said. Another that Koos considered to be one of his prize pieces was the large sun-face on the ceiling of the kitchen. It was a very tricky job, involving lying on his back on scaffolding, while the glass with which he was working kept falling into his eyes. When he had finished, Miss Helen lay down flat on the kitchen floor and, looking up, exclaimed, 'I think, Koos, this is your best work!'

Koos Malgas spent twelve years in Helen Martins' employ. Before he came to her he had been a farm labourer on a sheep farm in Newcastle. He first met Miss Helen when he arrived to help as an odd-job man at the Owl House. At that time he was assisting his father, whom Helen had employed to fix the roof of a bird-cage. Koos was then a man in his thirties, with a wife and three daughters. He had never made a statue in his life. Helen wanted help with her statue garden and she gave Koos a trial task in order to test his ability. He was given the

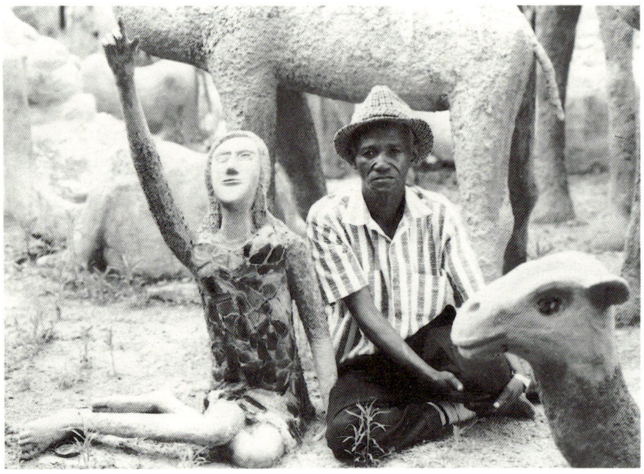

Koos Malgas sits beside the figure of Miss Helen that he made in the garden at the Owl House. Peggy Delport describes the working relationship between Helen and Koos: 'Koos would do more than carry out instructions. Miss Helen would describe something and he would create his own elegance. He was very gifted. We always said to her: "This man is incredibly gifted." The interpretive process and the forms with their particular elegance were his. She was very excited to see the things made by Koos, very stimulated. But she would always give him a departure point.'

sardine tin in which he was instructed to model his very first version of the woman from the illustration on the box of headache powders. Miss Helen must have been satisfied for he stayed on as a permanent employee at the Owl House, giving up sheep shearing as an occupation in order to devote himself to building statues in Miss Helen's back yard. In fact she greatly admired the talent Koos displayed, according to Peggy Delport: '... she would praise Koos very highly. She would be very excited and very generous in her praise of him.'

Most of the garden sculpture which still exists was built by Koos. He made whatever Helen requested of him. He once told a newspaper reporter:

> *I don't sell these things. I make them purely as a hobby and because my madam likes them in the garden. They are just there for our enjoyment.*

Miss Helen would show him a picture or an ornament, or merely describe something to him and this would give Koos his initial impetus. Peggy Delport observed the progress of his work over the years:

> *She would give him a departure point, and then he would go off with it. But one or two of the ideas were really completely his own from the conception, especially as he gained confidence. She would show him a picture or a little thing, but the point is he wasn't reproducing her visions — they generated his own. He definitely had his own ideas ... People see her as a creative artist and so she was. But I see Koos as the sculptor. That kind of silence and serenity of his, especially towards the end. She was the creative thinker, but still she didn't make these things. She didn't put a finger on them; and the actual material process is something different. So I see her as a creative personality, an enormously energetic creative personality. But I see*

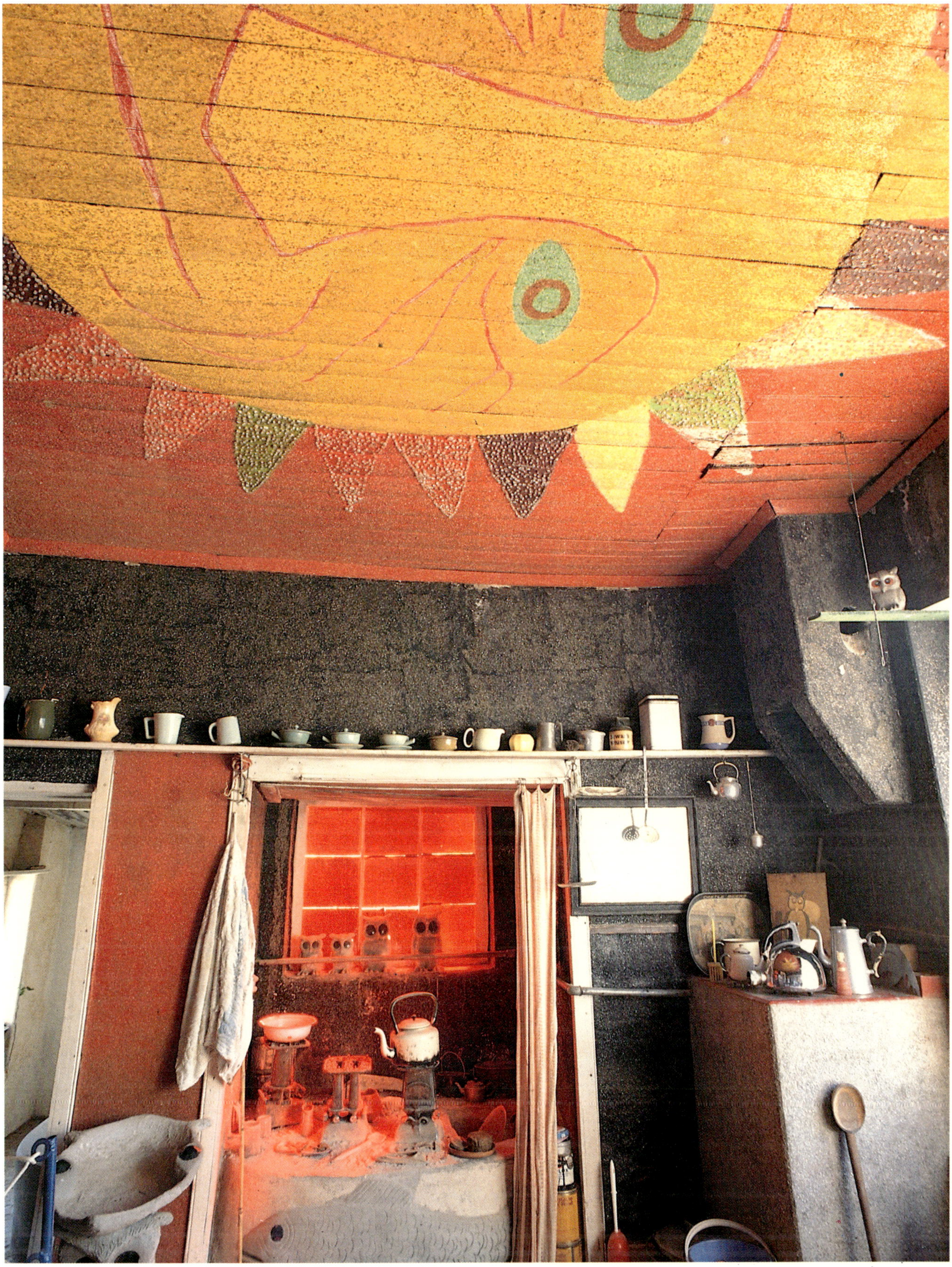

An enormous sun, spanning the entire kitchen ceiling, beams downwards. A tricky piece to do, Koos thinks of it as one of his finest suns. The sun shows up to best advantage at night, when the face of crushed glass sparkles in lamp and candle light. It is one of the many paradoxical reversals at *the Owl* **HOUSE**, that the sun on the kitchen ceiling only truly shines at night. *The Owl* **HOUSE** kitchen has primitive cooking arrangements. A couple of oil-burning cooking rings, standing in for a stove, rest on a cement slab. They are bathed in an unearthly red light that comes through the alcove window. Miss Helen referred to her stove arrangement as her 'little devil'. Across the front of the cement slab is the image of a swimming fish. Koos remembers that Helen intended the alcove to be another dammetjie. Alongside the alcove is the top of one of the double-faced concave owls that Helen intended as seats.

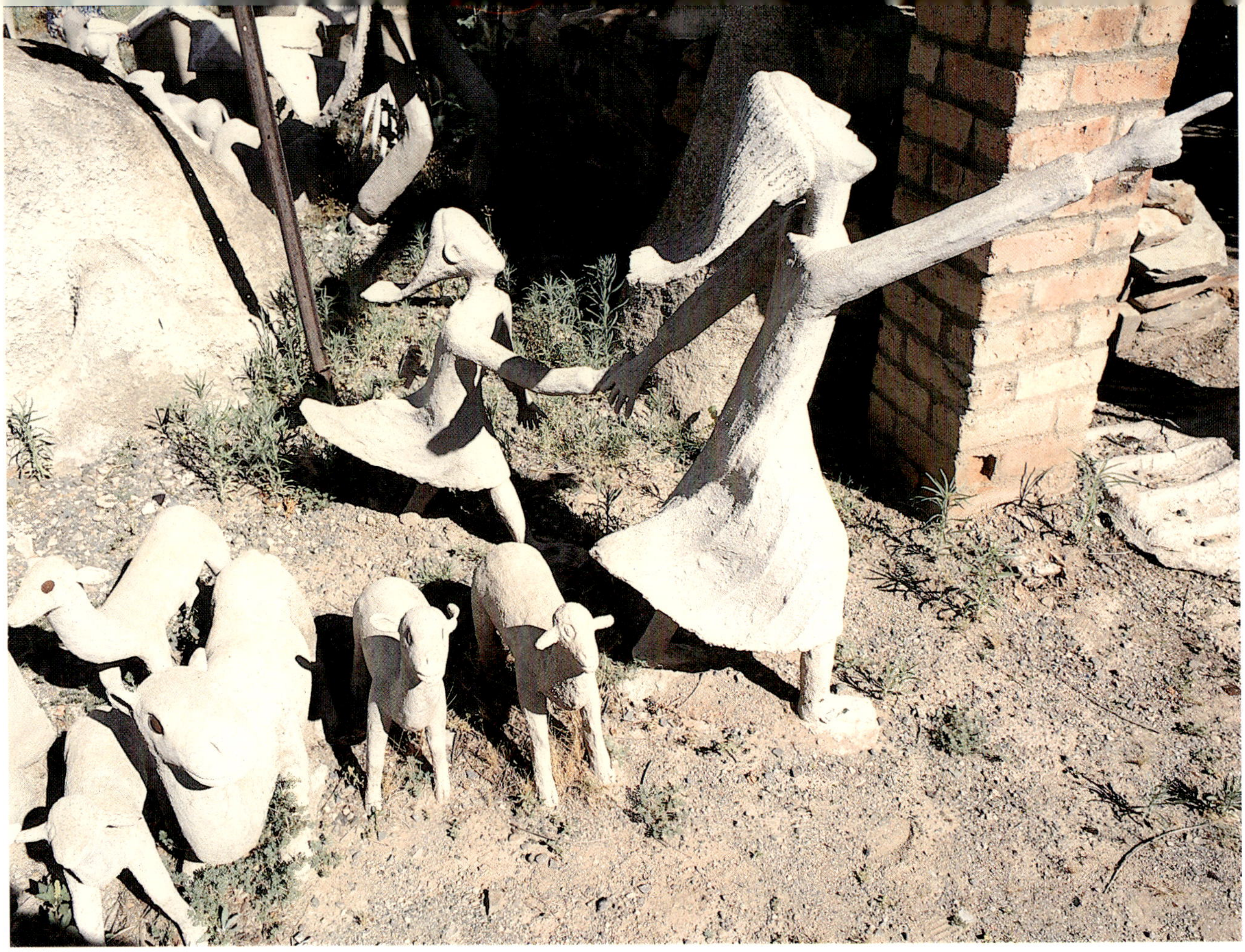

Koos, who made these two running girls, describes this as the only piece in the garden that he initiated himself, without Miss Helen's instructions. The two girls are his daughters, and the idea of including them in the garden pilgrimage occurred to him one day when they came to visit him at *the Owl* **HOUSE**. Miss Helen had her own interpretation of the piece. She saw it as herself excitedly tugging Jill around the garden. When showing the sculpture to Jill Wenman for the first time, she commented with satisfaction, 'Now you will never leave my garden.'

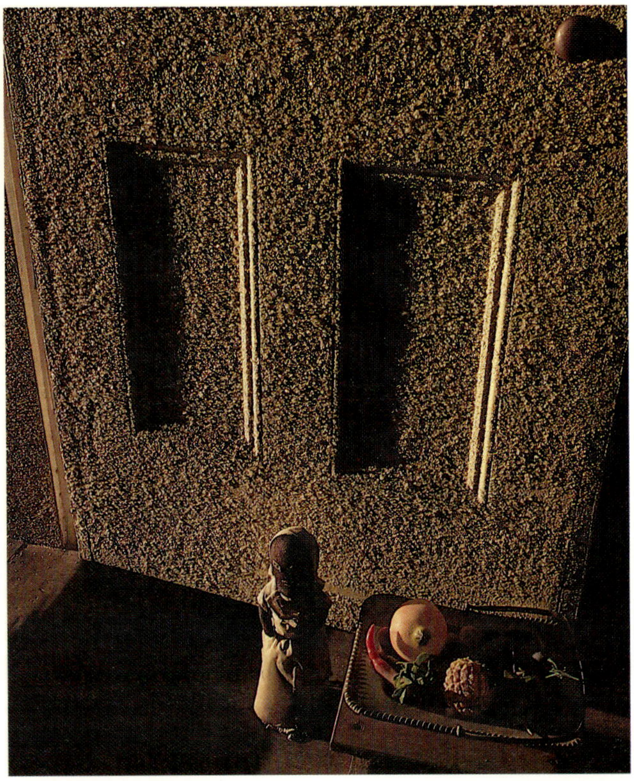

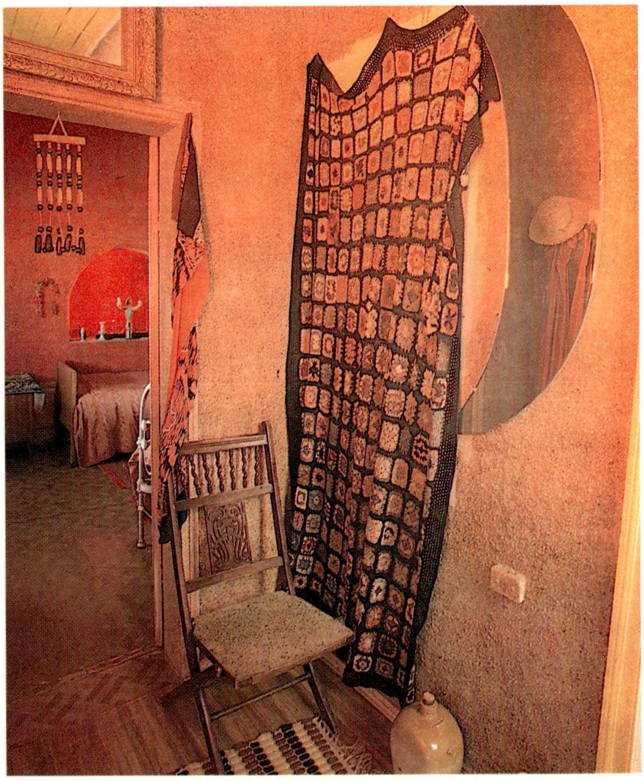

Miss Helen created a glittering but hazardous interior. She coated almost every surface with crushed glass. Doorways sparkle but are prickly to the touch, and even chair seats have been liberally sprinkled with a dusting of sharp glass particles, making them entirely unusable. Alongside the chair in the hall is a crocheted blanket where a Persian carpet once hung. The hall has been depleted of much of its original contents. It was Miss Helen's intention that it should evoke an Eastern bazaar, such as is visible in the picture of the Eastern carpet seller which hangs on a wall in the main living-room.

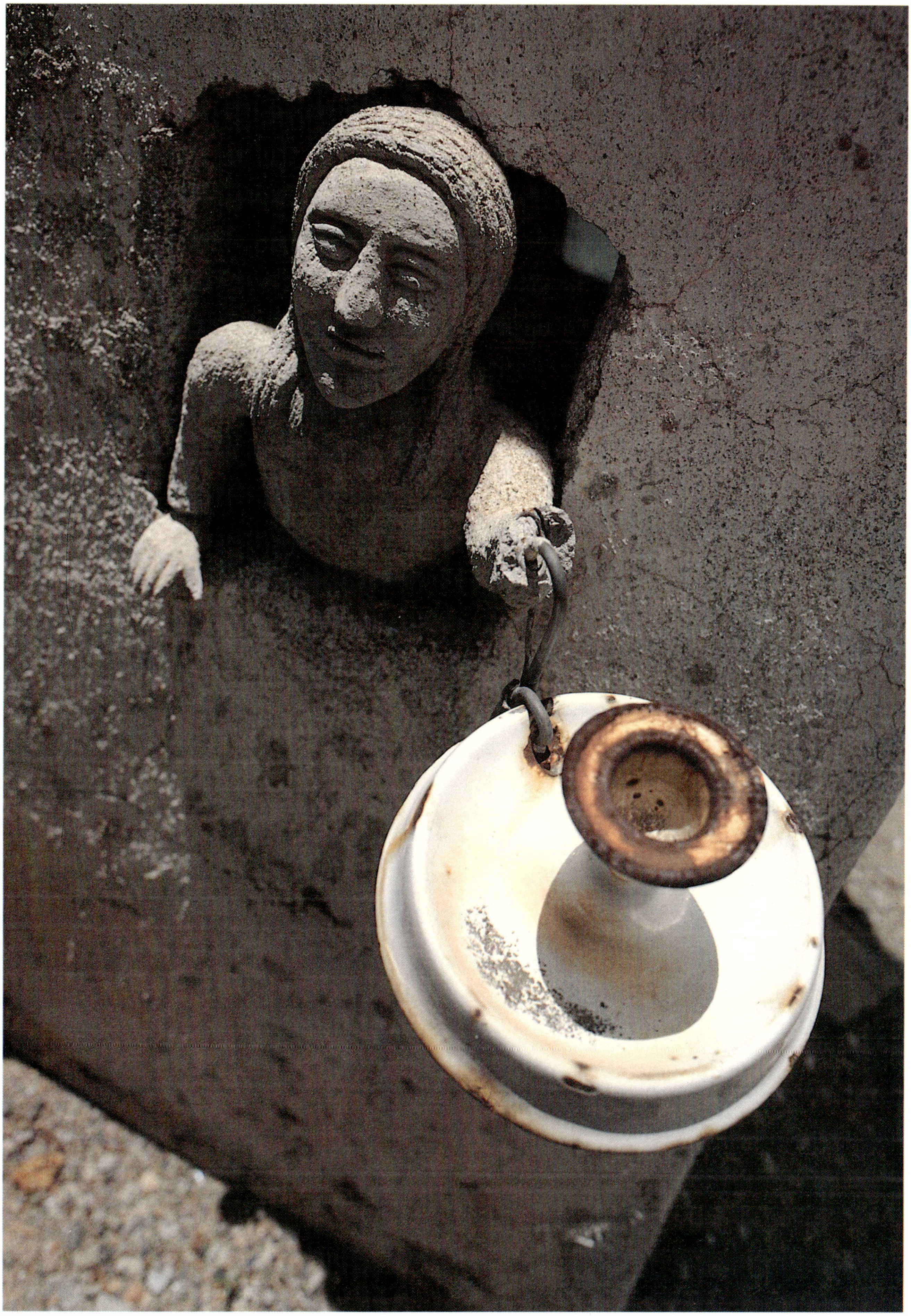

The sculpture garden contains many delightful narrative details. Here, as if lighting the way, a lady with a candle holder, leans from the window of a church spire.

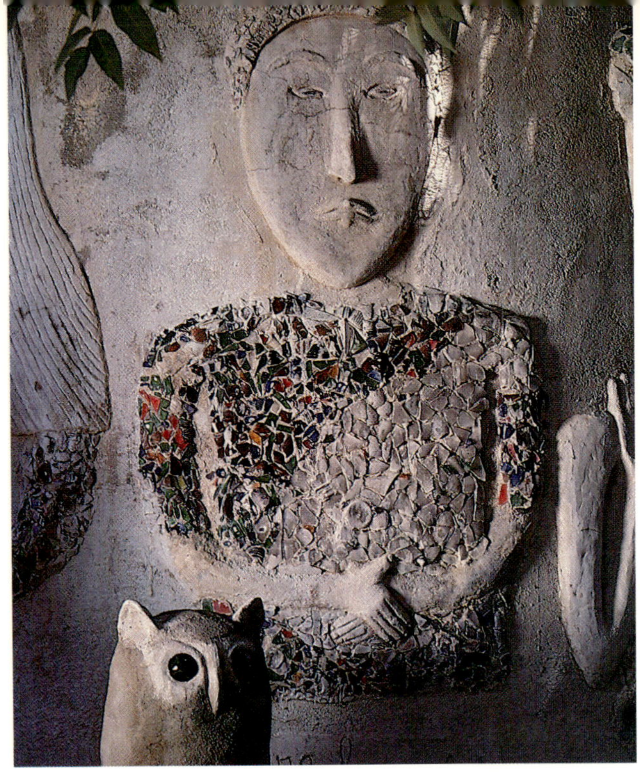

Written into the cement beneath this figure on the water tank are the words *A Young Lady of South China*. Helen was enamoured with exotic-sounding far-off places, and the East held a particular allure for her. The owl in front of the Chinese lady was one of the very first owls in the garden. It was made by Piet van der Merwe, but the begging hands are a later addition, and were constructed by Koos Malgas. Koos remembers how Miss Helen always left a coin lying in the owl's outstretched hands. The owl, he explains, is 'asking for donations'.

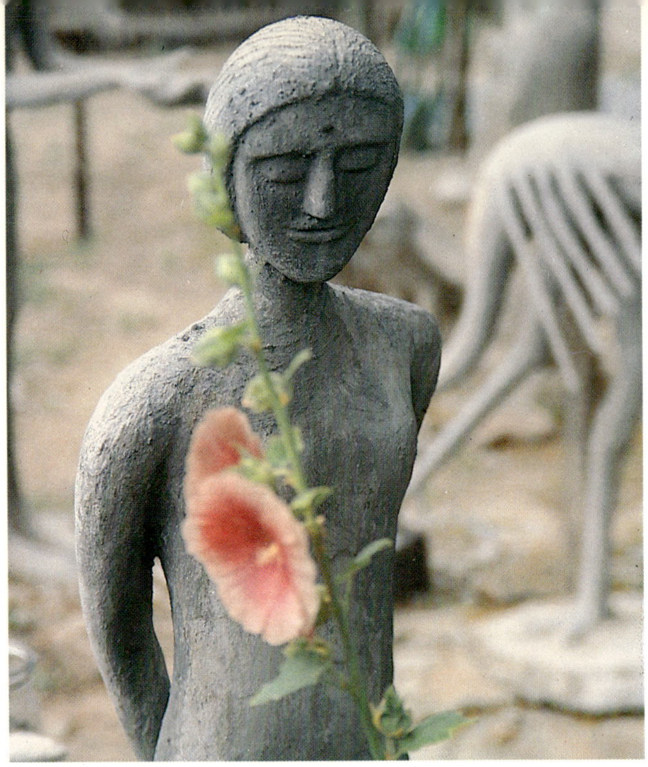

The nude figure of a woman gazes down, contemplatively. She is looking into one of the bottle-lined dammetjies, which were always kept filled with water. Here, as elsewhere in the garden, the mirror-like surface of the water implied self-reflection. The circular dammetjies, with their radiating array of bottles, form mandala patterns, the mandala being a symbol of psychic wholeness. The sculpture garden charts a personal, spiritual journey. There are numerous indications that, for Miss Helen, the inward-turning process of self-reflection, as suggested by this meditative figure, was a crucial component of her inner journey. (*Photograph*: **ANNE EMSLIE**)

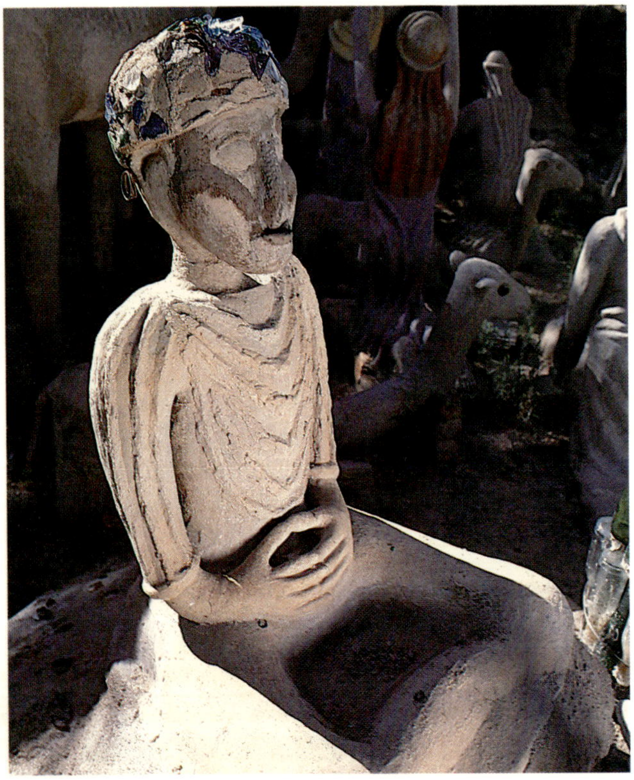

An Eastern figure wears an ornate turban, impregnated with glass. He sits meditating in the customary pose, legs crossed. The gap between his legs forms a dammetjie. Miss Helen always ensured that the garden dammetjies were filled with water. Koos Malgas, who made this piece in accordance with Miss Helen's instructions, believed at the time that he was building a statue of an African woman in traditional turbaned regalia.

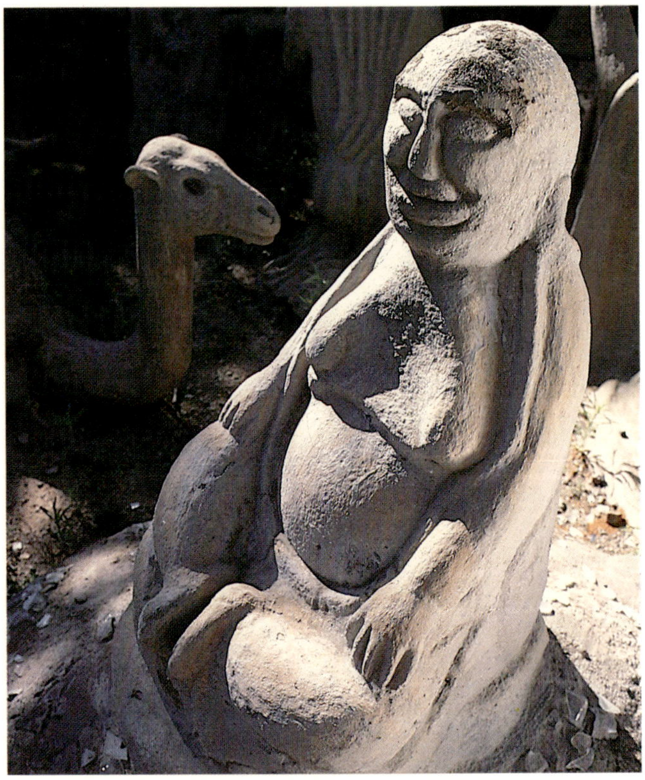

A chubby Buddha tranquilly occupies a corner of the garden. He calmly sits amidst the frenzy of travelling pilgrims. His presence is indicative of Helen's eclectic borrowing from disparate religious sources.

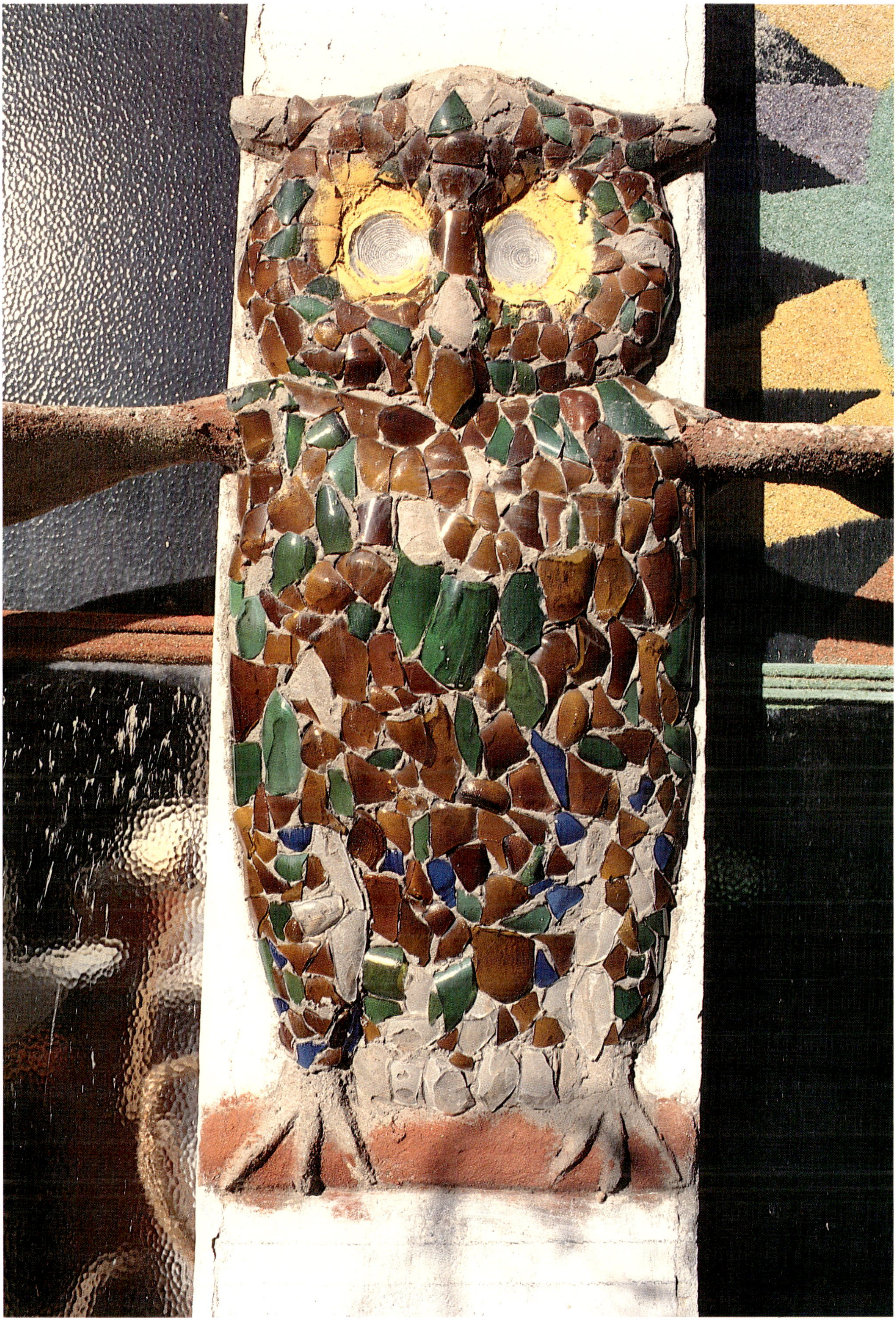

A large, glass-encrusted owl is a watchful presence on the patio.

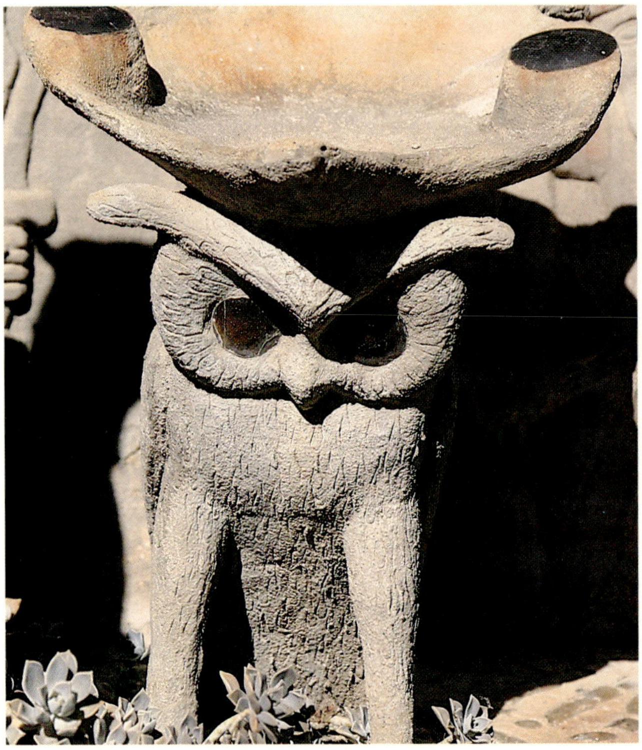

A double-faced owl stands in the patio area. The top face is concave and was conceived, here, as a planter for the type of succulents that can now be seen at its base. Other double-faced owls, positioned elsewhere in the house and garden, serve as birdbaths, or simply as seats.

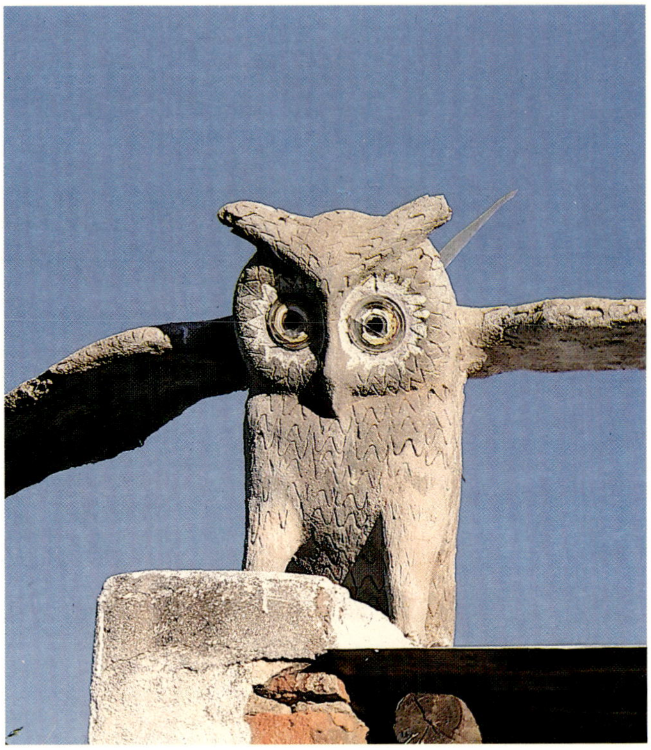

An owl with outstretched wings, as if ready to swoop, peers down from the rooftop.

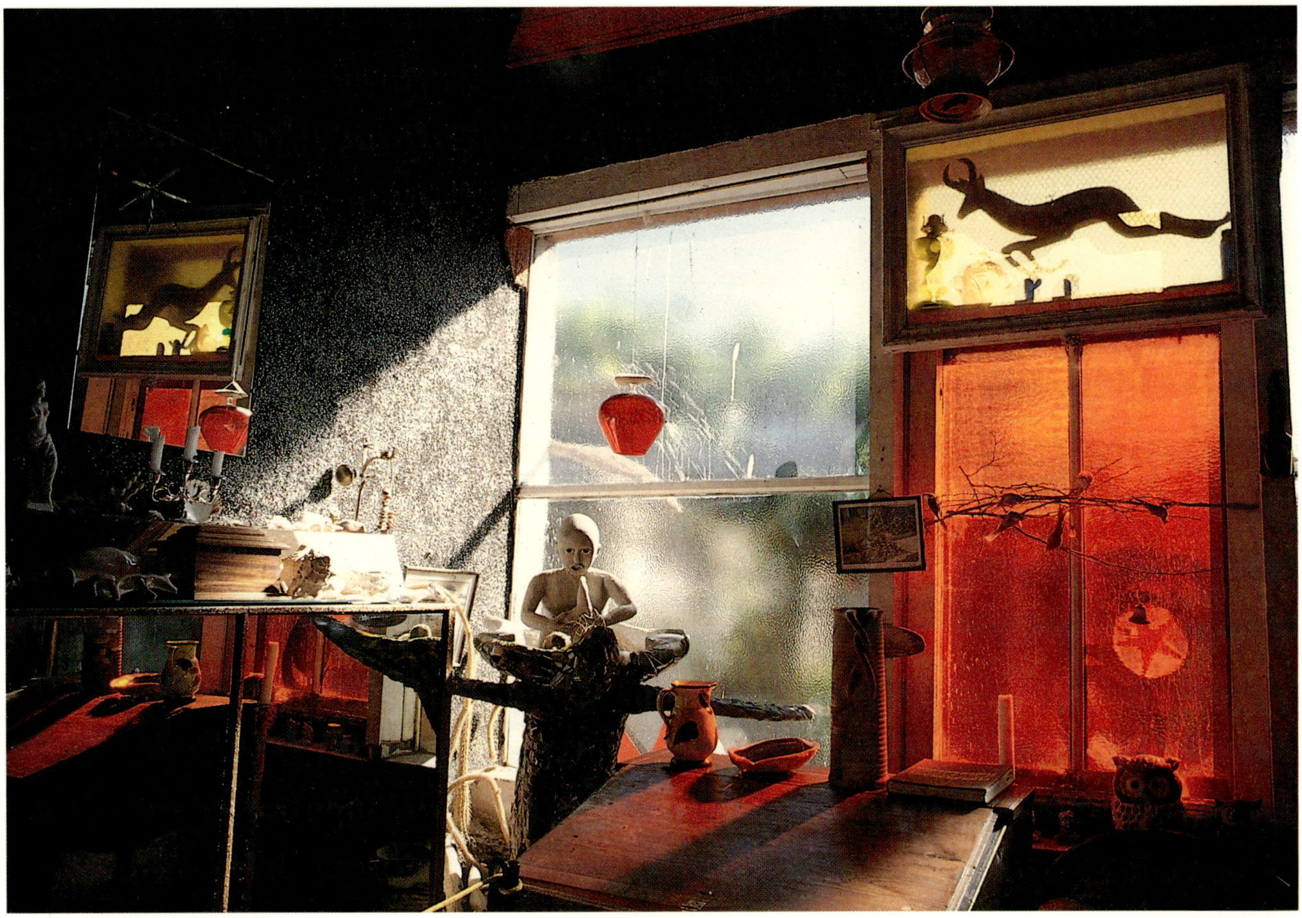

In a corner of the main living-room is a concave-faced owl. The owl's face forms a type of nest in which a baby sits. The baby is trying to get its toes into its mouth.

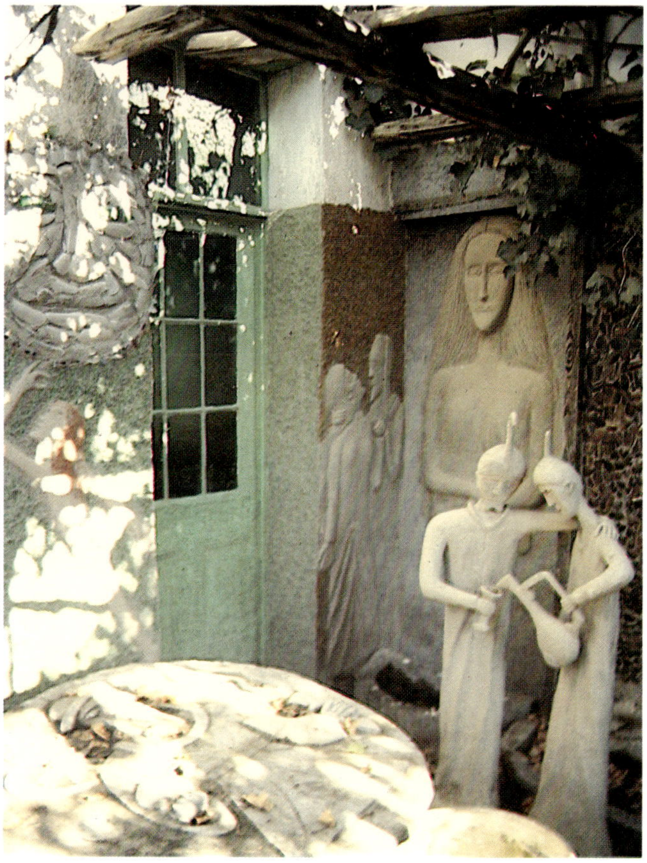

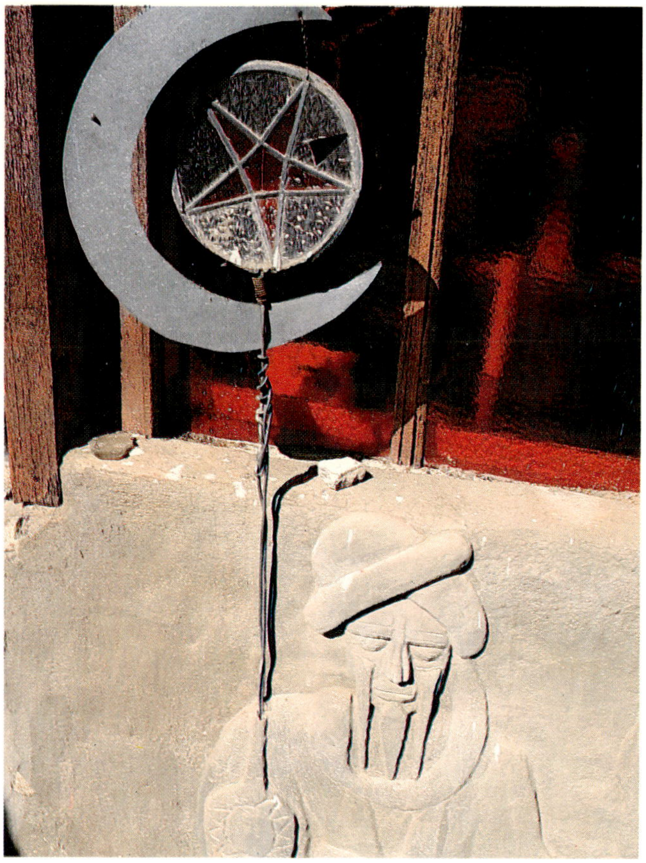

Beneath the vine, near the back door, is a table with a base that is coiled to resemble a snake. The top of the table holds an image, which is also visible, in modified form, on the nearby patio wall. It is the figure of a turbaned magician-like man who carries fire in one hand and the cosmic sun, moon and star in the other. A variation of the figure also appears in relief on the wall of the back patio. The image illustrates a verse from the *Rubáiyát*:

I sent my Soul through the Invisible,
Some letter of that After-life to spell
And after many days my soul return'd
And said, 'Behold, Myself am Heav'n and, Hell.'

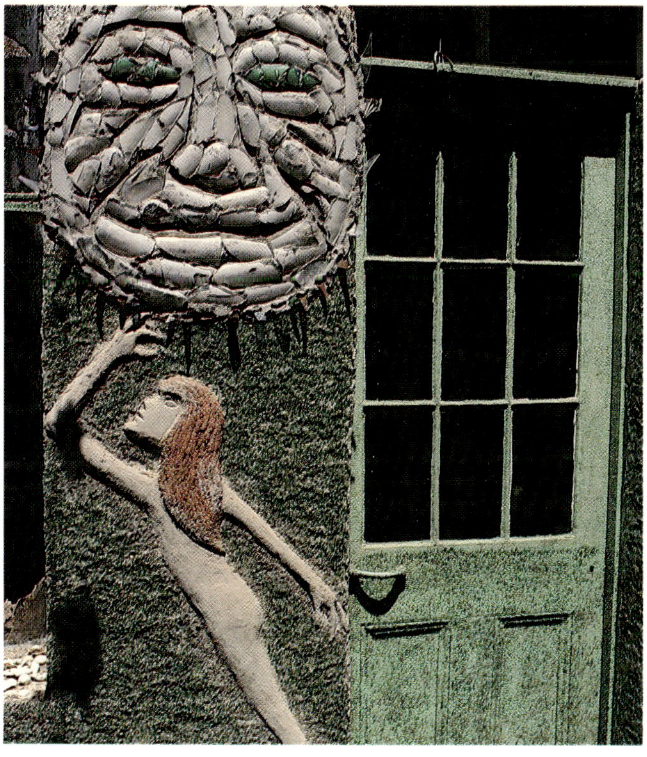

Mural-work on the wall of the patio depicts, in conjunction, an anthropomorphised sun and an underwater swimmer. The fiery and the aqueous realms are deliberately contrasted. Helen liked to play opposites off against each other. The sun, light, air and the masculine principle, as one polarity, are often juxtaposed against moon imagery, night, water and the female principle.

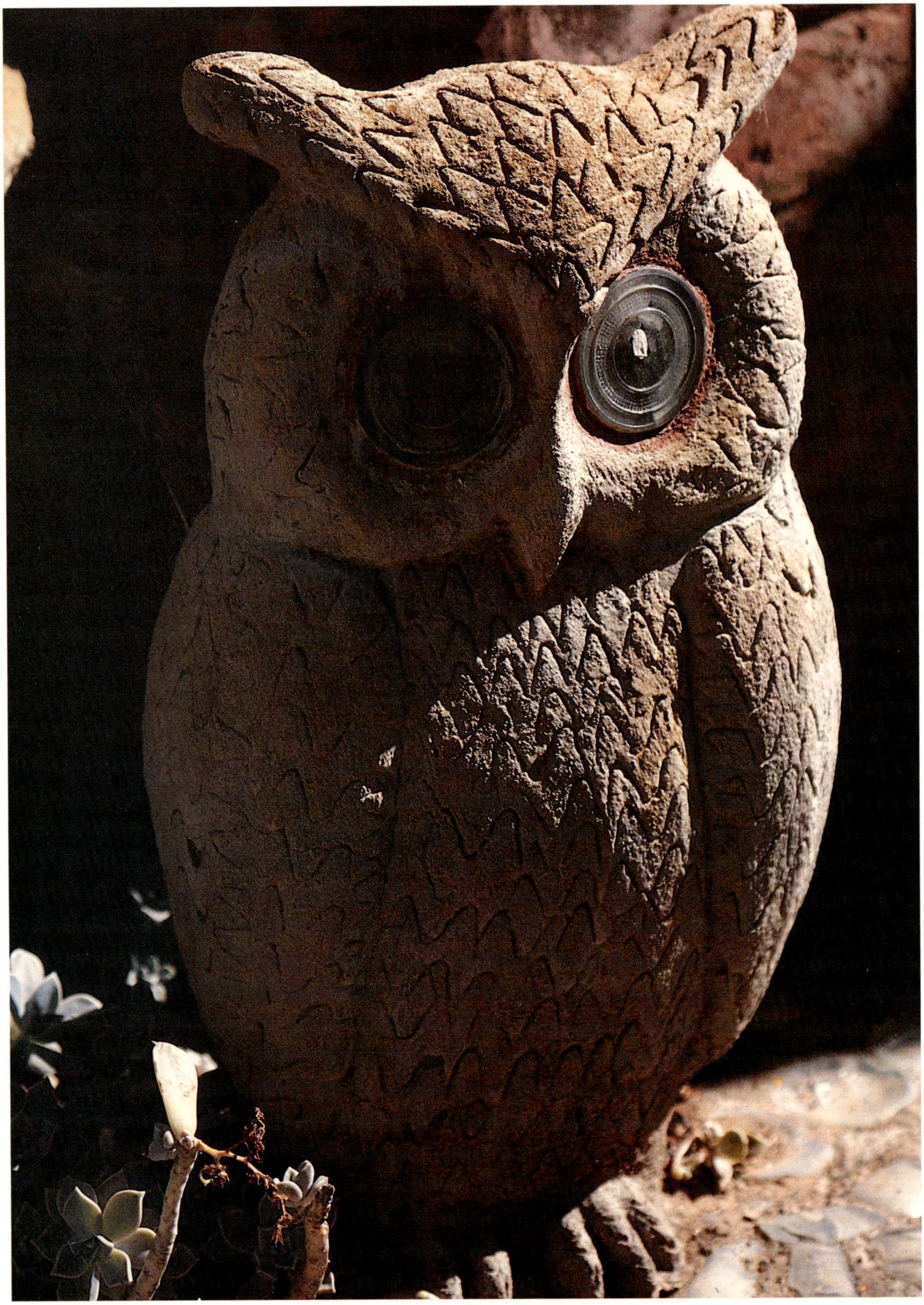

Helen's favourite owl, Oswald, has eyes that are made from the lids of preserve jars. He stands outside the kitchen door. Helen placed a bone across his feet, which has now gone. It was Helen's wish that after her death her ashes should be mixed with the precious red ground glass, kept on the larder shelf, and then glued to Oswald. This never happened, but she would have liked to have become part of his plumage, and thus remain in the sculpture garden.

Koos as the artist— which I don't think anyone else did really.

Who was the artist, Koos Malgas or Helen Martins? Koos, with characteristic modesty, would not take the credit:

Miss Helen used to say to me: 'Koos, do you not see what beautiful work you are doing?' But no, I'm no artist. I'm not clever enough for that. Miss Helen was very smart. She was the one who could think things out.

The question as to who the artist was throws into focus their respective contributions: Miss Helen as the conceptualiser, Koos as the craftsman. They were a team. Putting aside the notion that an artwork must be accredited to an individual, both Koos and Helen must be acknowledged for their separate accomplishments. It is clear that Koos was much more than merely a pair of hands for Helen Martins. He was involved in the intricate procedure of building sculptures. The working process involved an infinite number of finely judged, aesthetic decisions along the way. It was Koos who frequently decided such matters as the exact length of an arm or twist of a torso. Although Miss Helen had the ideas, and was most specific about what she wanted, his were the actual forms.

The method of working that Koos followed was first to build a wire armature onto which he would then pack his cement mix, modelling it as he went along. Building an armature was a tricky business.

First I bend my wire. But it is not a question of just bending the wire and then you are finished. You have to look carefully at the picture, at what the statue looks like on paper. You have to judge things like the length of an arm. It must look like an arm. You must first get your wire a hundred per cent right.

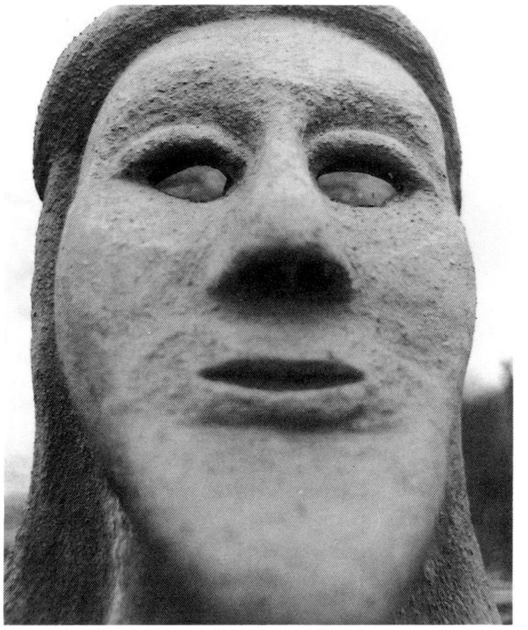

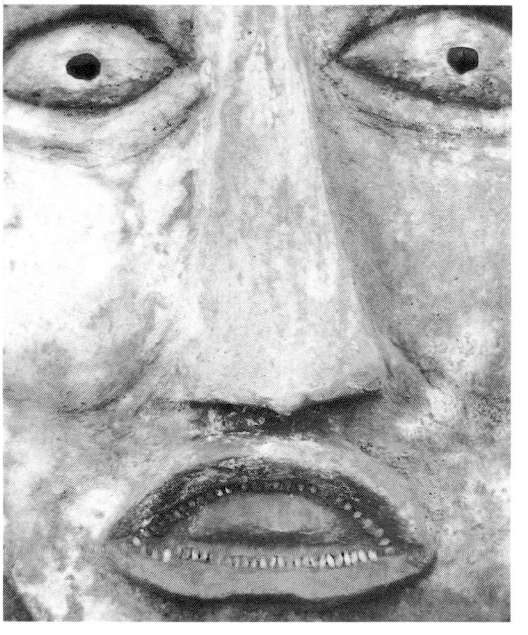

Two faces modelled by Koos. One shows the modelled features of the pilgrim who directs travellers towards the East. Koos was particularly proud of this face, feeling that he delineated the features very clearly. The other face is modelled in relief onto the water tank. According to the caption inscribed in the cement beneath, it possesses healing powers. (Photographs: Johann Potgieter)

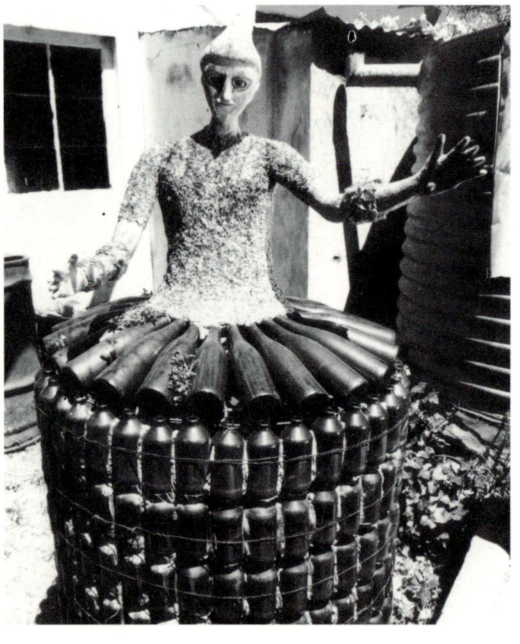

This is the last sculpture that Koos Malgas made at the Owl House. A garden hostess, or meisie, she directs the visitor onwards towards the patio area. Koos was working on this piece when Miss Helen died. He returned to complete it, feeling that he could not leave unfinished work.

He had a technique for working with cement:

> *I use a small thin trowel for the cement. Then I finish off with a brush dipped in a mixture of water and cement.*

Perhaps, for Koos, the most intricate part of the process of his sculpture building, was modelling the faces.

> *When I was making the faces, Miss Helen would not let anyone come and bother me. It is very precise work that you are doing.*

If the surface of a piece was to be encrusted with glass, Koos would press in the glass particles and shards while the cement was still wet. Alternatively, if Miss Helen decided that a piece ought to be covered with glass when the cement was already dry, he would roughen the surface, apply a layer of wet cement and then insert the glass. He became expert at building with bottles, and devised a method for creating the bottle-shrines using tiers of superimposed bottles held firm by a wire framework.

The skirts of the garden hostesses were created in a similar manner. These were the very last pieces he made in the garden. He was working on one of them, the hostess who is pointing the way to the kitchen door, when Helen committed suicide. Feeling that this piece could not remain incomplete, Koos returned to the house a week after her death, and spent a number of days finishing it off. This marked the end of his career as a sculptor. After Miss Helen's death he took a job with the local post office, servicing telephone wires in the district, but he was not happy as the job kept him away from home too much. He was also sensitive to what he perceived to be a certain degree of local hostility. 'The white people were saying that Miss Helen wasted her money on me building all these statues.'

Some of the white villagers did indeed believe that Miss

Helen's financial destitution might have contributed to her decision to take her life, and they were certainly critical of her spending her money on Koos. There was a feeling, too, that Koos perhaps exploited the situation, as Gertie Retief elaborated: 'The boy who worked for her exploited her, perhaps; took too much of her money, more than she could afford.'

Koos decided to take his family and leave Nieu Bethesda. They settled in Worcester, where he found employment, first as a factory worker and later as a gardener at Worcester Showground. He described his years with Miss Helen as the happiest of his life.

In January 1991 Koos Malgas returned to Nieu Bethesda to commence work on the restoration of the Owl House and the Camel Yard he once helped to create.

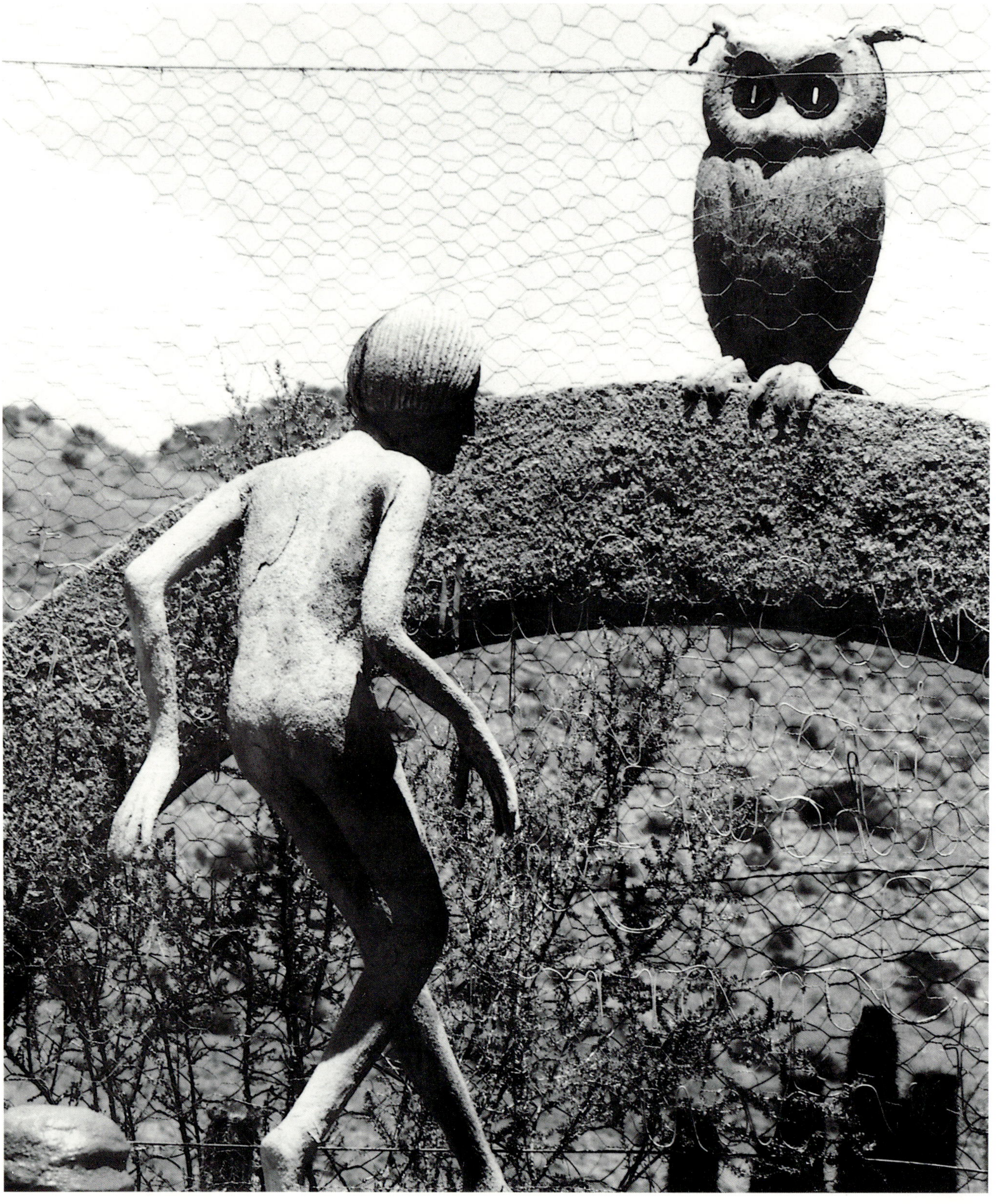

Koos used a photograph which hangs on the wall of the house as the departure point for this airborne, tiptoeing figure. He describes it as 'walking on air'.

Part Three: AN INNER JOURNEY

It was Helen Martins' wish that, after her death, her ashes be mixed with her most precious, red, ground glass. This she kept in one of the preserve jars on the larder shelf. She wanted the mixture of glass and ashes to be glued to her favourite owl, Oswald, which stood outside the kitchen door, with a bone across his feet. In effect she wanted to become a part of his plumage. When drawing up her will with the help of Jill Wenman, she had commented:

> *Come, darling, what should we do with the ashes? I've often thought it would be nice to have Koos mix them with that beautiful, precious, red glass in the pantry, and then have them glued to my owl called Oswald. But the dominee would be upset. He is worried about me enough as it is!*

Her wish was never heeded, and her ashes, to this day, remain in a casket on a shelf in the house, but her bizarre desire highlights an important point about the role of the owls at the Owl House. All the owls, not only Oswald, were *alter egos* for Helen Martins. She identified with them, saw them as an extension of herself. Her desire to remain in the garden and become immortalised in the red glass of Oswald's plumage was a natural progression of the intensely autobiographical nature of the space she created.

One of the ways in which the Owl House can be understood is to see it as a sort of personal diary. On one level, Helen populated the garden with many of the people she knew. There is the rendition of Oupa Frans, an

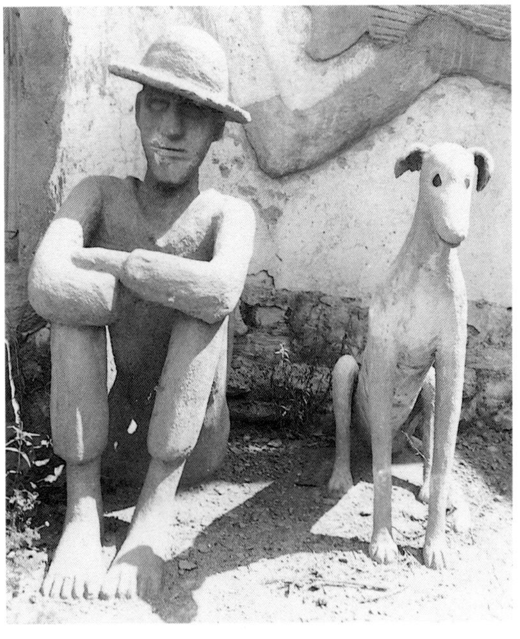

Oom Piet Meyer, with his dog, sits beside the steps to the Lion's Den. (Photograph: Johann Potgieter)

old man in the village. A crudely modelled giant of a man, this was amongst the first pieces to be made. Then there is Oom Piet Meyer who sits beside the steps of the room she called The Lion's Den. He can be identified by the walking-stick in the crook of his arm. As an elderly man, Piet Meyer always walked with the aid of a stick. He lived in the house directly across the river from the Owl House and he and his family always maintained good relations with Miss Helen. His daughter Matie remembers how, when her father was old and bedridden, Miss Helen would walk over to their home early every morning with a little basket of eggs for Piet's breakfast.

Koos Malgas's own two daughters are there too, holding hands and rushing headlong towards the East. Miss Helen also claimed sometimes that this piece represented herself and her friend Jill, with Helen enthusiastically leading Jill around the yard. When she showed Jill the two figures once Koos had completed them, she said with satisfaction: 'Now you will never leave my garden.'

However, on another level, the environment does more than record outward events and the people she knew. It is also about her most intimate and deeply felt yearnings, desires, hopes and intuitions. It records Helen Martins' inner state. It speaks of her urgent need for transcendence and her intensely religious promptings.

Her imagery encapsulates her very personal thoughts and longings and, as already described, it is derived from a number of sources. She used ready-made images, such as the Mona Lisa prints and mermaid ornaments, making straight copies of these images in the relief murals and garden mermaids. She also used highly original imagery of her own. The element of repetition in her work was her way of reinforcing the importance these images had for her. The same images appear and reappear in new and various combinations in different parts of the environment. In this way she elaborates upon their significance to her.

Art works were another major source of inspiration. If the Mona Lisa is an obvious example, so too was the

Rubáiyát of Omar Khayyám she owned. The illustrations in the book inspired numerous wall murals and free-standing sculptural pieces. Helen's art used existing art, finding inspiration in the art of others. Yet the environment retains validity and uniqueness because of her personal interpretation of her sources and the individualised context in which she sites objects. A formal inventiveness is evident, too, in a number of pieces, the double-faced owls, for example, and the metamorphosed camel-owl, and the bag with the cloven hoof. Together, her entire gambit of imagery creates a personal realm of myth which reflects her world-view. Myth, in this context, is used in its fundamental sense to suggest that, embodied in the imagery and narrative elements of the Owl House environment there exists a compelling vision, a cosmogonic paradigm of the order of things. Her vision is personal and unorthodox. It is infused with a deep spirituality, but does not adhere to the tenets of any one religious order. Mrs Cloete remembers an occasion when her husband, Dominee Cloete, asked Helen about her religious beliefs:

> *Once when my husband and I visited, he asked her directly [about her religion] and she said, well, that she was no atheist, but that she was not a conformist to religion, as most people express it. Going to church and such things were not for her. But I think, actually, her religion meant something to her, only not as a believer, as ordinary people who go to church every Sunday. That's not the way she did it.*

It was as if she flitted here and there in her religious searching, gleaning elements from varied and disparate places. It is typical that a fat Buddha in the garden sits in close proximity to the wise men travelling towards the star in the East, and that churches stand side by side with the structures which Helen called her Meccas. These edifices, built from tiers of beer bottles, were inspired by Islamic

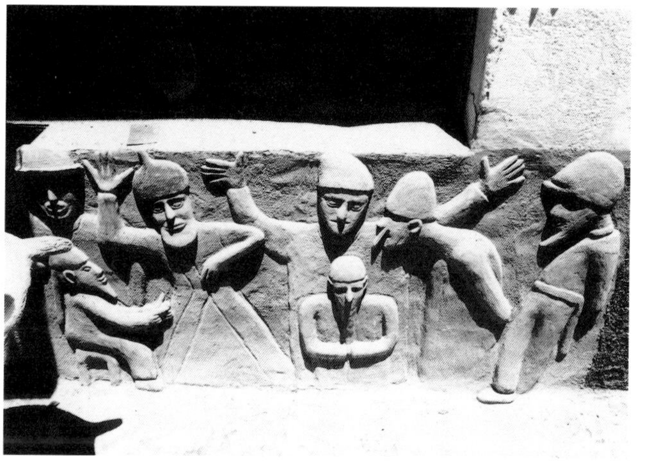

The *Rubáiyát of Omar Khayyám* had a profound influence on Helen Martins' work. A version she owned had illustrations by R S Sherriffs, which Koos was shown and asked to copy. Here, on the wall of the patio, he has depicted quatrain 27:

Myself when young did eagerly frequent
Doctor and Saint, and heard great Argument
About it and about, but evermore
Came out by the same door as in I went.

architecture. Helen at one time engaged in a prolonged correspondence with the Young Islamics' Association, who might have thought they had a potential convert. Her interest in Islam, however, although avid, was unorthodox, and at times subtly undermining. It amused her, for instance, that her Meccas were built out of beer bottles in the light of the strictly held Islamic beliefs about the prohibition of alcohol. She had no wish to embrace in its totality a single religious or philosophical system. A true eclectic, she built her vision from numerous sources.

Her spiritual quest can be understood partly as a response to her perception of the inadequacies and imperfections of her world. Thoughts of this nature are encapsulated in a verse from the *Rubáiyát*, which she asked Koos to write on the fence in a corner of the Camel Yard:

Ah Love! could Thou and I with Fate conspire
To grasp this sorry scheme of Things entire
Would not we shatter it to bits — and then
Re-mould it nearer to the Heart's Desire!

This verse, bent into shape with ordinary fencing wire, stands behind Helen's depiction of Adam and Eve's fall from Grace, the prelude to their expulsion from Paradise, the myth about man as an outcast in an imperfect world. This perception of the imperfection of things is the root of the strong element of wishfulness and wish projection in the Owl House environment. It exists in numerous forms. The Pool of Healing fed by the water tank is also a wishing well. The mermaids beckon passersby and indicate that coins are to be thrown into the water. When she was alive Helen always ensured that there was a coin in the palm of the mermaid who sits on the front edge of the pool.

The evocation of the exotic and the gorgeous was also a preoccupation of Helen Martins'. The glamorous aura of far-off places and the splendour of fine furbishings and rich attire were other elements of the environment that embodied a strong craving for a world and a wealth

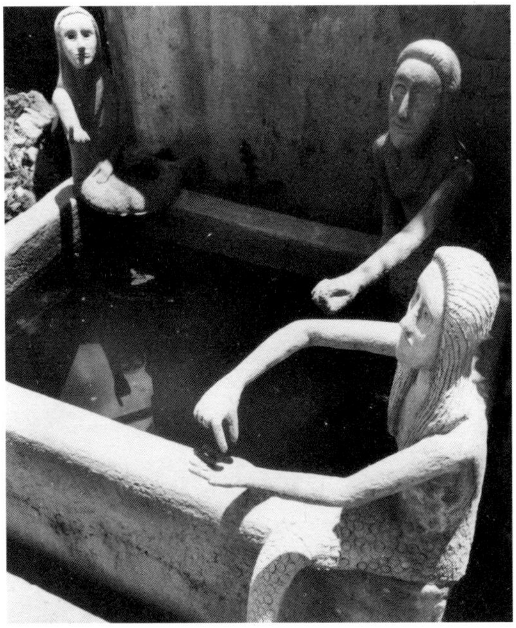

Three mermaids sit on the edge of the pool beside the water tank. This was where Helen always washed the glass she used. The pool was also a wishing well. The mermaids beckon. One of them asks for money. 'She is indicating that money should be thrown into the pool,' says Koos, who made the three mermaids.

beyond her reach.

In the garden, a carpet seller lies dreaming on the ground beneath his Persian rugs. These, hanging on the fence, are ingeniously constructed from ground glass embedded in sheets of cement. The scene is taken from a picture hanging on the wall of the house, accompanied by the following text:

> *Dreaming of the golden road to Samarkand. A Moroccan carpet seller, careless of his wares, takes his midday siesta beneath the burning sun.*

The carpet dealer, neglecting his worldly business, turns his thoughts to the mythical golden road of his dreams.

The picture held a considerable romantic allure for Helen, for not only did she portray it outside against the fence, but she also attempted to create a sumptuous Eastern bazaar in her entrance hall. For her it represented the abundance of riches and worldly possessions, while at the same time pointing to the ultimate poverty of purely material wealth. That the interior decor in the hall was once intended to suggest this Eastern bazaar is no longer obvious, as after Helen Martins' death, it was stripped of a Persian rug and various other oddments that contributed to the calculated recreation of the scene in the picture.

The fine clothing that hangs from the rack in the hall, as well as much of the clothing in the cupboards, made from silks, satins and lace, and never worn by Helen herself, are there only for display. The clothes, like the recreated Eastern bazaar, create a sense of the abundance of luxury worldly goods. They are also part of a repertoire of imagery at the Owl House used to draw attention to the seductive realm of feminine charm and beauty. This is a theme taken up by the many dressing-tables in the house. With their collections of soaps, cosmetics and personal adornments, they are shrines to the ideal of female beauty. Similarly, the richly bejewelled garden hostesses project an aura of ornate glamour, beauty, wealth and splendour,

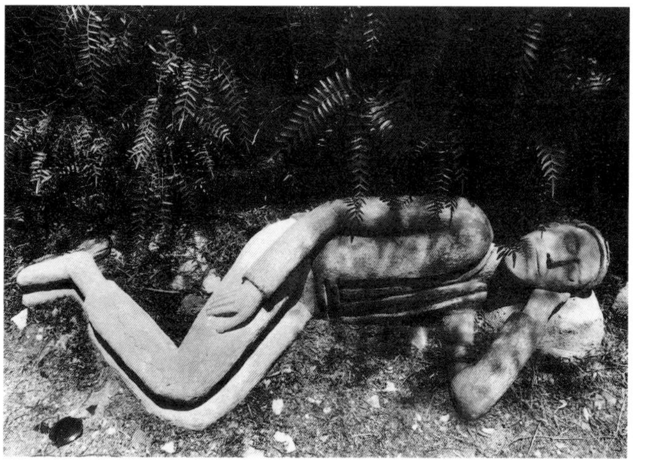

Sleeping beneath the midday sun, this carpet seller is part of a cement rendition of a picture of an Eastern bazaar that hangs on the wall of the main living-room. Above him, attached to the fence and made from cement embedded with shards of glass, are his rugs. The text accompanying the picture reveals that the carpet seller, heedless of his wares, is dreaming of the golden road to Samarkand.

in sharp contrast to Helen's own financially constricted, limited and narrow life.

But it is not just the desire for riches and the glamorous and gorgeous things of this world that the Owl House reflects. The imagery speaks also of an overpowering urge to uncover and claim spiritual wealth: to discover the 'golden road' that supersedes the way of worldly wealth. This 'golden road' can be equated with the alchemists' search for the true, the pure gold. 'Our gold is not the common gold,' profound thinkers among the alchemists stated. Their preoccupation with the chemical transformation of matter had a parallel psychic and spiritual dimension. A principal symbol for alchemical gold, as well as for the sought-after treasure, the indestructible philosopher's stone, was the circle or mandala.

The evocation of ostensible wealth and splendour in the Owl House environment always has a parallel higher dimension to it. Re-enacted in the garden is the story of Christ's birth in which the wise men bring expensive and precious gifts to celebrate the birth of a Divine child: a child who will bring light to the world and whose destiny it is to save mankind. These gifts, embodying worldly wealth, symbolise, too, the spiritual wealth that the holy child will bring to the world.

The frequent evidence of the mandala symbol is another indication that, like the alchemists, Helen Martins sought 'not the common gold'. Like the alchemists,the psychological equivalent of the quest she undertook is the individuation process whereby the contents of the unconscious become integrated. The individual arrives at a new level of self-awareness, called the *unio mentalis* by the alchemists. The circular mandala is frequently used, pictorially, to represent this state of psychic wholeness, suggesting a parallel between the achievement of the *unio mentalis* and the attainment of the alchemical gold.

Mandala imagery at the Owl House takes on many forms. The mandala is seen, architecturally, in the shape of the Moon Gate, as well as the ground plan of the numerous bottle shrines. The Moon Gate was used to symbolise the separation between worlds — the world outside the garden and the world within, the unknown versus the known, day versus night — as well as the divide between this life and the next. The shape of the gate suggests that a psychic completeness has been reached at this point, the divide between life and death. It is the natural end-point of the garden. An exit from the garden through the Moon Gate suggests a rite of passage to a supernatural realm. Adjacent sculptural pieces reinforce the idea of leavetaking. There is a woman standing in a dammetjie, the cement filaments of her hair drifting out behind her as if in a breeze. She blows across the palm of one hand, while waving with the other. Jill Wenman recalls the blowing of kisses and waving as Miss Helen's own manner of saying farewell to departing guests: 'It was a ritual we went through,' she said.

Also near the Moon Gate is a pelican sitting up against the gate, its head on its chest. This bird allegorically represents the crucifixion of Christ. The story goes that it so loved its offspring that it pecked open its own breast to feed them from its blood. The presence of the pelican reminds the viewer of the blood of Christ, symbol of a promised afterlife. Riding towards the gate, as if to pass through, is a wise man on a camel. Accompanying him is an owl. It rests on his shoulder, a symbol of the wisdom he has acquired regarding the approach of death. Another bird, this time a heron, known in Egyptian mythology as the phoenix or Bennu bird that rose from the ashes, flies above a sun on the adjacent wall. Its presence indicates the promise of transcendence and rebirth. The phoenix in medieval alchemy was emblematic of the last stages of the sought-after transformation base metal into gold on the material plane and, on a spiritual plane, salvation. It is not clear whether Helen Martins would have been aware of the alchemical or even the Egyptian significance of the phoenix bird. In general, it is difficult to establish to what extent she was aware of the intrinsic symbolic content of

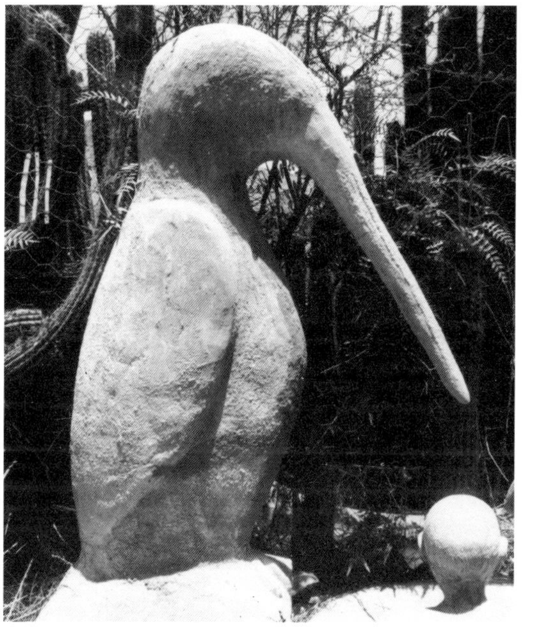

A pelican sits beneath the Moon Gate. The bird is used allegorically to represent the sacrifice of Christ upon the cross and His subsequent resurrection. The placement of the pelican at this point of the garden suggests that death can be transcended.

the imagery she used. However, the manner in which she uses her imagery, while personal, is in accord with many of the meanings ascribed to these images in history and mythology. It is plausible that in the process of creating her environment, under isolated circumstances, she gained access to a rich vein of archetypal imagery within herself. In the words of Jung:

> *Figuratively speaking, it is a kind of immersion in ourselves (isolation and reclusiveness) that leads to the living gem of our wholeness. The practice of this immersion is mythological fundamentalism and the end result of such practice is that our eyes having been opened to the images that stream out of the ground, we find we have returned to the place where the two .... absolute and relative coincide.*[1]

Helen Martins' particular use of imagery has to be understood in her personal context. However, she developed a private mythology which yields up much of its meaning when analysed in terms of the universal archetypes, such as the mandala images.

The mandala-shaped bottle shrines or Meccas are sacred dwellings. In architecture, the circle is frequently an underlying form in sacred buildings or cities. These Meccas were designed as contemplation spaces, their mandala form suggesting a link between inner reflection and psychic growth. That they are intended as contemplation or prayer shrines is indicated by the presence, in one of them, of a stool and a dammetjie. The dammetjie, when filled with water, reflects images. Sitting on the stool and gazing into the water, one would, as in the Narcissus myth, encounter one's own reflection, indicating a play on the idea of self-reflection. The bottles of the shrines have been built into shapes resembling beehives. The bottles themselves create a pattern that suggests the cellular-like arrangement of cells in a honeycomb and filter to the interior an amber or honey coloured light. Because the bee extracts its nectar from selected flowers, flying hither and thither in search of them, both the bee and the honey it makes have come to symbolise the inspirational ability to discern the essence of life, to see below the surface of existence. Intrinsic to the act of self-reflection and the contemplation process, is the attempt to delve beneath the surface of experience and discern the essence of things. The hive-like associations that the shrines provide are eminently suitable for a dwelling in which inspiration and insight are to be found.

The shrines, in addition to their beehive forms, look like giant bottles built from smaller bottle units. The particular bottles used all at one time contained alcoholic beverages, suggesting a connection between the shrines and the consumption of alcohol. Alcohol has been used since ancient times to facilitate breaking down inhibitions and help access the hidden dimension of the unconscious. Alcohol, in the form of wine, mead, soma and ambrosia, is known mythologically to be a 'vital fluid'. Substances known as 'vital fluids' symbolise an increase in libido, the feeling of being alive and the flow of vital interests to and from the subconscious.

A relationship between the intake of alcoholic or 'vital fluids' and the mandala image, appears in another combination at the Owl House, that of the circular, bottle-lined dammetjies. These dammetjies were filled with water for the birds, but the manner in which the bottles lining the dammetjies, are tilted downwards, implies that their contents are being drained into the pools, suggesting that the water is also wine or beer. Thus, metaphorically speaking, the birds in the garden were all tipsy — watered with alcohol, the 'vital fluid' that symbolically aided them in accessing the realm of the unconscious. The water which used to fill the dammetjies can also be understood as the 'water of life' or 'living water'. This is related to the other 'vital fluids' and is used, as in Christian baptism, as a symbol of spiritual renewal.

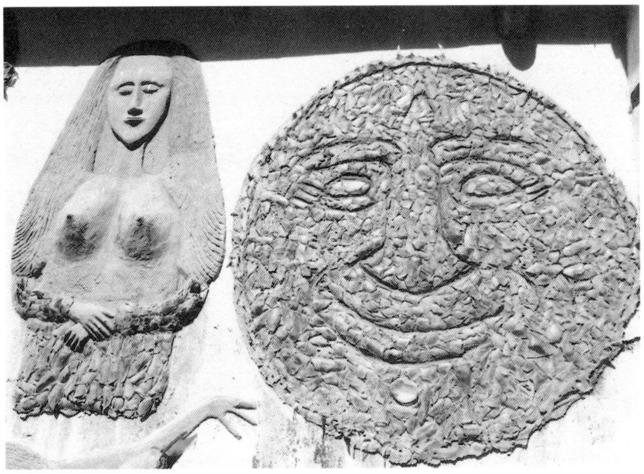

Helen Martins frequently juxtaposed male and female, solar and lunar imagery. On the exterior wall of the Lion's Den a sun, identified with the masculine principle, has been positioned alongside a mural rendition of the Mona Lisa, a feminine image.

Two important sources of mandala imagery that Helen Martins used frequently were the sun and the moon, and an understanding of the symbolism relating to the solar and lunar icons is central to the meaning of her work. Although both are light sources and, as the major alternating sources of light in the universe, have become mythological personifications for the abstract idea of imaginative power, they are each affiliated with certain distinct notions. Suns appear 'looking in' at the windows of the house; they appear in the shapes of mirrors and as foil cut-outs attached to poles in the garden. There are also a number of glittering sun-murals created from ground glass. Almost without exception the suns are anthropomorphised. Almost all have human faces. The lid of a Cobra polish tin was the source of inspiration for many of Helen's sun faces. These suns take on human characteristics, even sometimes displaying emotion. The sun with 'jealous eyes' stares into the Honeymoon Room, while others like the image on the polish tin, beam forth with broad, optimistic smiles. They bring to mind the bright, clear light of day. Mankind has always identified the sun with the masculine principle. It is seen as the visible father of the world and stands for the great generative force of nature and the luminous world of consciousness.

Helen's suns, affiliated with the male principle, are set against the female realm, embodied by the lunar imagery. The moon has traditionally been associated with the feminine, believed since time immemorial to be the force regulating the rhythm of the ocean tides as well as the rhythm of the female menstrual cycle. Many traditional myths accord the moon the power to regulate the fecundity of the earth, as well as the fertility of women. The romantic affiliation of the moon with love is related to this. The connection between the moon and human love is an association Helen strongly establishes at the Owl House. It is evident, for example, in her use of a moon-shaped window in the room she called the Honeymoon Room. Certain of her frequently repeated cement creatures, as well as architectural elements, are related to the sphere of the moon, and hence also the female realm. Chief amongst these is the owl, a nocturnal bird, and a bird associated with the lunar realm. The uterine shape of the owl's belly traditionally connotes a feminine aspect.

As the moon stands in opposition to the sun, so the camel stands in opposition to the owl. The camel is the creature most used by Helen Martins to embody the masculine and the daylight principle. The camel can be regarded as a horse of the desert, a beast of burden associated with relentless heat and wilderness terrain, as well as the patriarchal world of trade and transport. At the Owl House the Camel Yard is the chief domain of the camel, while the owl motif dominates in the house, hence its name. There are the owls on the stoep, the cement owls that sit along window ledges, the owl candle-holders, the two-faced owl seats and numerous owl ornaments.

The owl, for Helen Martins, represented both true and false wisdom. Many of her owls are two-faced and this has a double meaning: Helen's owls were creatures of deception and at the same time creatures of great vision. In their positive aspect, their extraordinary two-way vision is in accord with the traditional role of birds in myths and legends as creatures of intuition, creatures who perceive clearly what others fail to see. In addition, birds, such as owls, which can see at night, symbolise an ability to recognise contents of the unconscious. In this realm they demonstrate their wisdom. The double-facing of the owls relates to Helen's broader portrayal of her female subjects as either dangerous and deceptive or benign and hospitable. In these two opposite roles are the typical characteristics of the archetypal 'Great Mother' in both her good and her destructive form. The work of Helen Martins deals with the archetypal 'Great Mother' complex in both of her guises.

The Owl House itself, like the double-faced owls, is a manifestation of the 'Great Mother'. As a refuge from the elements, a place of homecoming where both shelter and

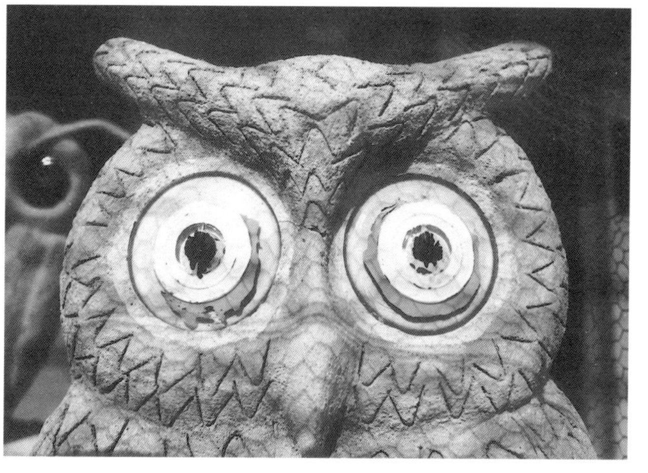

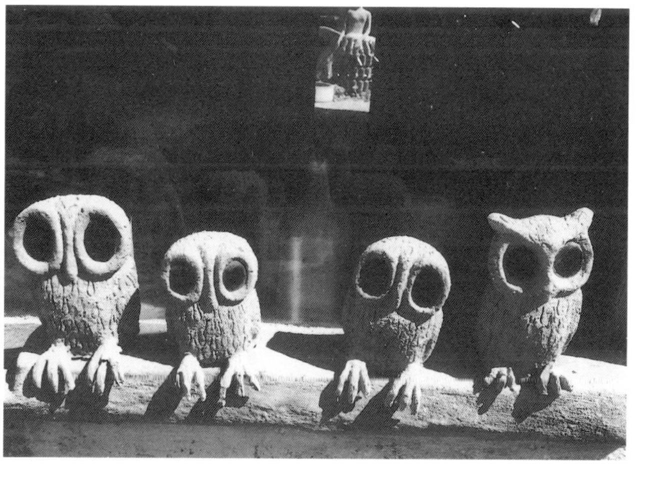

The owl is one of Helen Martins' most frequently repeated motifs. Owls stare at one from all corners of the house and yard.

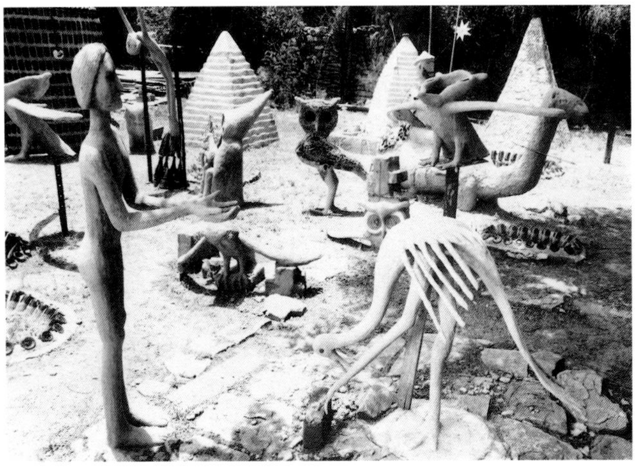

This female figure, who stands in the portion of the yard that was once a bird-cage, cups her hands. Her gesture shows that she is feeding the heron who bows low in gratitude. The cupped hands form a nest in which the birds could lay their eggs. Koos Malgas, who made this piece, explains: 'You must make a person exactly as it is. If it is a woman, then it must look like one.' Miss Helen wished this nude to be female, so he carefully included the genital details.

sustenance can be found, it reveals the positive aspects of the archetype. But there is, too, in the claustrophobic clutter of objects, a sense of suffocation permeating the interior. The mirrors intensify the clutter by doubling it in their reflective surfaces. The many mirrors also create a sense of duplicity, falsifying the space by suggesting other spaces that are not really there. At night, in the unpredictable flickering light of candles and lamps, the wavering shadows create an even greater sense of spatial ambivalence. The glittering glass particles on the walls and other surfaces, while beautifying the interior, are sharp and dangerous at the same time. It is these aspects of the Owl House that reveal its other side — ambiguous, stifling and hazardous. The 'Great Mother' is the protector and nourisher, but she can also be the terrible one. Those whom she protects are at her mercy.

The 'Great Mother' appears again in her benign aspect in the form of the hospitable garden hostesses, with their spreading bell-shaped, beer bottle skirts. They provide alcoholic beverages as refreshments, and serve to show visitors the way. The enclosed garden, like the house, is another image of the archetypal 'Great Mother'. Surrounded by a high fence, and once roofed over with wire, it was a protective space for birds that was both hostile and nurturing. While trapping them within its perimeters, it was also a place of nourishment and safety. The continually replenished pools of water and the abundance of food for the birds created a form of bird haven during the years that Helen Martins lived at the Owl House. This aspect of the garden is still evident in the gestures of two female figures with cupped hands, who are feeding the birds. In front of one girlish figure a heron bows low. It is a posture of reverence, as if in thanks for the food being provided.

Helen's mermaids are like the owls and the house and the garden, full of ambivalence. They fall between the polarities of deception and truth. Alluring and seductive creatures, they are half amphibian and half human. One mermaid sits in her dammetjie and combs her long hair with a yellow plastic comb. The dammetjie, when filled with water, reflects her image as a mirror would. These overt attentions to her personal toilet mark her as a creature of vanity and feminine attraction. There are many stories of mermaids who have lured men to their deaths through their fatal charms and the possibility exists that these mermaids might do likewise. Some beckon seductively and point the way. One of the pointing mermaids, according to Koos Malgas, is showing the way to the kitchen where Miss Helen could be found, while other dammetjie mermaids are beckoning to the geese to come into the water and swim. However, in accord with the traditional dual function of the mermaid, their intentions and actions are not entirely innocent. Mythologically, mermaids are known to be both true and false guides. Likewise, these mermaids cannot be altogether trusted. Their gestures are somewhat too enticing for comfort.

The mermaids sometimes appear in trios, such as the three dammetjie mermaids and the three who preside over the wishing pool. This is in accord with many mythological depictions of females. The three Fates of Greek mythology controlled the destiny of every man, while the classical Hecate, an underworld goddess, and the Celtic Morrigan are known to have appeared in triplicate in the form of owls or ravens. On the back of the water-tank at the Owl House is a relief group of three owls, while on the front there are three female heads. The number three frequently comes across where the female protagonists at the Owl House are concerned, most noticeably in their roles as temptresses.

The three garden sphinxes, one of which is blind, are also creatures of deception. Koos Malgas's two smaller sphinxes were modelled on the image of the lion taken from a brand of matchbox. However, at Miss Helen's insistence, he tried to make the faces look both animal and human. Mythologically, the sphinx is a monster with the head of a woman and the body of a lioness. Like the sphinx of Oedipus, it is an enigmatic creature that pro-

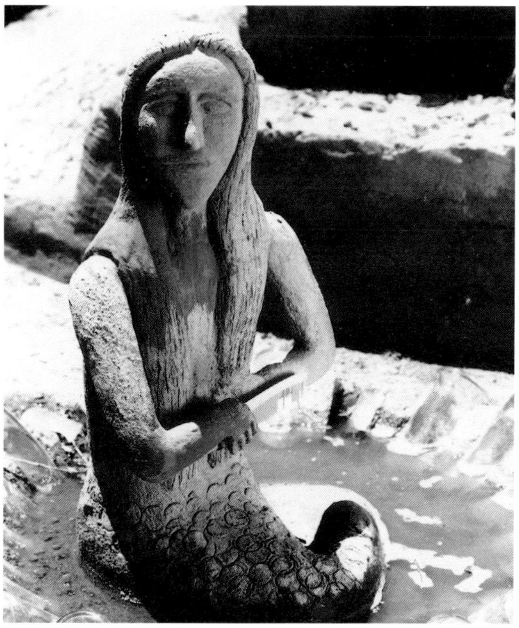

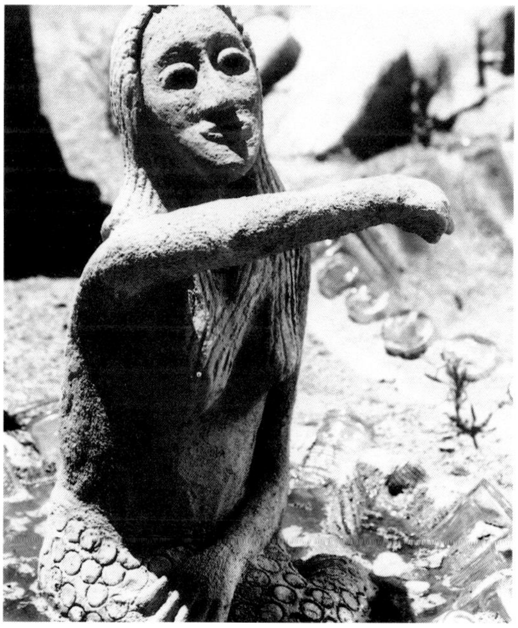

Two of a trio of Miss Helen's mermaids sit side by side in their respective dammetjies.

poses tricky riddles to travellers and inevitably destroys those who cannot solve them. The sphinx represents the relentless forces of fate which can play cruel tricks upon the unwary, catapulting them to their doom. The Camel Yard sphinx that cannot see appropriately inhabits a realm of darkness as the creature who prophesies the blind march of fate.

Perhaps the most disturbing image of the destructive and devouring feminine force or 'Terrible Mother' at the Owl House is the bag body, made from the skin of a buck, which lies on the floor of the Green Bedroom. It has neither head nor arms. Only two cement legs protrude, one with a human foot and the other an animal foot, or cloven hoof. Beside this creature, which like the mermaids and the sphinxes, is half human and half not, lies a silver spoon. The spoon suggests that the bag body is a type of stomach that requires feeding. It is a devouring creature. There is a terrifying aspect to this image, headless and hungry, human and inhuman. Koos recalls how Miss Helen used to chuckle to herself about this piece. It amused her. And on the most mundane of levels, she used it as a doorstop when she wished to keep open the door behind it. Helen's own deformed feet, the source of so much pain to her, make it not inconceivable that there is an autobiographical element in this half human, half bestial image with its cloven hoof.

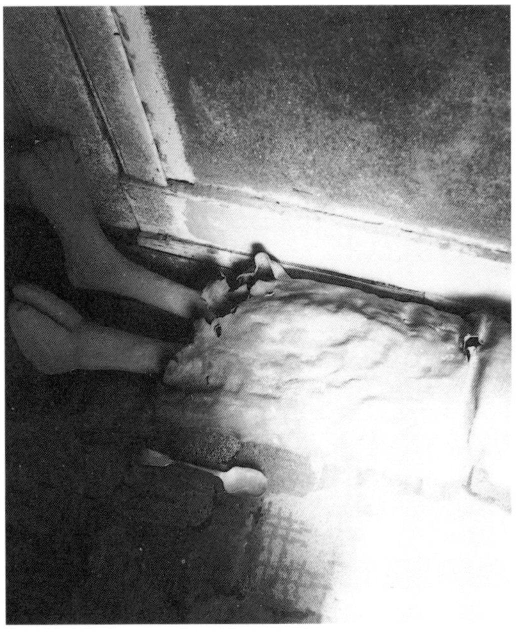

Lying on the floor of the Green Bedroom is a half-human, decapitated sculpture. The bag body is made from buck skin. Protruding from it are two legs. One has a human foot and the other, devil-like, a cloven hoof. The animal hoof is that of a buck, according to Koos who made it. A silver spoon lies beside this enigmatic, headless creature. It is a powerful and disturbing sculptural piece. It appears to be one of Helen Martins' personalised images of the archetypal 'Terrible Mother'. The spoon and the bag stomach suggest its devouring nature. Yet there are contradictions. It is a sealed and isolated image. There are no apertures, no mouth for feeding. In a lighter vein, Miss Helen used it as a doorstop, to prevent the door behind from slamming in the wind, and she frequently chuckled to herself about the monstrous form on her floor.

There are frequent occurrences, in the art environment, of opposites being brought into play against one another. The benign and the destructive aspects of the 'Great Mother' archetype is one example. Other important polarities are the realm of the sun and the realm of the moon, the interior and the exterior, the masculine and the feminine. It has been suggested that an equation exists between the masculine, the exterior and the sun, while the feminine, the interior and the moon are, similarly, linked. A major theme in the work is an exploration of the divide between these polarities, and a possible resolution in the coming together of opposites, a *mysterium coniunctionis.*

The Honeymoon Room is one which explores this theme. A divide between the interior of the room and the exterior is indicated by the sun which peers into the room. The sun belongs to the exterior and the realm of daylight, whereas the interior, with its half-moon window knocked into one of the inside walls of the house, belongs to the nocturnal dimension. The walls are coated in bands of ground glass, the predominant colour being red, the colour of passion. There are two single beds in this room, separated by a wardrobe. Above one of the beds hangs a picture of a young girl sleeping, flowers strewn on her pillow. It is the sleep of innocence. Above the other bed is a mirror in the shape of a cross. The mirrored surface, which reflects the image of those who look at it, suggests the viewer's involvement in the death and resurrection of Christ. It is a symbol, too, of spiritual conciliation and union between man and God. However, the Honeymoon Room also suggests that a physical union between the sexes is not possible. In the Honeymoon Room the masculine and the feminine realms remain distinct.

They appear, however, to come together in another place. There is a cement creature in the garden which is part owl and part camel. It has a camel's body, but the wings and face of an owl, a union of the two animals which symbolise the opposite principles of male and female, night and day. The outspread owl wings imply flight, as if this creature is about to soar heavenwards. On the back of this fantastical beast is a woman, facing in the direction of the Moon Gate.

She is Helen Martins' equivalent of the mythological 'Lady of the Beasts'. Universally, in myth and legend, the female has been represented in relation to the animal realm, indicating her affiliation with the forces of the unconscious. In the process of mastering the unconscious, and gaining conscious power, she appears in different forms. At the lowest level she assumes the form of the beast, be it fish, owl or sphinx. Later she appears accompanied by animals, such as Helen Martins' water-bearer flanked by two owls. Finally, she rides the beast, indicating her domination of the animal kingdom and the flowering of consciousness. Helen's female rider has mastered the beast. She stands, holding up her hands in a protective gesture. Koos Malgas, who made this sculpture, describes the pose: 'She shields her eyes from the overwhelming brightness of the light.'

Helen, in her imagination, was fascinated by the meaning of light. Light symbolism became a core component of her work and her fascination with it can be traced back to her childhood. She is reported to have once said:

> *There was very little brightness in my childhood. As soon as I was able to I began to express the brightness around me.*

The meaning of light, for Miss Helen, was bound up with an apprehension of the Divine. As in mysticism, her inwardly perceived vision of the Divine was often manifested as sun or light. This equating of light with a Divine principle, a universal tendency, is evident in a notebook entry, found in the Owl House.

> *Light ahead! the star was coming their way, and it was growing round like the sun, growing bigger every minute; so bright that it was a white blaze, the white centre of eternity, with time streaming from its spears. That was God, His face was going to show in that white light.*

The worship of light, as well as the pursuit of the light that guides the way to the Divine source, is a central concern of the sculpture environment. Figures, which Miss Helen called her 'sun-worshippers', bend gracefully backwards in prayerful ecstasy. Rather than bend their heads forward in prayer, as is conventionally done, Helen explained her intention to have them facing the source of the Godhead by bending backwards. These figures face in the direction of the rising and the setting sun: they honour its departure, at sunset, and its symbolic rebirth at sunrise.

A guiding heavenly light, the Star of Bethlehem, is a repeated motif. The journey towards the star in the East signifies a journey towards the mystery of eternity and rebirth, and is a focus of the garden pilgrimage. It appears on a pole adjacent to the sign on the fence depicting 'East'. It also appears in the form of a head-lamp on the hut known as the Stable of Bethlehem and it used to be suspended above the glass roof of the Nativity.

In Helen Martins' creative imagination there existed a correlation between the Divine and the erotic. Divine love has frequently been expressed and experienced by mystics through a vision of erotic love. Similarly, Helen turns to the erotic in order symbolically to heighten the experience of the Divine. The ecstatic, naked figures of the backward-bending sun-worshippers derive from a semi-erotic nude photograph that hangs in the house. Another photograph, also a nude study and faintly pornographic, inspired the figure of the woman who rides on the back of the half-camel, half-owl fantastical animal. Helen delighted in pointing out a titillating feature of the naked woman, namely her ruby nipples, as if she had been very daring, and rather naughty, in her design. This sexually erotic detail, added to a figure who is blinded by the intensity of the Divine light, indicates a connection between sexual and spiritual arousal, a theme also evident in the Honeymoon Room.

The relationship between love and death at the Owl House is an interesting one. The mirrored cross, as well as the presence of another cross in the garden, recall the biblical belief that God so loved the world He gave His only begotten Son to be sacrificed upon the cross. Love led to a sacrificial death that brought with it a promise for man, in the resurrection, of renewed life. On one wall of the house there hangs a picture of the Angel of Death. Embracing him, as she is being swept up to heaven, is a young maiden. The inscription beneath the picture reads,

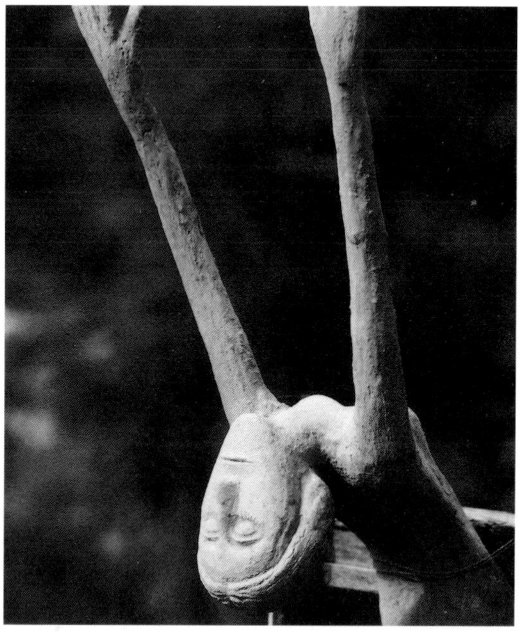

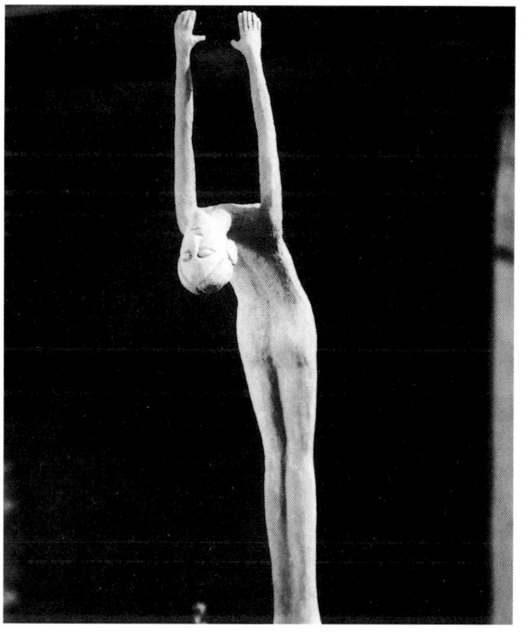

Nudes arabesque backwards in worshipful ecstasy. They are two of the figures Helen called her sun-worshippers. Typically unconventional, she felt that these praying figures should arch their heads reverently backwards, rather than bow them forwards. She thought that it was important that they should be made to face the source of the Divinity.

'Not Death, but Love'. In the Honeymoon Room the cross, emblem of the crucifixion and of death, hangs above a single bed, emblem of frustrated love. Again, the two, love and death, are paired.

Elsewhere the notions of the imperfections of human love versus the power of Divine love are linked.

The Honeymoon Room and the camel-owl creature are both manifestations of the manner in which Helen Martins played with the conjunction of the opposite realms of male and female, and night and day. Standing in the corner of the main living-room is another significant sculptural piece, an elaboration upon Helen's concave-faced owls that are used elsewhere as pools, planters or seats. This piece is all three. Sitting in the hollow of the female owl face is a baby boy. The owl face is also a planter. There are grasses growing in it. Nestling among the grasses are a few small china crocodiles, indicating that this place is to be understood as a watery and swamp-like environment. Koos Malgas confirmed this when he described his brief for building the sculpture:

> *She never said why she wanted me to make this owl, but she liked it very much... She wished me to make the owl with a dammetjie in which a baby sits. The baby wants to put his toe into his mouth.*

The primeval origins of life are associated with water and with swamps. Here, a male child has been gestated. The nocturnal owl has become the archetypal maternal vessel, protective and nurturing. The mosaic surface of coloured glass with which the owl is encrusted has a jewelled quality, implying precious riches. The heart-like shape of its face cavity symbolises its cherishing nature, while the eyes at each side guard and protect the baby.

The owl, with its wings outstretched, is the same as the design used for the owls inside Helen's bird-cages. Within the cages, the outstretched wings served as branches upon which the birds could build their nests. The owl thus becomes a form of tree, with a central trunk and side branches. Here, the tree-owl stands upon a mound of stones, an indoor rockery. The baby is holding its foot up to its mouth, as if attempting to suck its toes, in a posture reminiscent of the ouroborus snake, tail in mouth. The ouroborus serpent, continually eating itself, refers to the refining transformational process that occurs through the re-digestion of experience. Self-renewal and rebirth are implied.

There are indications that the scene incorporating the baby and the owl should be interpreted as a birth, but no ordinary birth. Mythologically speaking, it is the birth of a Divine child, a luminous son — the birth of a hero.

In alchemy, the significance of birth from a tree relates to the emergence of a luminous quality of consciousness and is the end result of transformational processes which cannot be assigned to the sphere of animal instinct. The origins of a hero or god child are always miraculous. He may spring from a rock or from an immaculate conception. The elements and the heavenly bodies fanfare the arrival, as in the story of Buddha's birth:

Maya the queen ...
Dreamed a strange dream; dreamed that a star from heaven
Splendid, six rayed, in colour rosy pearl,
Whereof the token was an Elephant,
Six tusked and white as milk of Kamadhuk —
Shot through the void, and, shining into her
Entered her womb upon the right.

During the conception
A wind blew
With unknown freshness over land and seas
After the birth of the four genies of the East, West, North and South come to offer their services as palanquin bearers. (Told by Sir Edwin Arnold)

The coming into the world of a powerful religious figure needs to be metaphorically expressed, so as to indicate that this is the birth of no mere mortal. It is the birth of a being of 'superman' stature who symbolises the ideas, forms and forces which grip and mould the soul. The newborn child becomes the protagonist of God's transformation in man. The birth story draws upon primordial images which express the 'extraordinarily potent'. The maternal owl, bearing her baby in the nest of her face, is such an image. On the night-black wall, beside the baby, there used to hang a large star mirror. This disappeared from the Owl House after Helen Martins' death.

The heavenly light, a feature of Buddha's birth, appears to have been an accompaniment to the birth of the baby in the owl face. It was also a feature of the birth of Christ as it was portrayed in the sculpture garden, although the star which used to be suspended above the nativity group has long since fallen down. The significance of the East as the direction of the rising sun, the birth of the great luminous principle of the world, plays its part in the Christ story, as it also plays its part in this birth from the maternal owl. The owl is positioned against the east window of the house. Behind it, large panes of glass admit the early morning sunlight. The adjacent star mirror and the black wall counteract the daylight principle, creating a tension between the polarities of light and dark.

Another baby, also attempting to suck its toes like the baby in the vessel of the owl, sits on a rock beside a dammetjie close to the Moon Gate, and, again, this repeated motif signifies the presence of a luminous son. The repeated theme at the Owl House of the birth of a Divine child is indicative of Helen's abiding fascination with the idea of the emergence of the luminous sphere of consciousness out of the maternal depth of the unconscious. Again, this baby who tries to put its toes in its mouth, posturally forming a circle, conjures up the image of the ouroborus. The circular pose also calls to mind the mandala symbol. The mandala signifies the self as a totality. These images carry the suggestion that, as psychology and religion confirm, the self is an *imago Dei*, an image of the Divine. Carl Jung records a dream in which this insight came to him:

> *Yesterday I had a marvellous dream: one bluish diamond, like a star high in heaven, reflected in a round quiet pool — heaven above, heaven below. The* imago Dei *in the darkness of the earth. This is myself.*[2]

In its way, the broader structure of the Camel Yard, with its own heaven below heaven, suggests this truth. Helen Martins' own cut-out, metallic stars shimmer at night beneath the stars of the cosmos. Her round, bottle-lined pools of water, like reflective mirrors, carry the image of the stars in their depths.

In a pool beside the rock upon which the baby sits, is another baby. Its arms are uplifted. Koos Malgas describes it:

> *... It is the same baby. It can now stand on its own. But it is lifting up its arms, asking to be picked up by its mother.*

The baby in its circular pool is close to the Moon Gate. It is the portion of the yard which deals thematically with death and spiritual rebirth. The baby's mother is not tangibly present, for she is the 'Great Mother' or 'Great Round', also symbolised by the Moon Gate. The Moon Gate embraces those who pass through it into the arms of death, but the cross, the rising sun-mural, the phoenix and the ibis all symbolise a rebirth. The Moon Gate and indeed the entire ceremonial structure of the Owl House and its Camel Yard — which leads one back to the point at which one started, is like the metaphorical ring of rings spoken of by Nietzsche in *Thus Spake Zarathustra*:

O how should I not burn for eternity and for the nuptial ring of rings— the ring of return! Never yet did I find the woman from whom I desired children, unless it be this woman whom I love: for I love thee, O Eternity (Translated by Common)

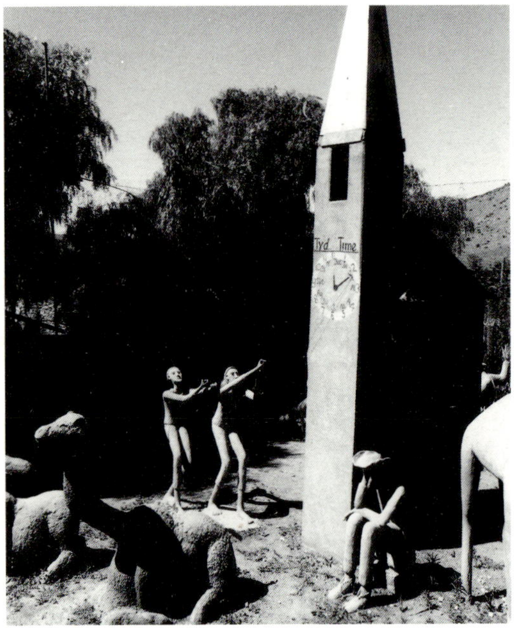

Two youths try to hold back the hands on the church clock, so as to halt the passage of time.

The problem of grasping eternity, for man caught up in the temporary nature of existence, is embodied in an elaborately narrative sculptured scenario that, like the baby who is both at and in the pool, represents different time frames simultaneously. On one side of a church spire at the Owl House is a clock. Where one would normally expect to find the numerals, Helen Martins had the clock face marked out with the twelve months of the year. Two youths stand alongside the steeple. They are dragging on a piece of wire attached to the clock dials, in an apparent attempt to stop the advance of time. An old man sits beneath the clock, head in hands. He is contemplating the passage of time. There was another small statue which completed the scenario, although this has since vanished from the garden. It was a crawling baby. The scene thus charts the passage of time in the old man's life. Koos comments:

The old man thinks back over the years. He was once a baby and then a young man. He cannot turn back the clock. He is now old.

Change is a condition of life. Near this church, another sculpture reinforces this concept. A caterpillar crawls up an oak leaf, while upon another leaf the caterpillar has turned into a chrysalis (the next stage, not depicted, being the emergence of the butterfly, in this cyclic drama of nature). This chrysalis, however, has a human face and it resembles an infant in swaddling clothes. The scene has been copied from a William Blake illustration, from his small book *The Gates of Paradise*, later expanded and reissued under the title *For the Sexes*. Behind the chrysalis, on the pillar of the arched gateway, which can be understood as Helen Martins' depiction of *The Gates of Paradise*, is the verse which accompanies Blake's engraving.

> *What is man!*
> *The sun's light when he unfolds it*
> *Depends on the organ that beholds it.*

Man is a mortal worm and a sleeping butterfly. His ability to transcend this earthly existence is implied. The meaning of the sun's light depends upon the beholder, but can perhaps be found in these images if they are perceived with a spiritual eye. Near the chrysalis on its oak leaf 'cradle' is another sculpture, also copied from a Blake engraving. A crouched figure with a crook sits on the ground beneath a tree, presumably an oak, encircled by a long worm. Blake's accompanying text reads:

> *I have said to the Worm: Thou*
> *art my mother and my sister*

In the Blake engraving the heads of three bodies melt back into the ground, dust unto dust, claimed by death. The worm emerges from the earth, spirals around the sitting figure, cowled Death, and returns to the earth. The encircling worm, metaphorically, forms Nietzsche's 'ring of return'. It is likely that Blake's figure is 'Eno aged Mother ... Sitting beneath the eternal oak', who appears on the frontispiece of *The Book of Los* in a similar guise, lamenting the loss of a remote time of innocence and purity.

The Camel Yard's sculptural depiction of the hooded figure and encircling worm, unlike the Blake engraving, does not include the decaying heads. Also, the pointed stick that cowled Death holds in the Blake illustration has become a shepherd's crook. The crouched figure of Death, in the protective robe, here takes on the Christ-like role of the shepherd of men, and this figure resembles the other hunched shepherds in the garden who care for their

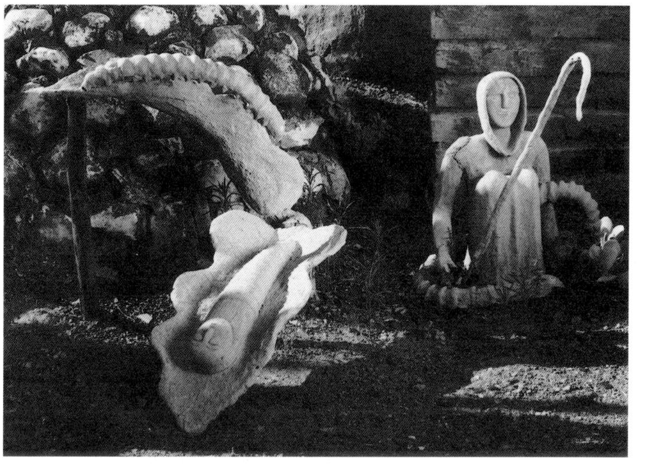

A caterpillar crawls up the side of an oak leaf. Another oak leaf cradles a cocoon that bears a human face. Seated a little way apart, is a huddled and hooded figure, encircled by a worm. The worm emerges out of the earth and returns to it. The cyclic nature of life, dust unto dust, is depicted in these images that derive from a Blake engraving. In the Blake illustration the cowled figure holds a pointed stick. Miss Helen has substituted this for a crook, thereby identifying the figure with her other shepherds in the garden.

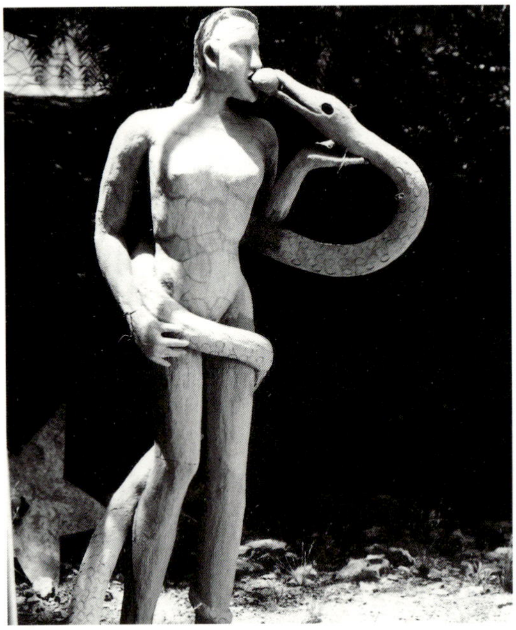

The snake tempts Eve to take a bite from the apple. The image of the snake, entwining itself around the figure of Eve, comes from a Blake drawing that Koos Malgas remembers Miss Helen receiving as a Christmas card.

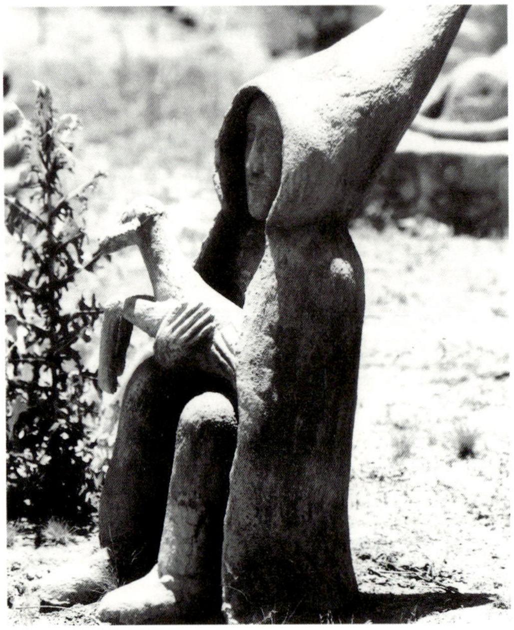

One of the shepherds, with his protective cape and pointed hood, holds a lamb on his lap.

flock. These also wear protective, hooded cloaks.

This part of the garden, with the youths attempting to hold back time and the two scenes from Blake, deals with man's mortality and his hopes of immortality. Another scene, close by, is thematically related. It is the depiction of the Temptation of Eve and the resultant expulsion from the Garden of Eden, the entry of sin, and hence death, into the world. The serpent entwines the figure of Eve. In its mouth it holds an apple, with which it tempts her. Adam has his hands in the air, which in the Blake drawing from which the scene derives, appears to be a gesture of wonderment at the beauty of Paradise, although Koos Malgas, the sculptor, describes his version as carrying a heavy load. The depiction of the original fall of humanity, symbolically the moment when time and mortality broke into eternity, again focuses upon the fleeting nature of man's earthly sojourn. In close proximity to this scenario, the theme is taken up in the lettering upon the fence:

And the caravan moves north, O make haste

This is the first line of the *Rubáiyát* quatrain which continues:

One moment in Annihilation's waste,
One moment, of the well of Life to taste —
The stars are setting and the Caravan
Starts for the Dawn of Nothing — Oh make haste

The caravan journey towards the 'Dawn of Nothing' appears to be represented by the adjacent stately wise man, with his glass-bejewelled headdress, who rides on a camel's back. An imposing and kingly figure, he was apparently Miss Helen's favourite wise man. He is riding in the direction of another scene, which again is narratively linked. It shows a rider leaning against his camel, staring into the distance, the direction of the setting sun. He has arrived at the fence of the Camel Yard and can go no further. This scene comes from an illustration by Sherriffs in Helen's copy of the *Rubáiyát.* Beside the man is his faithful dog. Dogs, through the ages, have borne certain funerary associations. In the Zoroastrian tradition, from which the *Rubáiyát* arose, a priest and his dog are always summoned to a death-bed to dispel the supposed evil nature of the dead body. This is in accordance with the ancient belief that a dog's stare can drive away the demons from a corpse, which led to funeral processions being headed by a priest and a dog. The dog, who guides and guards his flock like the priest, is also an allegory of faith. It is possible, in the Camel Yard, to see the dog and his master as heading a vast funeral procession of the entire pilgrimage that travels through the garden. An accompanying verse to the scene with the journeying camel-man and his dog, cut-out letters of tin, is attached to the fence of the yard:

Ah Moon of my Delight who Know'st no wane,
The moon of Heav'n is rising once again;
How oft hereafter rising shall she look
Through this same garden after me in vain!

The lines have an autobiographical ring, as if Helen Martins foresaw the time when the moon, rising over her garden, would find her no longer there. Acutely aware of her own mortality, she made elaborate plans for her death, one of which was to participate, in her own way, in the garden's funerary procession. She expressed a wish to have her body taken out of the back door and carried through the Camel Yard to the zinc gate, which is positioned at the start and the culmination of the garden's layout. Jill Wenman remembers the occasion upon which she voiced this request. It was the last time they were together, and they were drafting her will.

We spent most of the three days drinking endless cups of tea, while wrapped up together in her bed

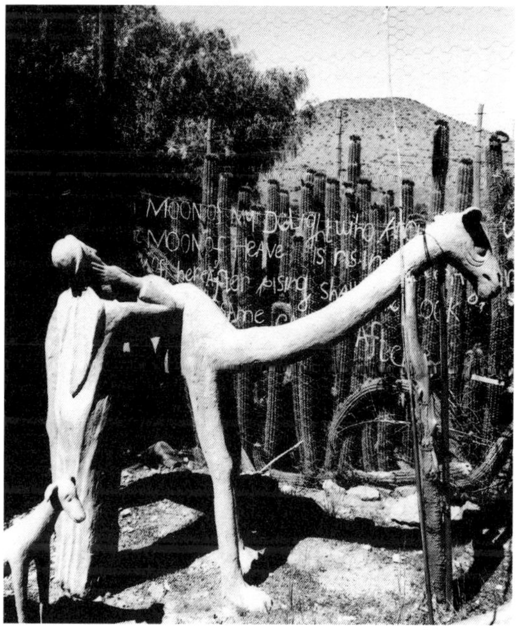

A travelling pilgrim has reached a culmination point in his journey. He has arrived at the fence of the Camel Yard. Leaning against his camel, he gazes towards the hills.

> *in the long, green room. In Clause 2 she wanted her body removed through the back door and out through the zinc gate. Not through the front gate. 'I have my reasons,' she said.*

When Jill asked her to elaborate she was given a flippant answer, which nevertheless reflected Helen's desire to preserve her precious Owl House.

> *My darling, the people in this village are so careless you wouldn't believe it. If they carted my body out through the front door and walked through the house, they would rub all my precious glass off the walls.*

The other reason, to participate in the funerary drama that she had created, can only be deduced. However, it seems a natural extension of the autobiographical nature of her work, her intensely felt identification with it, and her desire to be an integral part of the world she made. This was expressed in her other wish — that her ashes be mixed with ground glass and glued to Oswald, the owl.

The 'Moon of my Delight who Know'st no wane' refers to the full moon. In the verse on the fence the moon is personified. She will search through the garden in vain, an intermediary between heaven and earth. It is the moon as she is depicted in the Moon Gate, full and round and, symbolically, the intermediate gateway between this world and the next. The Moon Gate faces the direction in which the sun sets behind the nearby hills. At sunset, the setting sun can be seen through the circular perimeter of the Moon Gate. The two draw parallel, as if in union. In *Isaiah* 30:26, the prophecy of the salvation of mankind is expressed through the union of sun and moon.

> *Moreover the light of the moon shall be as the light of the sun, and the light of the sun shall be sevenfold, as the light of seven days, in the day that the*

Lord bindeth up the breach of his people, and healeth the stroke of their wound.
(King James Version)

The Moon Gate, like the sun mural with the flying phoenix, the statue of the ibis, the rendition of Christ's cross, and much other imagery in this corner of the garden, expresses the idea of salvation and rebirth.

The heavenly union of sun and moon is a universal, mythological motif denoting cosmic unity. It has its parallel, on the earthly plane, in the union of male and female. Again, biblically, the marriage of the sexes is used as a metaphor for the union between Christ and the Church. Christ is referred to as the groom, his Church the bride — a bond which brings salvation to his people.

Helen Martins' preoccupation with the conjugal image is often evident. There is the Honeymoon Room, and the profusion of heart-shaped mirrors. There is also the wall relief on the back patio depicting two lovers clasped in each other's embrace. Here and elsewhere, when the union of lovers occurs at the Owl House, it takes on a metaphysical as well as a physical meaning. Nietzsche's 'nuptial ring of rings, the ring of return' finds expression in Helen's images of the oneness of lovers. The lovers know the secret of salvation. They hold the key to eternity. The patio relief shows the lovers from quatrain 57 of the *Rubáiyát.*

You know, my Friends, how bravely in my House
For a new Marriage I did make Carrouse:
Divorced old barren Reason from my Bed,
And took the Daughter of the Vine to Spouse.

The 'Daughter of the Vine' is, of course, a reference to wine, and this relief is tucked away beneath the patio vine. It is close to another sculptured scene, that of the wine-pourer, the dark angel from quatrain 89 of the *Rubáiyát.*

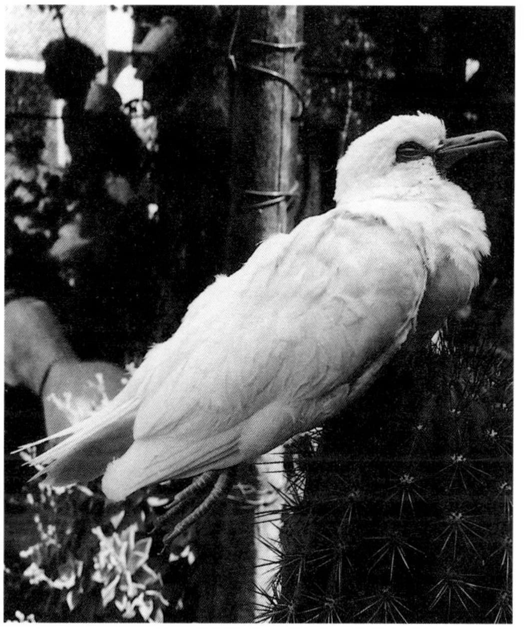

Visiting Miss Helen, Johann Potgieter noticed that she had deliberately impaled a dead dove on one of the long thorns of a cactus plant. This striking image has its parallel in Miss Helen's interest in the crucifixion story of Christ. Situated in a corner of the garden, there stands a cross studded with glass. That it depicts the cross upon which Christ was crucified is clear from the use of the red glass, to indicate blood, at the points where the nails went through hands and feet. In a personal reworking of the crucifixion theme, the cactus thorn, which penetrates the bird, brings to mind the crown of thorns which Jesus wore upon His head, while the dove is a traditional symbol of the Holy Spirit. The Crucifixion prefigures the story of the Resurrection of Christ, which embodies the hope of eternal life. Helen Martins continually manipulated her imagery to draw attention to the great divide between life and death, and the possible existence of an afterlife.

So when at last the Angel of the darker drink
Of Darkness finds you by the river-brink,
And, proffering his Cup, invites your Soul
Forth to your Lips to quaff it — do not shrink.

The significance attached to wine is an important feature of both the relief and the depiction of the dark angel. Wine, as one of the so-called 'vital fluids', is a life-enhancing substance, an elixir of life. It bears this meaning in the Christian Communion service, where it symbolises the blood of Christ, spilt, so that man might taste eternal life. In the *Rubáiyát* wine carries the same promise of eternal life. In quatrain 89, when the dark angel of death 'proffers his Cup', his companion is urged not to shrink. Wine, used here as a metaphor for death, holds out the hope of the life to come.

The wine in quatrain 57, illustrated by the lovers, takes on other associations. It is a metaphor for the spirit and for faith, in contrast to 'old barren Reason'. The 'Daughter of the Vine' is not only a reference to wine, but also to the bride. The idea of a marriage to 'the Daughter of the Vine' is synonymous with the consumption of the symbolic wine of the spiritual life.

Helen Martins wanted her own patio vine to be permanently fruitful. She suspended a bunch of cement grapes from one of the branches of the overhanging patio vine, so that the fruit on the vine would remain all year round. The image of the garden of fruitfulness she wished to create, is an image of paradise. It is analogous to the mythical Persian garden Iram, created by Shaddad bin Ad in the Arabian desert, which is described in quatrain 5 of the *Rubáiyát.*

Iram indeed is gone with all His Rose,
And Jamshyd's Sev'n Ring'd Cup where no one knows
But still a ruby kindles in the Vine,
And many a garden by the water blows.

The *Song of Songs* contains a passage describing another paradisiacal garden.

Awake! Oh north wind,
And come, wind of the south;
Make my garden breathe out fragrance,
Let its spices be wafted abroad.
May my beloved come into his garden
And eat its choice fruits.

In some respects the enclosed Camel Yard is the mythical paradise garden. There is fruit. There is water. There are the Gates of Paradise. There is also wind, a frequently described feature of the paradise garden, which Helen Martins visually portrays in a number of sculptural pieces — the nude figure who stands in her dammetjie of water and blows kisses has hair that has been whipped backwards in the wind. Several wise men riding camels have capes flowing and billowing in the breeze. As in the *Song of Songs*, the enclosed garden is commonly the mythical meeting place of lovers, the place of the consummation of marriages. Helen Martins uses it as such in the wall relief showing the embracing lovers. The bird and its song are another feature of the mythical garden of delight, paradise. A verse from the *Rubáiyát* incorporates this idea.

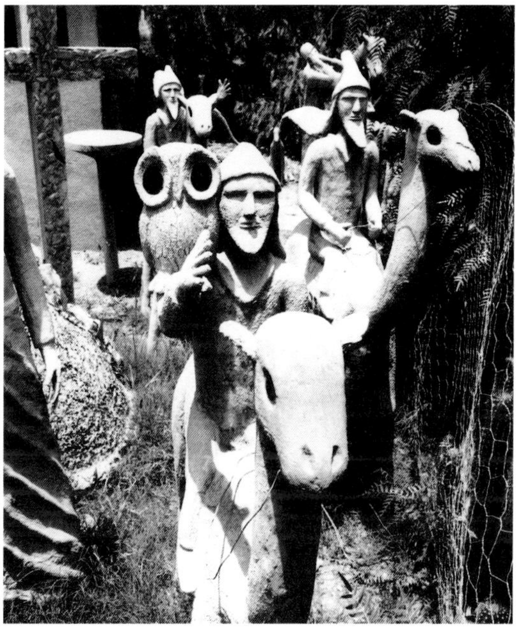

A wise man on camel back, in that part of the garden thematically devoted to approaching death. He rides towards the Moon Gate. The companion owl, resting upon his shoulder, denotes the attainment of wisdom regarding matters of life and death.

A Book of Verses underneath the Bough,
A Jug of Wine, a loaf of Bread — and Thou
Beside me singing in the Wilderness —
Oh, Wilderness were Paradise enow!

This is quatrain 12, which in the Fitzgerald translation owned by Helen, is accompanied by an illustration. This Koos Malgas copied for Miss Helen in cement and it occupies a portion of the garden. Beneath a fruit tree in the Camel Yard sits a woman with a long veil. She holds a jug with a spout that has metamorphosed into the head of a bird. Beside her is a loaf of bread. Above her, sitting on one of the branches of the tree, is a small cement bird, its beak wide open as if in full-throated song. The verse equates the bird and its song with 'Paradise'. The Camel Yard, with its profusion of cement birds, and once with its many live birds, is a garden of birds, an image of paradise.

The woman has a bird jug that holds 'wine'. Here the bird is affiliated with the wine. A similar association occurs with Helen Martins' bottle-lined dammetjies where the birds immerse themselves in, and partake of, the water that is symbolically wine. The conjunction of the bird, known mythologically as a creature capable of transcendental access, and the wine, an elixir of life, suggests a spiritual rebirth as the means of gaining entry to 'Paradise'. Like the 'Daughter of the Vine' in quatrain 57, the woman with her veil is a bride. The meaning of this sculptured scenario connects with that of the lovers on the patio wall, in that wine becomes a medium of spiritual attainment, and the conjugal image is used to suggest a metaphysical marriage.

The relief image of the embracing lovers is one of several images in close proximity that deal with the coming together of opposites. There is also the underwater swimmer, wearing flippers, against the wall of the house, with the large, anthropomorphised sun-face above it. Here, in one format, the watery female realm is contrasted with the fiery male realm.

But perhaps the most interesting and complete image of the conjunction of opposites is the snake table. Here the coils of a snake form the supporting base for the circular top of a table. An image, modelled into the tabletop, depicts an imposing turbaned figure, holding a flaming stake in one hand. In the palm of the other he balances the symbols of the cosmos — sun, moon and stars. It is an image of totality, combining many opposites — the earthly stake and the aerial fire, as well as the lunar and the solar realms and their corresponding personifications as masculine and feminine. The circular format of the table, a mandala symbol, is the shape of both the sun and the full moon. The supporting snake is an androgynous symbol, being at the same time phallic and associated with the mother earth upon which it crawls. The turbaned figure comes from Sherriffs' illustration of quatrain 71 of the *Rubáiyát.*

I sent my Soul through the Invisible,
Some letter of the After-life to spell;
And after many days my soul return'd
And said, "Behold, Myself am Heav'n and, Hell."

The image of the self as the cosmic totality, the union of heaven and hell, sun and moon, good and evil, masculine and feminine: this is a profound realisation and one which Helen Martins explored in many of its complex facets. Her thoughts, spelt out in glass and concrete, make tangible her intuitions and insights into the nature of this life and the beyond.

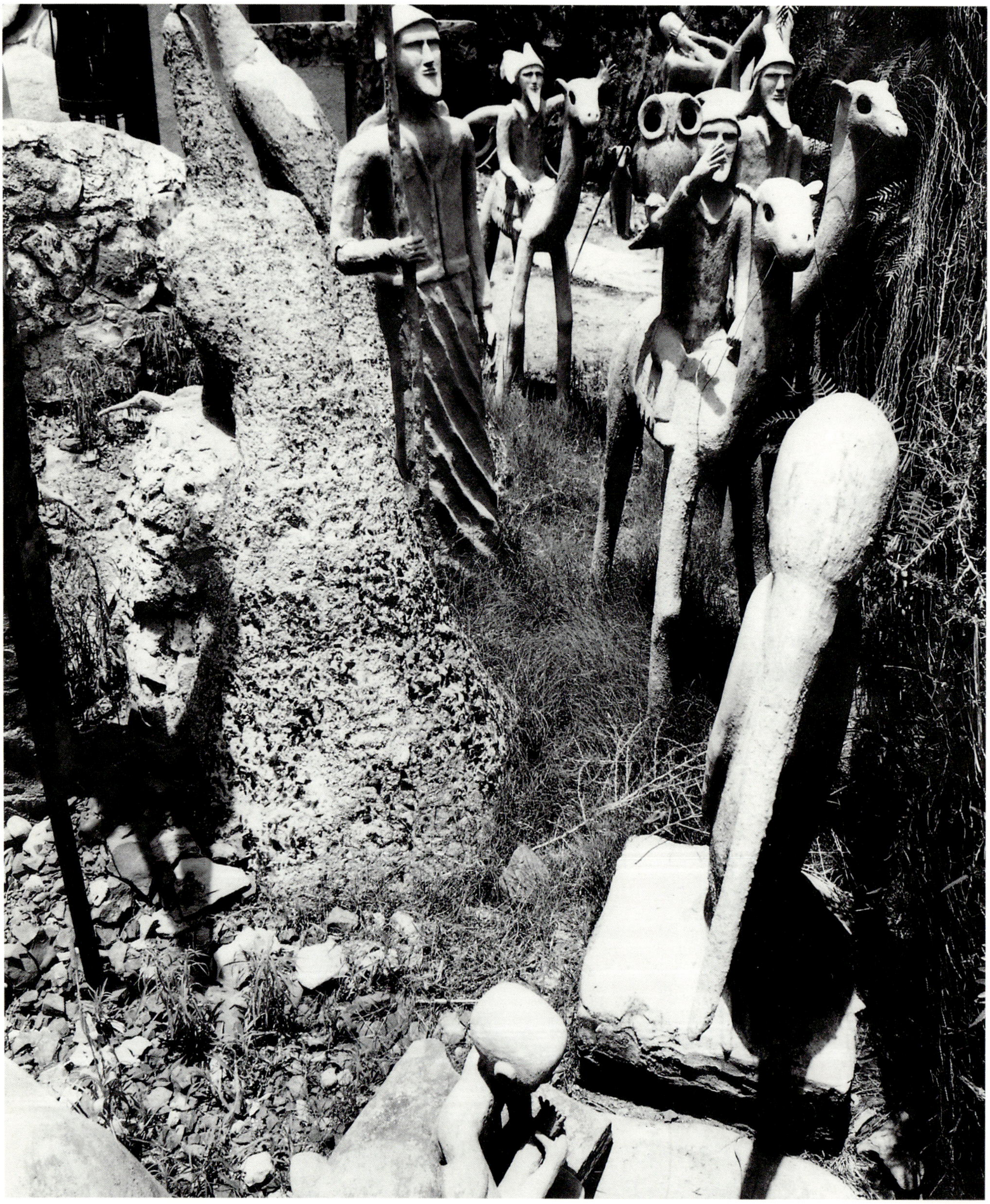

Pilgrims travel towards the Moon Gate while, sitting in a dammetjie in the foreground, a baby attempts to suck its toes.

Postscript: **A PERSONAL APPRAISAL**

What, ultimately, is the worth of the Owl House? How much more is it than a dusty, eccentric Karoo backyard? One that is filled with garden statuary, some of it looking suspiciously like gnomes run amok? And the house, bizarre, glass-encrusted and claustrophobically cluttered with sentimental oddities — has it a worth beyond that of a spectacle of mere novelty value?

And what about Helen Martins herself, reclusive and highly eccentric (some would say dotty or even mad)? How does one evaluate her? Do her efforts embody anything greater than an obsessive and somewhat vulgar love affair with home decoration, prettifying and personalising her environment?

It is clear, on a close examination of her work, that what might have started out as a mere decorative urge to brighten up her home and decorate her garden soon transcended such limited objectives. The house, as it took on its interior casing of glass and its symbolically resonant clutter of knick-knacks and kitsch ornaments, extended well beyond any typical notion of interior decoration. Similarly, the sculpture garden, as it grew, took on a life and a meaning of its own. Helen found expressive and symbolic possibilities in her work. She exploited these and the scope of her work increased. One thing led to another, and ideas generated new ideas to form what can rightly be described as an art statement. The work displays thematic consistency. Naive and untutored as it may appear, the meanings run deep. The art environment is far too coherent and complex to have been created by a mad person.

Helen Martins was only mad in the sense that all true artists are mad. Possessed by the gods and demons of creativity, she was driven by a type of obsessive mania to give formal expression to her intuitions, apprehensions, visions, dreams and desires.

Her work is not always easy to understand and appreciate. Its apparent simplicity is illusory. It is built upon elaborate iconic juxtaposition. So whereas, individually, certain pieces may seem stereotyped, crudely made and resembling even the kitsch statuary that populates many a suburban garden, they must be viewed in their context and specific place in the garden. Also, like other artists toying with the inherent possibilities of thematic concerns, the work is full of repetition. Far from being monotonous and facile, however, this repetitive element reveals an artist at work, teasing out new possibilities within her chosen repertoire of images.

The fact that Helen did little with her own hands, leaving the making and building to Koos, Piet, Jonas and others, has become a stumbling block to those who feel that there is, consequently, something fraudulent about the work. I take the view that an artist can legitimately employ the labours of others. For me this is not a problem. The problem arises in trying to assess the independent contributions of apprentices and employees. In Helen's case, to what extent ought Piet, Jonas and most especially Koos, be accredited as co-creators of the space? I feel most comfortable acknowledging the Owl House as fundamentally the work of Helen Martins, for although Koos and others left significant personal signatures upon the space, it was Helen who visualised it all. It was her mind and her thoughts that breathed life and significance into the work and made the separate elements and images hold together as a coherent art environment.

In the final analysis, what I perceive to be Helen's greatest accomplishment is her ability to transcend the limitations of her circumscribed life, as well as to create an art statement that in itself transcends limitations. She did this with the material she used. Geographic isolation and relative poverty restricted her choice of materials to what was cheap and readily available. With little more than glass, paint and cement she created a wonder-world. It was always her way to use what was at hand. It is entirely characteristic that she should even choose to commit suicide with what was at hand, the caustic soda that she kept on her larder shelf to clean her floors. Her ability to adapt available materials to her own end lent a spontaneous inventiveness, and even at times wit, to the work. To suddenly discover, for instance, that the eyes of an owl are actually the lids of preserve bottles, or that the eyes of a lion are ordinary car head-lamps, ingeniously recontextualised, is delightful and amusing. The art is full of charm, humour and whimsy.

Living in a remote and conservative community she was able, too, to transcend the culture boundaries of her background. She looked to the East and to the West. Bottle shrines or 'Meccas' stand cheek to jowl with churches, and a Buddha sits amongst biblical pilgrims with their flowing robes. She looked back in time to ancient and archaic cultures, and she looked to the present. It is typical that a pyramid is surmounted by a modern wind pump, and that the star of Bethlehem is depicted as a large-globed searchlight. Stepping across barriers of religion and thought, with easy agility, she created an art environment that is eclectic as it is universal.

Helen Martins must, in my view, be accepted as an artist and her creation, the Owl House, acknowledged as a work of art characterised by irony and insight, by passionate and profound yearning. The universality of Helen's themes is at once heightened and belied by the ordinariness of their setting, a juxtaposition of which she was not only aware but which she exploited with subtlety and humour in the accomplishment of her meaning.

REFERENCES

Part One

1 **ROBERT HUGHES:** *The Shock of the New: art and the century of change*, p 220. (London: *BBC*, 1981)

2 **ROBERT HUGHES:** *The Shock of the New: art and the century of change*, pp 229-31. (London: Balding and Mansell, 1980)

3 **BEVERLEY MARKS:** *The Uses of Visual Mythology in Contemporary South African Art.* Unpublished Masters dissertation, University of the Witwatersrand, 1987, p 168.

4 **ROGER CARDINAL:** *Outsider Art*, p 65. (London: Studio Vista, 1972)

5 **ROGER CARDINAL:** *Outsider Art*, p 68. (London: Studio Vista, 1972)

6 **GAVIN YOUNGE:** *Art of the South African Townships*, pp 84-5. (London: Thames and Hudson Ltd, 1988)

7 Testimonial, written in High Dutch, found among Helen Martins' papers after her death.

Part Three

1 **CARL JUNG:** *Essays on a Science of Mythology*, p 10. Translated by R C F Hull. (New York: Bollingon Series, Pantheon Books, 1942)

2 **CARL JUNG:** *Word and Image*, pp 102-103. Edited by A Jaffe. (Bollingon Series, XCVII: 2, Princeton University Press, 1979)